John N. Deely (26 April 1942–2017 January 7)

This painting by Margaret Footit is based on a 1989 photo of John,
when he was a Fulbright professor in Brazil.

i

John N. Deely

(26 April 1942–2017 January 7)

When John Deely, Editor-in-Chief of *The American Journal of Semiotics*, passed away on January 7, 2017, the world lost one of its keenest philosophical minds. Members of the Semiotic Society of America know how central John was to its history. The story of his life is a spiral of semiosis that blazed brightly from the founding of the SSA to its flourishing.

Born in Chicago on April 26, 1942, John was educated at the Pontifical Faculty of Philosophy of the Aquinas Institute of Theology in River Forest, Illinois, receiving a Ph.D. in 1967. After briefly holding several academic posts, John's first major career accomplishment was his close work with Mortimer Adler at the Institute for Philosophical Research from 1969 to 1974. A fruitful disagreement between John and Mortimer over key issues in semiotics resulted in John going his own way in order to continue unhampered his investigations into the history of semiotics in the Middle Ages. "I am indebted to him and regret that unresolved differences of opinion between us about certain aspects of a theory that we otherwise share prevent him from associating his name with mine in the authorship of this book", wrote Adler in the preface to *Some Questions about Language: A Theory of Human Discourse and Its Objects* (Chicago: Open Court, 1976), which they had originally begun writing together in collaboration.

John continued his intense and innovative work in semiotics as he went on from Adler's Institute for Philosophical Research to work as full Professor at Loras College in Dubuque, Iowa (1976–1999). John's academic career had an international impact, as it was a career that included service as a Fulbright scholar-professor in Brazil (1988–1989), Mexico (1994–1995), and Bulgaria (2005). He was also a visiting scholar-professor at the University of Helsinki in Finland and at the University of Tartu in Estonia. As a founding member, John worked with Thomas Sebeok from the outset of the Semiotic Society of America in 1975, was involved in the drafting of its constitution, and has played a central role in its academic activity ever since, including much diligent work on its yearbook and journal.

ISSN 0277-7126
doi: 10.5840/ajs2016321/44

The American Journal of Semiotics 32.1–4 (2016), iii–v.

In 1999, John became a professor of philosophy at the Center for Thomistic Studies at the University of St. Thomas in Houston, Texas, and went on to hold the Rudman Chair of Graduate Philosophy there from 2007 to 2015. From 2015 to the time of his death, John was Philosopher in Residence at St. Vincent Archabbey College and Seminary in Latrobe, Pennsylvania, the oldest Benedictine institution in North America.

His books, over thirty in number, are complemented by over 200 articles and a number of book series that he edited. Two of his most important achievements, both produced at Loras College, are his bilingual edition of John Poinsot's *Tractatus de Signis*, which upon publication received the featured book review in *The New York Times* (Easter, 1986), and his *Four Ages of Understanding* (2001), which presents a full-scale demonstration of the centrality of the theory of signs to the history of philosophy, rigorously establishing a semiotic philosophical perspective for the twenty-first century.

As a philosopher, John developed this prospective semiotic viewpoint in the fertile soil of the Catholic intellectual tradition. The influence of Jacques Maritain was immense, not only in John's professional life, but also deeply within his personal life. His most treasured photograph was a picture of a very young John with Maritain himself. John was among the founding members of the American Maritain Association, of which he remained a devoted member throughout his life.

Most importantly, John met his wife Brooke Williams Deely, herself a noted Maritain scholar, at a meeting of the American Maritain Association. Throughout their married life, John and Brooke remained close collaborators in John's philosophical work. Brooke's devotion to John's vocation as a philosopher is a moving testimony to a wife's deep and mature love.

John's seminal legacy is his lifelong promotion of the works of John Poinsot (also known as John of St. Thomas) as an explicit link between Baroque Thomism and the current emerging worldview of semiotics. It is a legacy that ties John's efforts not only to the work of semioticians such as Charles S. Peirce and Thomas Sebeok, but also to the historic Benedictine Order. The Abbey of Solesmes is the publisher of the critical edition of Poinsot's writings. John's move near the end of his life to St. Vincent College and Seminary was an act that joined together both his devotion to Dominican scholasticism and the ancient Benedictine order. It thereby paralleled the intellectual-spiritual union of these two religious orders in the lives of St. Thomas Aquinas and

Jacques Maritain, himself a Benedictine Oblate for whom Poinsot was the Thomistic commentator with whom he fell in love.

Though aware of his own philosophical accomplishments, John did not desire to have his life trumpeted in a grand, eulogistic manner. When recently asked whom he would like to be his eulogist, he conceded only slight ground to the request—he desired his eulogist to be his faithful canine companion, Bruno. In response, Bruno is reportedly working with John and Brooke's other rescue dog, Bella, on the next translation of John's masterful introduction to semiotics, *Basics of Semiotics*, a foundational text which has been published around the world in nine different editions and translated from English into Portuguese, Romanian, Japanese, Spanish, Ukrainian, Italian, Estonian, Chinese, Russian, and French.

With contributions from an earlier obituary written by Gary Shank and published in the Greensburg Tribune Review *on Jan 12, 2017.*

Photo of John, 1989, when he was a Fulbright professor in Mexico.

TAJS 32.1–4 (2016)

CONTENTS

Special Issue:
SEMIOTIC ANIMAL

Richard Currie Smith, Guest Editor

Introduction by the Guest Editor

Richard Currie Smith

Case Western Reserve University and Kent State University

On a warm summer day in 2015, in the living room of John Deely and his wife Brooke's summer home in Dubuque, Iowa, I suggested that John's *semiotic animal* definition for humankind was the pinnacle expression and culmination of his prodigious work. I explained that I'd come to this conclusion after much reflection and through discussions I had with him intermittently for what was now over a decade. He responded, "And not the *Four Ages?*" in reference to his brilliant history of semiotics within the "great conversation" of Western philosophy beginning with the Greeks to the present. I responded that in my view as an ecological anthropologist the monumental book was only a precursor, as were all his other writings. Furthermore, I felt it was the semiotic animal for which he would be most remembered and that I had begun writing an article on my contention.

My wife Maggie and I departed later that afternoon, and while we were driving back to my family home in Sioux City I received a call from John on my cell phone. He said that he thought I may be on to something and wondered if I would consider being the guest editor of a special issue of *The American Journal of Semiotics* on the semiotic animal. My article would appear with other authors of my choosing that I thought would best contribute to the topic, and if I would like, he would assist me in acquiring some of the best semioticians in the world that he saw as ideal for the project. Moreover, the journal's highly accomplished managing editor, Chris Morrissey, if he agreed to the special issue project, would be there to offer advice. I enthusiastically agreed with Deely's proposal, as did Morrissey. The issue you are reading today is the result of Deely's vision.

To help place the readings included alphabetically in this special issue in context, I will briefly mention what led me that summer day to my assertions about the importance of the semiotic animal concept, and I will leave it to

ISSN 0277-7126

doi: 10.5840/ajs2016321/42

The American Journal of Semiotics 32.1–4 (2016), ix–xi.

my article to present the crux of the argument. Two major contentions that arose from my understanding and application of the complementary notions of Deely and that of the ecological and semiotic anthropologist Gregory Bateson underlay my valuation. First, after 350 years of ontological domination in Western culture by Descartes's inherently flawed *thinking thing* definition of human being, Deely's semiotic animal was the first truly worthy replacement. Secondly, the importance of this replacement to humanity and to life on earth as we know it is immense; its consequence frankly cannot be overstated. This is because while the thinking thing definition propelled modernity and its marvelous technological and scientific achievements around the world, its globalization also served to deleteriously frame the natural environment.

This flawed orientation toward the natural world included the indigenous, animistic, foraging members of our species that through an ontology embedded in nature had co-existed within their environments in an essentially sustainable fashion for 190,000 years. Our Paleolithic ancestors, as well as some in the Neolithic and Ancient eras, survived by developing intimate respectful relationships in varying degrees of consonance with the grand tapestry of diverse animals and plants in the ecosystems around the globe they inhabited.

Indigenous peoples' animistic relational ontology and their natural environments were not of value to modern thinking things; they were deemed as lesser, inherently unknowable, and expendable in the ineluctable march of material progress and planetary commodification. Framing traditional cultures, nature, and even humankind's "animal-like" bodies as adversaries to be controlled and dominated by our supreme rational intellect led to our present global materialistic monoculture, an epidemic of depressive and anxiety-related diseases, along with devastating climate change and massive biodiversity loss that threaten our species' very survival.

Deely's semiotic animal definition, on the other hand, while still incorporating the value of technological and scientific advance, replaces Descartes's thinking thing with a view of the human being as embedded like all other animals within the knowable semiotic or communicative matrix of life. For Deely, we have become semiotic animals through understanding that we are the only animal that is both engaged in sign production and interpretation while being aware of this process of semiosis, a process grounded upon the reality of relational being. Furthermore, along with being unique in our recently formed awareness of the semiotic processes of life comes an appreciation of our semioethical responsibility to the preservation and restoration of the natural environment.

Moreover, in writing the historical chronology for my article, I came to realize that Deely's semiotic animal was not only the culmination of his work, it was the culmination of 2500 years of semiotic development beginning with Hippocrates. *With the development of the semiotic animal as the apex of philosophy's long quest for wisdom, semiotics becomes the great conversation within the great conversation.* Finally, this development came when it was most needed and most able to be propagated through the global information network of the Internet, and even *as the thinking thing ushered in the Enlightenment and the Modern Age, so the semiotic animal ushers in the Semiotic Age to replace modernity.*

While this vision may seem too bold, the reader is asked to consider these possibilities when reflecting upon the following articles, which further clarify and operationalize the semiotic animal definition of human, for our species' sustainability crisis requires nothing less than inspired transformative insights.

From Maritain's Thoughts on the Micro-sign to the Science of Semiotics

Edward J. (Ted) Baenziger, CSB

University of St. Thomas

Abstract: Jacques Maritain's discussion of the micro-sign leads us to question how signs get interpreted, from the least to the most complex forms of communication, while John Deely's treatment of both cenoscopic and ideoscopic interpretation lies in the distinction between attraction, repulsion, and indifference. I add the key concept of inter-reaction, symbiosis, that allows for cooperation within and among all organisms. Using quantum physics and cathexis to delve the mystery of cellular sign values and beyond, we, the semiotic animal, better comprehend our own nature and that of the living world through semiotics.

Keywords: Cathexis, cell functions, cenoscopy, ideoscopy, Jacques Maritain, John Deely, micro-sign, quanta, semiotic animal, symbiosis

Seated beside the unlit fireplace, facing John Deely on a warm July evening in 2016, I asked about the photo of Jacques Maritain behind him, prominent among other important figures in his and Brooke's life. "Beatified soon," he said, eyes a-twinkle, "with Raïssa." The Deelys have a long history of admiration and respect for this French philosopher and his wife; John had met him as a young scholar, and Brooke had used Maritain's writings as the subject of her doctoral thesis.

From Deely to Maritain, from philosophy to genetics, let us stretch our minds to take in concepts not readily available to most of us. I propose we

ISSN 0277-7126

doi: 10.5840/ajs2016122818

Online First: December 29, 2016

The American Journal of Semiotics 32.1–4 (2016), 1–16.

look at the littlest of things and see a bigger picture. The paper is in three parts: the brief examination of a fascicule by Jacques Maritain, a discussion of some life forces as micro-signs, and a reconciliation of Deely's *Semiotic Animal* with cenoscopic and ideoscopic science.

Part One

First of all, there was my own project, to read and understand a text from Jacques Maritain that seemed arcane and private, an address he gave to the Little Brothers of Jesus in formation (referred to hereafter as the LBJ) in 1964.[1] In 1973, after Maritain's death, LBJ gave this pamphlet (sixteen pages in French) to a young professor named John Deely, who had made a visit to the then-Brother Jacques himself in 1972, and in the same House of Formation, at the end of the latter's life. When I borrowed the text, I read it but did not "get" what Maritain was saying. I had to translate it, carefully, in order to understand what was going on in the little speech he gave.[2]

Illustration 1: Here is Jacques Maritain in the 1970s;
he was 88 when he entered the Little Brothers of Jesus.

---

[1] All translations are mine. The text in English is twelve pages

[2] That translation was used in 2007, in a subsequent class for students to read, to explain to them what contemplation was and how it related to Maritain's concept of a micro-sign. Dr. Brooke Williams Deely and I were team-teaching this text in France. The course was concerned with semiotics and the science of signs. The same text also formed part of an address I made to the Maritain Association in 2008, as well as an article of hers (see Williams Deely 2013), entitled "Contemplation Overflowing the Roads of the World."

The reasoning he developed in his address was that the Little Brothers of Jesus were neither an active community, like diocesan priests, nor a sequestered group of cenobites, but religious who would wear no visible sign of their calling.[3] They would be in the world of non-believers, would work with and love them, and, he says, such a vocation was meant to be an invisible sign, so small it could not be seen, but which would bear fruit because of the care, the sharing that went into the life itself, while the brother remained deeply and calmly in the contemplative mode (i.e., all aspects of that life which lead to praying and adoring God in a different mode that the active life would seem to allow). Such contemplation takes a tremendous effort so that it is not a billboard but a micro-sign for others of God's love.[4]

Maritain's own project, summarized in the pamphlet and used on the LBJ's website[5] is the following: After the deaths of Raïssa and of her sister, Vera,[6] who lived with them, Jacques asked to be part of the group he had watched being formed some thirty years earlier. To be part of them, of course, was not to do their work but to be a humble brother himself, to live at the novitiate and take vows and live out the rest of his life in silence.[7] In his words:

> Frankly, isn't that the idea of following contemplative life in the world while not being of it that so enflamed Raïssa, Vera and me in the little flock we formed? These two women went right to the end of the road, in a complete gift of themselves, even to the pains of the Cross, while I just try to follow them, a craftsman of concepts, not bereft of talent maybe, which gives me a hypothetical basis for my (clumsy) living out of the thing. I believe they would approve my present decision freely taken, and that they will thank you so much more than I ever could to welcome me into your midst.

---

[3] They did have a habit, a uniform, in 1933, abandoned in favor of anonymous, ordinary dress (except in the monastery during prayer), after 1947.

[4] The interpretation is entirely mine. For another and better development of his ideas on contemplation, I strongly recommend the Brooke Williams Deely article (see note 2, above).

[5] **Little Brothers of Jesus**, founded in 1933, first superior was René Voillaume; Jacques Maritain knows of them from about 1934 (he is speaking in 1964). From Wikipedia: Their traditional habit was replaced with the appropriate plain clothes to help assimilate into their work and neighborhood roles. There are some 250 brothers in 40 different countries; See "https://en.wikipedia.org/w/index.php?title=Ren%C3%A9_Voillaume&action=edit&redlink=1"Voillaume

[6] Vera Ousmansoff (also spelled Ousmançoff, is his sister-in-law, born in 1886; baptized with Raïssa and Jacques in 1906; died in 1959).

[7] "J'ai une telle faim de silence." The word 'faim' is sometimes translated as 'thirst'; his word is 'hunger.' I translate it as "I am so starved for silence."

Illustration 2: Charles de Foucauld, René Voillaume,[8] and Jacques Maritain, from the website of the Little Brothers.

A few years prior to his becoming an LBJ himself, in December, 1964,[9] he spoke to the Brothers about their vocation, and the subtitles for his musings are very telling about how he saw these men:

1st section: The Two Meanings of the word "Apostolic".

2nd section: Living the Truth, and by this fact helping others to do it as well.

3rd section: Invisible witness, or nearly Invisible, and yet Visible.

4th section: The Immense Job for those who have nothing to do in the Church.

He is aiming at a semiotic meaning of the micro-sign, although he uses neither 'semiotics' nor 'semiosis' or any of its variables to get to his point. He references physics and psychology. On the scientific level he talks of the subconscious, hidden passages of the soul,[10] and micro-particles, the stuff of quantum physics. In each of the ten times he uses the term "micro-," he

---

[8] Charles de Foucauld (blessed) (1858 September 15—1 December 1916 [ca.]), Trappist from 1890—1897; hermit in the Holy Land, 1897–1900; ordained at Notre-Dame des Neiges in the Ardèche, summer of 1899; in Béni Abbès, Algeria 1901–1904, he builds a monastery but no-one joins him; friend of the Tuaregs at Tamanrasset, 1904–1916, not a single convert. On the first of December, 1916, he is assassinated. *René Voillaume* (1905 July 19–13 May 2003) founder of the Petits Frères de Jésus in 1933 (following the rule of Blessed Charles de Foucault, +1916); the Fraternity of Jesus Caritas in 1952, a secular institute; then founder of the Petites Sœurs de l'Évangile in 1963.

[9] "After living with the Little Brothers for nine years [as a teacher of philosophy], Jacques asked to be admitted to their Fraternity", Williams Deely 2013: 15.

[10] The soul is not an "unnatural" part of the human person, but constitutive. As for the subconscious, it forms part of our nature; he uses the example of subliminal advertising using "small unnoticed insinuations," which practice has become illegal in most countries, but which is quite effective, and insidious.

deepens the understanding: invisible, almost non-existent, but making a difference in the world. Philosophically, he ties it to love and to theological processes which I will not develop here, including the idea that one can be saved and still be a non-believer (in Christ, I mean; but the extension goes beyond that). He finds that the Brothers' vocation is to love: "To do this not using any large[r], visible means, but rather through the invisible or nearly invisible method of simple fraternal presence among the poor and abandoned." Further on:

> This witnessing comes about through signs—but by infinitely small signs, passing, imperceptible things which are written on the subconscious more than on the conscious mind. A look, a gesture, a friendly smile, and even less than that, a certain manner of listening or of paying attention to this or that, what we could call micro-signs. (Maritain 1964: 8)

Note here that the sign itself has no size, being immaterial, so that, strictly speaking all signs are the same size. He reduces the *size* of the *evidence* of the sign in perception ("infinitely"), and finds its importance in "infinitesimal things" that amount to an "aura" of contemplative love ... "micro-signs of redemptive love" (ibid.: 9). This effect, though, is not through willing or intending to create an impression; he says these are existential signs, resembling the signs that God places throughout creation to hint at, to indicate his existence: "being there, *Dasein*, existing with the people, with [ordinary] men and women" (ibid.)

From a website about the Little Brothers of Jesus we learn: "Before all projects, before all plans, before all works and actions is **being**. Being comfortable and alive in Christ interiorly (and exteriorly); being with and existing with others exteriorly (and interiorly)."[11] From the life of Charles de Foucauld, the thought of Maritain, and the very existence of the LBJ, we learn that relationships, at the hidden core of the self, manifest themselves imperceptibly. The authors continue:

> One of the greatest and longest reflections Jacques Maritain made in his life was on the place of the values, hidden within us, which manifest themselves externally, though perhaps in masked ways. It's not that the "interior life" is unmanifest on the outside. It is manifest, but it is manifest first as being, not as doing or planning or acting. With regards to contemplation itself this is true: Contemplation ... is frequently the treasure of persons hidden in the world ... souls who live by it in all simplicity, without visions, without miracles, but with such a flame of love for God and neighbour that good happens all around them without noise and without agitation.

---

[11] This and the following are taken from https://contemplativein themud.wordpress.com/2014/09/29before-all-else-being/ accessed September 25, 2015.

Contemplation, as an activity of the entire person, is present in many, if not all cultures; in India, Japan, Morocco, Russia, etc., but what it is exactly cannot be described merely as an inner conversation. It is both an awareness and a forgetting of self, a seeking within for that which transcends, the Other in its very nature, outside and yet intimately joined to the one who contemplates. Whether in the temple of the spirit or in that of nature, this process goes beyond analysis or deduction to attempt union, communion, erasing boundaries. Even so, contemplation is not, strictly speaking, either active or passive since it seeks while not moving as such, demanding concentration along with abandon. Maritain uses contemplation in a Christian context and regards it as transformative in his own life with Raïssa and Vera, and for the Brothers, in the tradition of the Christian mystics throughout the ages. What he brings to the table is this curious concept of micro-sign, something so tiny it is not seen, as a result of contemplation, a left-over as it were, or a surplus, an aura.

Part Two

Maritain's musings and those of the Brothers give us pause and lead me to present a plan of smallness, on a logarithmic scale, that I borrow from a book (Montenat et al. 1994) about the origin of life and its relationship to God's existence: *Pour lire la création dans l'évolution*, in which the authors examine objects from what can barely be seen (100 μm, [micrometers]), down to the invisible molecule of water, 1 angstrom unit: Å, below the threshold of life (see plate at end of main text).

Going from what can be seen to the realm of the unseen and unknown leads us to some interesting observations. On the one hand the smallest piece of life is either the cell or the virus, depending on what defines life; on the other, the smallest piece of information defined is the bit, four of which constitute a byte, infamous in computer circles. The bit is either on or off, although in quantum computers (can we call them the "wave" of the future?), the bit can be on or off or in between. In either case, the smallest is the key to all information and to all life, yet it is invisible to our sight, a micro-sign that comes to us through both ideoscopic and cenoscopic reality.[12]

---

[12] Deely 2007: 86: "Cenoscopy *precedes* but does not *supplant* ideoscopy" (italics are his). The distinction between that which is known through instruments and measurements (the sciences of today's STEM systems), namely cenoscopy, and that which is known through human experience and thought, (philosophy, logic, the premises of science) are inseparable, indeed essential to each other. For instance, the scientific community depends upon the work of others, previous to, but useful for, further exploration. A scientist must have faith in what has been accepted by the community of scientists (although calling it into question is a healthy

Here I would like to invoke John Deely, Brooke's husband, who resorts to mathematic notation, asserting that life proceeds this way: $(+)$, $(-)$, and (0), where plus $(+)$ indicates that which is desirable, either as food or sexual partner, while the negative $(-)$ is that which is to be avoided as a rival for either one or the antagonist that can eat me.[13] John adds the "0" to indicate that which may be safely ignored, indifferent to one's existence, having nothing to do with $-$ or $+$. Of course these categories can change according to the circumstances in the *umwelt* of any creature and a plus or a zero can become a definite and fatal minus. Indeed, if the creature makes a mistake in the calculation—for example, if the predator is sufficiently camouflaged and the prey does not see it—it may mean death. For the purposes of this discussion and for the fact of life in general, I add another symbol, plus AND minus: $(\pm)$, which indicates an essential part of all life. Far from being avoidance or attraction or simple indifference, life as we know it cannot exist without an interaction between organisms that do not involve either death $(-)$ or food and sex $(+)$ or lack of interest (0), but co-existence, an inter-reaction: $(\pm)$.

To illustrate this relativity in life, I present to you the cell. Prokaryotes are cells that have the DNA and RNA (sometimes only RNA) present in an undifferentiated mass in the cell, called a nucleoid; they are all unicellular and they reproduce usually by budding division, at an incredibly fast pace. In layman's terms, these are "microbes," that is, very small pieces of life, which cause infection, such as the flu or polio. Independent, they may create colonies and sense each other, and they are prey to many enemies, but they interpret their environment through their chemistry and their interior structure, which is very complex indeed. These include the two domains of *Archaea* and *Bacteria*.

Eukaryotes are cells that contain a nucleus (already a sort of symbiotic relationship), in which communication (exchange of signs) must be ongoing; but these cells also contain mitochondria, assisting in the respiration and other vital functions of the cell. The relation of these parts forms the base for all multicellular organisms, from yeast to right whale. Without the clear differentiation of these elements within the cell, most unicellular and all multicellular organisms would be incapable of exchanging and, as a

---

exercise, because reproducibility is vital to the scientific structure). We may conclude that scientific investigation is fundamentally *semiotic*, and I will develop the theme further in this paper.

[13] Personal communication with the author, who tells me his schema is not original except in the latter part, although the formula is found in Deely 2007: 66ff. in the discussion on the *quo / quod* fallacy, as well as in *Semiotic Animal* (2010): 94ff.

result, of storing information, except in the most basic of RNA and DNA functioning. As it is, the genetic information is NOT the organism, but the foundation of what is called the phenotype, the individual organism with all its originality and quirks.

Plant Cell Anatomy

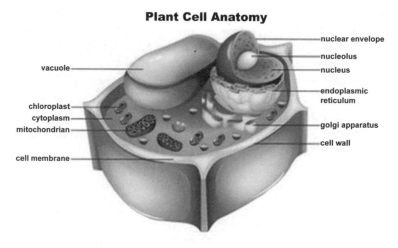

Illustration 3: The eukaryote cell (in a plant).

Let us return, briefly, to macro-reality. Semiotics needs the scientific method to prove that it (the science of the study of signs) is not an addendum to this reality but an integral part of the functioning of this (±) relationship: each part communicating by signs with the other, thereby making up a whole which functions as an individual exactly through the plus (+) by giving up some of its autonomy and, through the minus (−), by gaining an ability to reproduce and giving to the whole another positive aspect. Society, communication, the functioning of human communities all depend upon this give and take.

We know that, in the case of chlorophyll, chloroplasts have (pre-)historically come from elsewhere (probably photosynthetic bacteria that have become integral parts of plants), ceding their independence to become part of a larger, more productive whole. Interdependence is central to life as we know it. These relationships are of many types, from external attachment and little or no relation, to invasion and death through internal dissolution of the host; however, the most common form of relationship, and one essential for life, is the symbiotic pathway in which each organism gains and loses some function, thus the (±). The internal workings of eukaryote cells show at least three, and indeed many more, combinations; at the most primitive level it means that the nucleus, with its double membrane separating it from the cytoplasm, is a modified remnant of a previously independent organism that can no longer live outside of the cell, but which now co-directs the cell's functions. Add to this the mitochondria and other organelles in the cytoplasm and we have a community of survivors communicating and reproducing more or less in concert with the nucleus. This interaction is called *mutualism*, a cooperative activity that all life shares, even non-eukaryotic cells like virus and bacteria. The key to our understanding here is that mutualism is not the exception but the basis for cellular and intercellular relationships, and that the functions of life demand cooperation, that all life is semiosic, exchanging (triadic) signs.[14]

One case in point, one that drives all animal life, is the plant's production of food for itself and others (willingly or not, in the latter case). The complex chemical nature of the "machine"[15] that produces sugar on which most life of the planet depends (ourselves included, and all animals, and most of the fungi, bacteria and virus that we know, but not all) is called the chlorophyll (or Calvin[16]) cycle; and I propose we look more closely at the role of the micro-sign in that very process.

Plants are marvelous machines that use quantum mechanics in the most surprising ways. The chlorophyll molecule is the result of an ancient (3-billion-year?[17]) relationship that uses and measures the action of the particles called photons as well as the wave phase of light, thus both quantum forms. First, a little quantum theory can go a long way to help us understand. Light is both a wave and a particle, but we cannot measure the one without losing the information on the other, although we can prove that light acts in distinct "minimal packages" called quanta (singular quantum) = photons. Once we know the wave-length, the photon is no longer there. Once we see the results of the photon, the wave is gone; we cannot have both, according to quantum

---

[14] Cf. Zehr 2015: 1163–1164: "Symbiotic interactions are fundamental to life on Earth and were critical for the evolution of organelles that led to the success of eukaryotes on the planet. Such mutualistic interactions between unicellular micro-organisms and multicellular plants are pervasive in natural and agricultural ecosystems." The article then talks about acquiring endosymbionts (living parts "inside" the cell), and how it happens [including the science upholding the concept of (±)].

[15] Of course the cell is self-repairing and self-reproducing, which no machine can do, but alas, the mechanistic view of life prevails, even among the scientific community, with its reductionist tendencies.

[16] The process is named for Melvin Calvin, a chemistry professor in California, who received a Nobel for his work.

[17] **3.4 billion years ago**—First photosynthetic bacteria; **1.2 billion years ago**—Red and brown algae; *0.475 billion years ago*—First land plants, mosses and liverworts, according to *Scientific American*, April 7 2008.

mechanics (again that word "mechanics"), yet light has both properties, as seen in photosynthesis. With complex chemical and physical analysis, scientists have shown that the chloroplast receives enzymes and proteins from the nucleus, the cytoplasm and the Golgi bodies to produce a hypersensitive compound that reacts to light with an extremely high efficiency. As the photon strikes a portion of the chlorophyll molecule it is stored or transferred as energy, which has three possible effects: either the energy is transferred to phosphorescence (rare here, but existent in some fungi[18]), which is re-emitted light; or storage of the energy in the chlorophyll as heat; or thirdly, and most commonly, passage of the energy into an electron in a neighboring molecule pushing it a higher 'excited' state, which in turn will produce sugar.

In the third case, the action is to fix and reduce carbon dioxide (CO_2 with exterior energy, namely light) in an anaerobic environment (no oxygen, please!), which creates the base for sugars (CH_2O) + two byproducts: $O_2 + H_2O$. The source for this energy $E = hv$, is of course light, where Energy is the result of two factors: h, Planck's constant[19] ($6.62607004 \times 10^{-34} \, m^2 \, kg/s$) multiplied by v, (the letter "nu" in Greek) equal to the speed of light divided by the wavelength, which is the frequency of the radiation. Blue light has the most energy, highest frequency, while the far red end of the spectrum has much less. Photosynthetic plants use both ends, while reflecting most of the inefficient color back to the atmosphere, which is why most plants appear to us as various shades of green. The interesting part of this process, for our understanding, is that the plant chloroplast contains filters and pigments to capture the light quanta and transform the energy into food. For the rest of the action and reaction, I refer the reader to an excellent source,[20] but the reader may go to Wikipedia for a rather good summary.[21]

---

[18] *Armillaria mellea* (the honey mushroom) is only one of some eighty species of fungus that provide light, most likely from ingesting plant material, especially lignin. The purpose for luminescence is poorly understood. Wikipedia 2015: [https://en.wikipedia.org/wiki/List_of_bioluminescent_fungi [accessed Oct. 12], gives the figure 520–530 nm for the wavelength. From my personal experience (in a walk-in refrigerator, with some students), the light is greenish, and steady in living material. Another study underway is focusing on the phosphorescent stage of photosynthesis, dim as it is, to measure the level of activity of plants in remote areas, by satellite.

[19] Max Planck is the father of quantum physics. His constant is the size of one quantum, and his discovery revolutionized physics, as well as inspired the young Albert Einstein to ponder light and gravity together.

[20] Buchanan et al. 2000, Chapter 12: 568ff, is written by Richard Malkin and Krishna Niyogi (Department of Plant and Microbial Biology, University of California at Berkeley). My interest is, of course, orchids, whose photosynthesis is described (in most cases) as CAM photosynthesis, or Crassulacean Acid Metabolism, not germane to our discussion here, but following the same principles.

[21] https://en.wikipedia.org/wiki/Photosynthesis.

Even more interesting is the fact that plants can *sense* how much energy is being used, the periodicity (day-night quotients), the quantities of light and the wavelengths received, and from this *information* they create more or less of the pigments and multiply or subtract chloroplasts to respond. There is indeed signaling by micro-sign going on here and, in effect, the plant is reading both the wavelengths and the particles on a quantum level through the results it obtains. Even more amazing is that "within several picoseconds of the initial charge separation event of photosynthesis, the light energy conversion reaction is complete and chemical products have been formed" (Buchanan et al.: 585). What is a picosecond? An *extremely* small amount of time: 10^{-12} or $1/_{1,000,000,000,000}$ of one second.[22] Just to hammer the point home, the plant's chlorophyll can produce ~20 billion reactions in a single second, and can do so with an efficiency that surpasses any nerve or muscle activity (nearly 100%).[23] How can a plant "sense" this reaction? By its result, i.e., the amount of product released, a stream of information is recorded in the chemistry of the cells themselves, and serves to signal other functions in other parts of the cell that are also semi-independent, such as the Golgi apparatus (which produces the pigments and the energy transforming enzymes); the mitochondria (needed to get rid of the oxygen, poisonous to the chloroplasts); and the nucleus. To make the chlorophyll and the other pigments (including carotenes, which make carrots orange and maple leaves red) takes longer, of course, and the plant's growth goes so slowly in general that we cannot see it (another micro-sign), but the fact remains that the activity, invisible to us, is going on and changes the world around it.

The micro-sign, as we have seen, is also information, the smallest particle of which is the bit, that is, the smallest vehicle for information exchange, and thus, for us the smallest "sign" possible. Not the same as changing a letter in 'read' to 'red', this sign is analogous on a much reduced scale (again, that logarithmic measurement!).[24] If there is a theory of information that holds water, as it were, it must account for the transfer of this information by signs,

---

[22] https://en.wikipedia.org/wiki/Picosecond.

[23] Malkin and Niyogi (see above, note 20), p. 574, give what they call the quantum yield, dividing the number of products formed photo-chemically by the number of quanta absorbed $(= \Phi)$. $\Phi = 1.0$ indicates *every* absorbed photon is converted. Under optimum conditions it approaches 1.0, or 100%.

[24] DNA is so large a molecule but still invisible, that, unfolded, it would stretch longer than a football field. Of course it is packaged in the most ingenious way, twisted and folded, wound up and protected, destined to be ripped apart by subtle changes inside the cell and reproduced at 99.99% accuracy by RNA. It is at the same time a) the memory of past development, b) the blueprint for proteins of life and c) the source for new individuals or phenotypes. It is NOT the selfish gene that some would like, for it contains—but is not limited to—genes; it is the sign of life itself (it is a very stable compound, and we can "read" it thousands of years after it

not as noise (for noise destroys meaning), but as discrete quanta that carry meaning from a source (emitter), by a vehicle, that is interpreted by a third. Although unseen, or just barely perceived, the sign-vehicle is still enough to change the third's existence, through an immaterial relationship that we call semiosis.

I believe that here I am approaching unorthodoxy in semiotic circles when I talk of quanta, but is it not inescapable when we talk of impossible small things (micro- or pico-signs), and when we reach an irreducible quantity of information? Think of the smallest triangle possible, then think of it as immaterial, and then have it carry information that makes a difference. This is quantum semiosis, and it occurs every day that life continues, in every one of our billions of cells that make up our bodies.

Part Three

What has this quantum biology got to do with us, since it is hidden from our sight by its infinitesimal nature? Precisely because we are semiotic animals it makes all the difference in the world. Although Deely refuses to talk about phyto-semiosis in *Semiotic Animal*,[25] he does state that "animals are, along with plants, and nature itself, semiosic in being" (2010: 105); thus, semiotics needs the scientific method in order to understand life itself. As a science (of the action of signs), it must do so, not in a reductive sense, that is. In a mechanistic fashion, removing all responses of the organism and making it a machine, but in a truly semiotic manner, seeing the sign relationships through both the philosophical (cenoscopic) and brute observational (ideoscopic) methods. Here we must introduce another concept, that of cathexis to understand how the information can take place in a non-sentient being.

Very simply, cathetic relation is one of nearly immediate stimulus/response. In the case of many beings it is mediated by nerves or ganglia, as in the case of the "knee-jerk" that comes from striking just the right spot on a person's knee, a reflex. The mind, conscious or not, has nothing to do with the matter: it is the direct action of a force producing a response of muscle and nerve. In the case of beings without nerves, however, such as protozoa or bacteria or plants in general, the pathways are chemical, even to a quantum level, and do not depend on any network of organs that resemble nerves. Reflexes without appeal to a "nervous system" are called cathetic and do indeed take the stimulus as a meaning and react to the signal. As a result,

---

has ceased to be in a living creature). DNA is not alive, but it is that upon which multicellular life depends.
[25] Deely 2010: 95.

our equation of $(+)$, $(-)$ (0) and $(\pm)$ describes a semiosic process that can be rational, although rarely, but need not be more than cathetic. For example, we have a relationship in our inner organs through the biome, that allows us to digest certain foods and to resist other invasive organisms, above and beyond our biological immune system in the blood. Unaware of this colonization, but explicated to us through both cenoscopic and ideoscopic examination, we. as semiotic animals, come to understand the inner workings of the marvels of interaction and intercommunication, through signs, small as they might be. The Calvin cycle, using quantum mechanics and complex enzymes, an array of tubing and sophisticated assembly, is but one vital example of the cathetic mode of semiosis. In turn, says Deely,[26] these various modes of knowing are precursors that gave rise to zoösemiosis, which "makes possible in the first place anthroposemiosis as a *further* development species-specific in type—including those bodily modes without which anthroposemiosis would collapse like a house of cards, fall as flat as a balloon without air." Our civilization falls flat on its face without food, yet all our food comes (directly or indirectly) from solar energy transformed by lowly plants, who harness the quanta of the heavens through micro-signs.

To be sure, everything is based on physics, the interaction of mass and velocity, the quanta of existence; just as everything depends upon chemistry, the interaction of very small and very large molecules; just as everything depends upon biology, for if there is no life, there is no understanding of the two former 'sciences,' and no one to ask questions about them. On another level, everything anthroposemiotic then depends upon *ethos*, the basis for culture, for without that we have no means of communicating; and, finally, everything anthroposemiotic depends upon spirit, which cannot be independent of all the others, but is of a different order. Immaterial spirit (as real as the persons we are and those we grow to love) leads us to question the universe and interpret the answers as meaningful signs, for we are semiotic *by our very nature*. This latter aspect leads us to contemplation of the extent and meaning of the semiotic web that is life itself, and beyond.

The micro-sign can help us pursue that investigation, even if it is invisible, for we can delve into the "infinitely small" through physics and chemistry and biology, and by using them wisely, arrive at a better understanding of our world and of ourselves as semiotic animal.

---

[26] Deely 2010: 105.

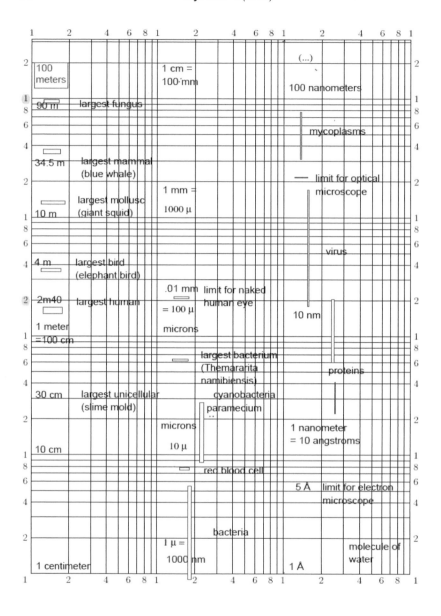

Logarithmic 3 cycles A4

Plate 1: A logarithmic scale of largest to smallest, from seen to unseen, from sign to micro-sign, to be read starting from the left, top to bottom, then the center, then the far right:

References

[All illustrations and the model for the logarithmic scale are in the public domain]

BUCHANAN, Bob B., Wilhelm GRUISSEM, and Russell L. JONES, Editors.
    2000. *Biochemistry and Molecular Biology of Plants* (Rockville, MD: The American Society of Plant Physiologists, 2000).

CALVIN, Melvin.
    1961. "The Path of Carbon in Photosynthesis", http://www.nobelprize.org/nobel_prizes/chemistry/laureates/1961/calvin-lecture.pdf, accessed Oct. 20, 2015. [His Nobel Lecture, December 11, 1961].

CALVIN, Melvin, and A. A. BENSON.
    1948. "The Path of Carbon in Photosynthesis" (Radiation Laboratory and Department of Chemistry, University of California, Berkeley). *Science* 107.2784 (May 7): 476–480.
    doi: https://doi.org/10.1126/science.107.2784.476

DEELY, John N.
    2007. *Intentionality and Semiotics: A Story of Mutual Fecundation (Approaches to Postmodernity) as told by John Deely* (Scranton and London: University of Scranton Press).
    2010. *Semiotic Animal: A Postmodern Definition of "Human Being" Transcending Patriarchy and Feminism* (South Bend, IN: St. Augustine's Press 2010).

MARITAIN, Jacques.
    1964. "A Propos de la Vocation des Petites Frères de Jesus", December 14, 1964, in René Page, [Prieur des Petits Frères de Jesus], 1973, "Introduction" to the fascicule published shortly after the death of Maritain, April 28, 1973, consisting of the following: Page's introduction "Frere Jacques Maritain (18.11.1882–28.4.1973)," pp. 1–3; remarks by Fr. Marie Michel Labourdette, O.P., from a conference at the Institut Catholique de Toulouse, dated 13.6.1973; a "Lettre de Jacques aux Frères" on the occasion of becoming himself one of the Little Brothers, dated July, 1970, p. 9; "Un mot du prieur, Frere René Page," accompanying the letter, p. 10; and concluding with Jacques' writing "A Propos de la Vocation des Petites Frères de Jesus," December 14, 1964.

MARITAIN, Raïssa.
    1921. *De mœurs divines* (Paris: Librairie de l'Art catholique).
    1949. *Les Grandes Amitiés*, coll. "Livre de vie" (Paris: Desclée de Brouwer, 1949).
    1962. *Journal de Raïssa* (Paris: Desclée de Brouwer). [published posthumously by permission of her husband, Jacques Maritain].
    2000. *Extraits des Grandes amitiés, de Raïssa Maritain* (Parole et Silence), "La vocation chrétienne est une vocation contemplative." http://www.croire.

com/Definitions/Vie-chretienne/Jacques-et-Raissa-Maritain/Textes-de-Raissa-Maritain, accessed Oct. 12, 2015.

MONTENAT, Christian, Luc PLATEAUX, and Pascal ROUX.
  1994.   *Pour lire la création dans l'évolution* (Paris: Les Editions du Cerf). [Èd. revue et augmentée]; 1st edition translated into English: *How to Read the World: Creation in Evolution* (Broché, 1985).

PAGE, René.
  1973.   "Prieur des Petits Frerès de Jesus." ["Introduction" to the fascicule published shortly after the death of Maritain, April 28, 1973; see above for Jacques Maritain].

PLANCK, Max.
  1900.   "Über eine Verbesserung der Wienschen Spektralgleichung". *Verhandlungen der Deutschen Physikalischen Gesellschaft* 2: 202–204; trans. D. ter Haar, "On an Improvement of Wien's Equation for the Spectrum," in *The Old Quantum Theory* (PDF) (Oxford: Pergamon Press, 1967), 79–81.

VOILLAUME, René.
  2005.   Entretiens sur la vie religieuses (Paris: Éditions du Cerf).

WIKIPEDIA.
  2015.   https://en.wikipedia.org/wiki/Photosynthesis
  2015a.   https://en.wikipedia.org/wiki/Picosecond
  2015b.   Association Famille Spirituelle Charles de Foucauld: http://www.charlesdefoucauld.org/fr/biographie.php, accessed Nov. 20.
  2015c.   Little Brothers of Jesus: From Wikipedia https://en.wikipedia.org/wiki/Little_Brothers_of_Jesus

WILLIAMS DEELY, Brooke.
  2013.   "Contemplation Overflowing the Roads of the World: Love and Friendship in the Lives of Jacques and Raïssa Maritain," in *Love and Friendship: Maritain and the Tradition*, ed. Montague Brown, American Maritain Association (distributed by the Catholic University of America Press, Washington DC), 3–19.

ZEHR, Jonathan P.
  2015.   "How Single Cells Work Together," *Science* 11 (September): 1163–1164.

The Unleashing of John Deely's "Semiotic Animal"

W. John Coletta
University of Wisconsin-Stevens Point

Seema Ladsaria
ISM Dhanbad

Dylan Couch
University of Wisconsin-Stevens Point

Abstract: Our purpose in this essay is twofold: to explore John Deely's "semiotic" or "contextualized animal" as also a "contextualizing animal", one that not only responds in context but one that changes first the context so as later to change itself—as all living things do; and to explore how this context-shifting "semiotic animal" has caused to emerge the very "signs upon which", as Deely writes, "the whole of life depends". Environmental ethics are inseparable from personal ethics, then, because (1) we are in fact ourselves environments for others, (2) we carry models of our environments within us (our genetic/ontogenetic selves), and (3) even our free will (the basis of ethical choice) is an "environmental" phenomenon, as Martin Heisenberg argues in *Nature* (14 May 2009: 164–165) and as Deely writes in *Semiotic Animal*: "signs do not fall strictly among the things objectified by perceptions of sense *but act prior to* that perception to enable it to reconstruct the physical environment along objective lines that are meaningful to the species" (*Semiotic Animal: A Postmodern Definition of Human Being Transcending Patriarchy and Feminism* [2010]: 119).

Keywords: Semiotic animal, semioethic animal, environmental ethics, Deely, Peirce, Petrilli

John Deely's "semiotic animal", as Deely himself writes, "displaces Descartes's notion of the isolated thinker with a contextualized animal whose behavior is distinctive in the realization that there are signs upon

ISSN 0277-7126

doi: 10.5840/ajs2016122817

Online First: December 29, 2016

The American Journal of Semiotics 32.1–4 (2016), 17–34.

which the whole of life depends for successful continuance" (2005: 156–157). Our purpose in this essay, then, is twofold: (1) to explore Deely's "contextualized animal" as also a "contextualizing animal", one that not only responds in context but one that, like the shape-shifter-character of science fiction that changes the context by changing first itself, changes first the context so as later to change itself—as all living things do; and (2) to explore how this context-shifting has caused to emerge the very "signs upon which", as Deely writes, "the whole of life depends". Indeed, the "semiotic animal", as we will show, is such a powerful "shape-shifting" formulation that it transforms (by increasing the spheres of relevance) everything it encounters, including, as we demonstrate, the Ten Commandments, allowing us to see them as always already a list of "signs upon which the whole of life depends". In this way, Deely's "semiotic animal" becomes, in Susan Petrilli's terms, the "semioethic animal" (2005); as such, Deely's "semiotic animal" is an example of, we would argue, Charles Sanders Peirce's Final Interpretant, which thereby evinces that kind of "final causation" "whereby the whole calls out its parts" (*Collected Papers* [CP] 1902: I.220). Or, we might say, whereby the *ecological* whole calls out its *sustainable* parts. As such, the "semiotic animal" is both contextualized and contextualizing, as it provides an interpretive context within which all around us, including the Ten Commandments, suddenly grow to have larger meanings. "Symbols [including that symbol of symbols, the Ten Commandments] grow", as Peirce tells us.

This essay, then, will offer a list of *Eleven Semioethic Directives*, as we dub them, with a conscious nod both to Buckminster Fuller's *Operating Manual for Spaceship Earth* (1968) and the "Prime Directive" of *Star Trek*. This list of "signs upon which the whole of life depends for successful continuance" may be seen, again, as an *interpretation* of, as an unleashing of, the always already latent potential of, in fact a celebration of the fecundity of, the Ten Commandments—that "living" compendium of *argumentative symbolic legisigns*. Such an interpretation is what Crystal Downing calls, in *Changing Signs of Truth: A Christian Introduction to the Semiotics of Communication*, the "resigning" (as in "resigned" to the "re-signing" or "re-assigning") of the Word, which is, of course, the very genius and "Spirit" of the "Word" (2012: 22–34). Thus, for example, in the context of Deely's "semiotic animal" and Susan Petrilli's "semioethic animal", "Thou shall not steal" clearly includes not merely refraining from, say, convenience store hoists or from stealing lunch money from your fellow students but also refraining from stealing (say by "assigning" nuclear waste with a half-life of hundreds of thousands of year to a native American reservation) from our children's children's children …, the proverbial "seventh generation", after which Iroquois concept a line of sustainable household products is named. Therefore, "Thou shalt not steal" may be interpreted to be, via Deely's "semiotic animal", a sign "upon which the whole of life depends for successful continuance". Or "Thou shalt not make unto thee any graven image, or any likeness *of any thing* that *is* in heaven above, or that *is* in the earth beneath, or that *is* in the water under the earth" could be interpreted (i.e., "re-assigned") as also (because the old value may still hold as well) a prohibition regarding genetically modified food (GMOs). The question is, how and to what extent and in what way do Deely's "semiotic animal" and Petrilli's "semioethic animal" condition such re-assigning, such re-contextualizing? That is, how do symbols grow? What governs the telos of "changing signs of truth"? We must ask these questions, because surely Deely's "semiotic animal" inaugurates a new age.

The cultural work that Deely's and Petrilli's semiotic-semioethic animal does, its power to re-assign the "signs of truth", derives from what we are calling "The Semioethic-Animal Principle", which principle, in fact, we have merely deduced from the work of Deely and Petrilli to begin with! First, the principle in its entirety; then we shall take up its elements one by one:

THE SEMIOETHIC-ANIMAL PRINCIPLE: CONCERNING HOW THE (Ecological) WHOLE OF THE "SEMIOTIC ANIMAL" CALLS OUT ITS (Sustainable) PARTS:

(1) Environmental ethics are personal ethics, and that is because **(2) we are in fact ourselves environments for others,** and because **(3) we carry models of our environments within us (our DNA), models that represent us as indexical signs of the very environments that we hope will interpret us into our shared future** ("the word or sign that man uses is the man himself" [Peirce]), and because **(4) even free will (the basis of ethical choice) is an "environmental" phenomenon,** as the benefit to individuals of an *environmental* advantage over *other* individuals led to an early emergence of a physiological strategy that privileges "behavioral output" over of "sensory input", a privileging that, according to Martin Heisenberg, is the neurological basis of "free will" (2009: 164–165) (as Deely writes, "signs do not fall strictly among the things objectified by perceptions of sense *but act prior to* that perception to enable it to reconstruct the physical environment along objective lines that are meaningful to the species" [2010: 119]).

By way of explanation, let us take each term of the principle in turn:

THE SEMIOETHIC-ANIMAL PRINCIPLE: CONCERNING HOW THE (ecological) WHOLE OF THE "SEMIOTIC ANIMAL" CALLS OUT ITS (sustainable) PARTS:

(1) Environmental ethics are in fact personal ethics

As John Deely writes in "Defining the Semiotic Animal", "whatever we are aware of, insofar as we are aware of it, is internal to our consciousness, not external to it. … The very idea of an 'external world' as modernity had proposed it soon enough manifested itself, to the eyes of inquirers into the action of signs, as a quasi-error, … a blunder *ab initio*" (2005: 147). Deely continues to show, in language that unites philosophy, literary criticism, and ecology, how the modernist logic of separation represents a naïve and scientifically inaccurate approach to understanding the organism-environment relationship, a naïve and inaccurate approach that has led most of us to believe that there is "an Environment" to which we adapt ourselves rather than environments being understood as individually inherited artifactual models of species-specific historically successful modes of living. As Deely writes in *The Semiotic Animal: A Postmodern Definition of Human Being Transcending Patriarchy and Feminism*, semiotics "recovers the *ens reale* insisted upon as knowable by scholastic realism; yet, at the same time, semiotics demonstrates the objectivity of *ens rationis* in the social construction of species-specific realities among biological organisms" (2010: 102 [emphasis added]). Indeed, Deely may be the first philosopher to provide an evolutionarily and ecologically accurate ontological basis for human "being in the world". In addition, Deely succeeds in outlining the ontology and epistemology of a true postmodern ecology. Thus, "Semiotics achieves not a return but an advance, the opening of a new era of intellectual culture […] for science and the humanities, wherein the split between nature and culture, inner and outer, self and other, is no longer the last word, because the quasi-fallacy of the external world has finally been laid to rest" (Deely 2010: 102).

Not only does Deely deconstruct the self-other binary looking outward from the individual to the whole of which it is a part, the outer Other; through his reference to endosemiotics, Deely also deconstructs the logic of the self-other binary by looking to our *inner* Other. As Deely writes, "Endosemiotics" is the study of organisms "whose maintenance of self-identity as individual substances depends intimately on our hosting of colonies and varieties of other organisms within our very bodies" (2010: 112). Here we find that the "ecology" within functions as a veritable second genome without. Indeed, a whole range of Peircean community-based ritualized habits (see the list below) shows the extent to which the "intimate hosting" that Deely mentions is inseparable from our so-called personal identity. Of course, as Peirce writes, "a person is not absolutely an individual" (CP 5.314). Note how in all of the following, the unstated implication is of our *constitution in community*; indeed, as Peirce writes, "[T]hat every thought is an external sign, proves that man is an external sign" (1868: 54), constituted by "COMMUNITY" (1868: 52). Thus, for example, (1) in drinking-cup sharing rituals, even / especially during the sacrament of the Eucharist, "spit is swapped" and microbes are communally shared; thus, when Deely speaks of "intimate hosting", we cannot help but think of the Holy Host—and thus the connection between hosting the Spirit and microbial hosting—or of Jacques Derrida's exploration of the host-hostile-hospitality semantic spectrum. As Downing writes, "True hospitality occurs when one welcomes in the allergens of society. Derrida thus echoes the teaching of Jesus: 'When you give a luncheon or a dinner, do not invite your friends or your brothers or your relatives or rich neighbors. ... But when you give a banquet, invite the poor, the crippled, the lame, and the blind' (Lk 14: 12–13) (2012: 183–184)". We are constituted by community, by the Other, by that which is hostile to us. Of course, the microbes that at least temporarily live within their "host" as "hostiles" may in fact be agents of their own "space exploration" and colonizing of other worlds / selves, as (2) in sneezing (which is initiated in some cases from within by the aforementioned hosted / hostile bacteria or viruses, microbial agents that initiate sneezing in the host as a transportation mechanism) and the *Gesundheit* ritual; or (3) in the wedding-cake feeding ritual, whereby the betrothed share bites of the same food and thus microbes (see "bacterial gifting" in Myra J. Hird 2009: 86); or (4) in barefooted wine crushing; or (5) in the experience that food that others cook tastes better—fostering communal eating and the sharing of microbes; or (6) during breast feeding and its direct transfer of immunity and taste (kids will like the foods the mother likes); or (7) in the bacterially conditioned smell of the mother's armpit for a breast-feeding baby; or (8) with respect to scent and sex (both proscriptive *and* prescriptive scents); (9) with respect to scent and illness (our inner selves, or others, that is, the microbes we host, cause *smells* to change their significance—a change that serves our hosted microbes' purpose in ways we don't yet fully understand); or (9) in the relationship between dreaming and digestion (see Scrooge, in *A Christmas Carol*)—how microbes influence our dreams; or (10) during kissing; or (11) in our evolutionary "deal" with the cold virus, which used to be much more deadly; or (12) with how ancestors of viviparous mammals evolved after accidental infection of an ancestor with (immune suppressor virus) ERV, which permitted the fetus to survive the immune system of the mother; or (13) by means of throwing up (often orchestrated by pathogens) and the cleaning-up rituals that follow; or (14) by infants picking up and eating stuff; or, finally, (15) by the history of lactose tolerance and intolerance. Such habits and rituals as those just cited foster community-individual identity, or "di-viduality", as Lady Victoria Welby puts it (quoted in Petrilli 2005: 76), and show the extent to which we are palimpsests, communities not persons—we are ourselves environments for others. Thus, according to principle one above, again, ENVIRONMENTAL ETHICS ARE PERSONAL ETHICS, since the "hosted" is also always "host", and vice versa. Indeed, facts such as that there are more bacteria in us than the cells we are made out of deconstruct the logic of the notion of the autonomous subject, of the person as an individual, replacing such logic with that of loving your neighbor as yourself—and your enemy as well: our religious texts, of course, are, in the context of Deely's "semiotic animal", ecological. Also, when Deely asserts that "there are signs upon which the whole of life depends for successful continuance" (2005: 157), all of the signs associated with the habits and rituals listed as 1–15 above must be seen as mediators of such continuance.

Speaking of loving the Other (your neighbor or your enemy), Aldo Leopold, the father of "environmental ethics" in America, writes, "I now suspect that just as a deer herd lives in mortal fear of its wolves, so does a mountain live in mortal fear of its deer". The self-enemy binary opposition makes little sense in the broader community ethic of the semioethic animal, for without the deer's "enemy", the wolf, the mountain dies from overgrazing and so the deer dies from malnutrition. Indeed, as Deely argues, whereas the conceptions of "Rational animal" and "*Res cogitans*" place man "'above' the rest of animal nature" and "above all material interactions of things", respectively (103), "[w]hat distinguishes the semiotic animal is the awareness of what ties its being with the whole of nature, what makes it a part of the unfolding cosmic whole" (103). Here, then, as we shall discuss in detail below, Professor Deely lays down another ontological floorboard for supporting the notion of environmental ethics as necessarily personal ethics. This is especially true if we are in fact environments for others ourselves. Here again is the ontology of Deely's and Petrilli's semioethic animal.

THE SEMIOETHIC-ANIMAL PRINCIPLE (continued): CONCERNING HOW THE (ecological) WHOLE OF THE "SEMIOTIC ANIMAL" CALLS OUT ITS (sustainable) PARTS:

(1) Environmental ethics are personal ethics, and that is because **(2) we are in fact ourselves already environments for others.**

Professor Deely continues to show how the older, classical ecology (that of the late nineteenth and early twentieth centuries and based on Cartesian principles) deconstructs itself, while he simultaneously outlines a postmodern, biosemiotic paradigm, inventing as he does a semiotic basis for an ethics of sustainability: again, "signs upon which the whole of life depends for continuance":

> The way of signs alone actually establishes the contacts and dependencies between human thought and action, on the one side, and the physical universe surrounding us as context for that thought and action, while at the same time accounting for the realization so dear to the moderns and, indeed, at the heart of modernity, the place for a social construction of reality as part and parcel of human experience. The discovery of what is distinctively human in the action of signs, it turns out, displaces Descartes' notion of the isolated thinker with a contextualized animal whose behavior is distinctive in the realization that there are signs upon which the whole of life depends for successful continuance. (2005: 156–157)

While Deely, drawing on Jacob von Uexküll, collapses the old outside-inside binary in terms both ecological and ontological, Susan Petrilli, in "From the Semiotic Animal to the Semioethic Animal" (2005), offers a Peircean deconstruction of modernist biological logic, a logic found both in the Central Dogma of genetics (that "DNA is destiny") and in what is termed, as mentioned above, classical ecology (which alternately brackets out or "blames" [as unnatural] the "human [not semiotic] animal"). She offers, then, a deconstruction of that same inside-outside binary opposition that Deely unpacks, a faulty logic best identified and characterized by Richard C. Lewontin: "the belief that individual autonomous units determine the properties of the collectivities in which they assemble" (1991: 94–95). In clear opposition to this faulty logic, Petrilli writes,

> As a developing sign, the subject emerges as a dialogic and relational entity, an open subject gradually delineated in the intrapersonal and interpersonal interrelationship with other signs and subjects. Therefore, the boundaries of the subject-sign are not defined once and for all, but rather emerge in dialogic encounters with other signs, and are never definitive. The human person develops in sociality, that is, in relation to the experiences of others and never in isolation. Indeed, the self, the subject is a community of selves obeying the laws of the logic of otherness. The self is a community of dialogically interrelated selves. If we interpret the word 'in-dividual' literally as meaning 'non-divided, non-divisible," we may claim with Peirce that 'a person is not absolutely an individual' (CP 5.314)". (2005: 75)

In *Semiotic Animal: A Postmodern Definition of Human Being Transcending Patriarchy and Feminism*, Deely writes, quoting Petrilli as well,

> In the semiotic animal, the modern experiment has passed its limits with the realization that rationality is by itself not yet reasonableness, for "reasonableness is the capacity to respond to the attraction exerted by the other," not the isolation of the self from the other. (2010: 116)

Thus, the "semiotic animal" supplants the "rational animal" for yet another reason: "Being" *in context*. Here, then, "I think; therefore I am" is replaced by "I am because my little dog knows me" (Gertrude Stein 1936). The "capacity to respond" is "response-ability" becomes "responsibility" becomes "responsivity and answerability" (Petrilli and Ponzio 2005: 89): openness to the other. (Remember who Jesus would have us invite to lunch.) It is useful to note in this context the preoccupation on the part of Descartes's "rational animal" with the nature and function of "reference" (as in important pairings such as Frege's distinction between "sense and reference"); indeed, before the work of Peirce and Deely and Ponzio and Petrilli, "reference" eclipsed in importance the epistemological and ontological role of "response", "response" being that range of interpretants ("proper significate outcomes") that constitute the cognitive and environmental relationships within which "reference" can even "make sense"—"making sense" understood both as making conceptual sense AND making a world that is capable of being sensed. As Peirce writes, "expression and thought are one", which is to say that we are not ontological black holes ("I think; therefore I am") but, rather, from the point of view of Pragmaticism, that we are made *by* our response, that, since for Peirce "the word or sign that man uses *is* the man himself", we are made *through* response, by the act of using signs, by the act of our signs using us. Is not our *flesh* inside and out energy "in formation": in-formation: information: a palimpsest of *response* codes? See Jesper Hoffmeyer and Claus Emmeche's "code duality", wherein we humans are constituted by *dual* response teams: we represent ourselves to the future both digitally (via our DNA) and analogically (via our behaviors, that are the currency of natural and sexual selection); indeed, Hoffmeyer and Emmeche demonstrate how, literally, "the word or sign that man uses *is* the man himself". And is not our skin a giant "touch screen"? Don't others "push our buttons"? Is it not the case that most of us have too many apps (response channels) open to respond generously to others? Not to mention the body's pheromone codes that condition our responses and the semiotic models that always already underlie fleshly perception and sensation, and thus render us response-able in the first place (Thomas Sebeok and Marcel Danesi 2000). And then the dietary, and dress, and "bro" and "girl" codes of the flesh, or the controlling "gaze", ... all of which condition and enable (or inhibit) our response-ability to others. That the self is made through response to others is revealed by the Peircean semiotician Edwina Taborsky, who characterizes "intentionality", the ontological space where response-ability meets responsibility, as follows:

> I think it is a mistake to consider intentionality within the framework of meaning that we have, in our 'western' minds, grown up with, i.e., the ego-centered, author-centered, monologic meaning
>
> ... my understanding of the term is the absolute requirement of an entity for 'reaching out', for contact with Otherness; this is an aspect of both indexicality and intentionality. But it isn't an intention with a 'final form' built into it; it is rather an action of reaching out, and the final form that action may take (final only in the semiotic act, i.e., that there will be more semiotic actions after that one) will be 'reasonably' open to input from other indexical 'reaching-outs' of other entities. (1995)

Coleridge embodies these thoughts poetically: "The body / Eternal Shadow of the finite soul / The Soul's self-symbol / its image of itself, / Its own yet not itself" (c.1810, from manuscript; not published in Coleridge's lifetime, but available in most "complete" Coleridge anthologies). Descartes takes us up to Coleridge's last line; Deely's "semiotic animal" allows us to process the last line. As Raimonda Modiano has written, "Only by acknowledging 'the action of kindred souls on each other' (C[oleridge's] L[etters], 2.1197), the fact that other beings modify our thoughts, will an individual attain self-consciousness and behave morally toward others" (1985: 75). This is precisely Petrilli's point when she writes that "reasonableness is the capacity to respond to the attraction exerted by the other".

Of course, being "reasonable", being the "reasonable animal", "makes sense", because not "to respond to the attraction exerted by the other" has little survival value—whether that "attraction" is the glint of the headlights of a car about to run you over, the lure of a potential mate, a person or animal in need, or a "beautiful idea". Thus Deely's "semiotic animal" is an instantiation of "concrete reasonableness"—not the abstract rationalism of Descartes's solipsistic "rational animal". Indeed, as E. San Juan, Jr., writes,

> For Peirce, "the word or sign that man uses *is* the man himself", hence "expression and thought are one", and "every thought is a sign" (1958, 381; Innis 1985, 2; compare Hjelmslev's theory in Hasan 1987)[.] Peirce's concept of semiosis is not the unwarranted extravaganza posited by Derrida because there is in it a continual reference to the object of the representamen/signifier existing in a world outside consciousness, a world manifested in the phenomena of experience mediated by signs. This referent is not a static

entity but a dynamic object, "an ever-developing cumulative definition of it, to be distinguished from the immediate object conjured up in any individual signification" (Potts 1996, 19; see also Eco 1995). Further, the exigencies of practical life, as well as the criteria of logical economy and "concrete reasonableness" (Thompson 1953, 255; Apel 1995, 89) circumscribe the actualization of the endless development of sign-production.

... Semiosis is thus rendered concretely determinate by the goal of "concrete reasonableness"; the latter phrase refers to the logically controlled use of signs in purposive thinking, with relevance to real problems of adaptation and adjustment of humans to their sociohistorical environment. (2004)

THE SEMIOETHIC-ANIMAL PRINCIPLE (continued): CONCERNING HOW THE (ecological) WHOLE OF THE "SEMIOTIC ANIMAL" CALLS OUT ITS (sustainable) PARTS:

(1) Environmental ethics are personal ethics, and that is because **(2) we are in fact ourselves environments for others,** and because **(3) we carry models of our environments within us (our DNA), models that represent us as indexical signs of those environments that we hope will interpret us into our shared futures** ("the word or sign that man uses is the man himself").

The Peircean logical precedence of *response* (of Thirdness, of the Interpretant, of "the proper significate outcome") over *reference* (of Firstness) for the semioethic animal, especially since the world is so complex that no iconic (referential) model of it can ever be complete, is overlooked by the Cartesian "rational animal" and the modernist scientific paradigm. However, (1) by monitoring how systems respond to our actions and thus adapting our actions to those system responses (the reasonable thing to do)—rather than falling into the endless rabbit hole of attempting to construct iconic models of dynamic objects and systems, and (2) by acting in ways that allow alternate versions of our environments to emerge, that encourage our environments to respond to us in different ways, the "semiotic animal" can better address "real problems of adaptation and adjustment of humans to their sociohistorical environment", as San Juan, above, writes.

Indeed, as Deely (2010) writes, what defines the "semiotic animal" is its abductive structure, its ability, when reasonable, to "act prior" to the referential tyranny of representation and perception:

the being of signs does not consist in anything sense-perceptible as such but wholly in the transcending, the 'supersubjective', relation as such tying together triadically what is sense-perceptible so as to form a meaningful world of objects. ... Semiotics showed that signs do not fall strictly among the things objectified by perceptions of sense but act prior to that perception to enable it to reconstruct the physical environment along objective lines that are meaningful to the species, into an Umwelt, as is now commonly said". (119)

This ability of the "sign" or "man-sign" to "act prior to" "the things objectified by perceptions of sense" might seem, at first, not to honor alterity; however, as we shall see, such "acting prior" represents a key survival strategy, one necessary to the creation of a sustainable future: quite simply, we must be able sometimes to act on prior hypotheses about the status of our environments before all the data are in—by which future time it might be too late. Deely's phrasing evokes also Martin Heisenberg, whose work along with Deely's helps us to see that responsibility often lies beyond mere response-ability—which can sometimes be merely an after-the-fact phenomenon. Responsibility, ultimately, requires us to respond *before* the fact, indeed, before reference, before the brute Secondness of indexicality. Heisenberg, in "Is Free Will an Illusion" (2009), writes about the "random walk" of the *E. coli* bacterium: it randomly "twitches" itself, sometimes irrespectively of any chemical index, into a new spatial orientation so as to achieve a new point of orientation from which to respond to its environment—or so to create a new environment; that is, the *a priori* evolutionary advantage for a single *E. coli* bacterium (and thus for all such bacterium in a general area) of being distributed in space is the "whole" that calls out of any given *E. coli* bacterium a proactive "twitch" at random moments. In acting in this random manner, the *E. coli* bacterium effectively puts a *behavioral output* ahead of *sensory input*, which sensory input generally guides the bacterium at other times. This *acting* ahead of *receiving* is, for Heisenberg, the ontological basis for free will, which he defines as an organism's proactivity being always already just a "step" or "twitch" ahead of its receptivity.

We might add, however, that this "twitch" is *not* completely random. Such a belief is an artifact, Marc Champagne has helped me to see, of a physicalist philosophical prejudice, a prejudice in which "[i]ndexicality is usually taken to be the direct mode of reference whereby language [or semiosis generally] comes into contact with whatever it denotes" (2014: 138). Consider, then, the "twitch" not as an effect of some indexical cause but rather as a "leap", an abductive, iconic "leap", a "(non)random leap" of the *E. coli* bacterium, a leap *resembling* any abductive "leap" of faith, a "leap" as icon of the unfolded openness (space, potentiality) into which it unfolds itself. These "leaps", then, may be understood as icons of spaciality—and "spatiality" as "environment" understood in its most elemental and abstract form: as "potentiality". As Peirce writes, "*Potentiality* is the absence of Determination (in the usual broad sense)[,] not a mere negative kind but a positive capacity to be Yea and to be

Nay; not ignorance but a state of being. It is therefore *Inchoateness of Being*. Nothing is the Egg of Being. It is self-contained ability to be this and that. Latent Being" (1908). Thus, what is often called *E. coli's* "random walk" is better understood as a "leap" of potential, wherein *E. coli* is both a "being in space" and a "space in being". Individual and environment (as icons and agents of each other, as Yea and Nay) make each other in a process that is the very ontological origin of "free will". Thus, behavioral output before sensory input evolved in living things by means of an *icon* of spatiality, of the environment: Thus, such "leaps" are free will in its most elemental form, and free will (the basis of ethical choice) is therefore an environmental phenomenon: as such "leaping" evolved so as to give a survival advantage to *individuals* who could create and use "space" to their advantage, which had to be achieved proactively. Thus signs, (life-signs), man-signs, the "semiotic animal" for Deely generally and *E. coli* for Heisenberg, are capable of "acting prior to that perception" (Firstness as prior to Secondness), a secondness that might otherwise fix them in place: signs (and the "semiotic animal") have free will, free will understood as an icon of "open" space, of "spatiality". This acting prior to sensing, then, is an instantiation of Peirce's idealism. As Peirce writes, "the true idealism, the pragmatistic idealism, is that reality consists in the *future*" (CP 8.284). Rather than "random indexical twitches", the term "prior iconic leaps" reflects how spatiality as an idealized environment creates the "real", thereby calling out its own and the E. coli's future. Again, Peirce writes, "The one intelligible theory of the universe is that of objective idealism, that matter is effete mind, inveterate habits becoming physical laws" (CP 6.24–5). So, environmental ethics are also personal ethics because "free will", i.e., acting prior to sensing, is itself an environmental phenomenon—derived as it is from the advantage that effective distribution in space exerts, as it were, from the future, as "real potential"—a freedom that enables the "semiotic animal" "to reconstruct the physical environment along objective lines that are meaningful to the species, into an Umwelt", in Deely's words, a freedom and a will that thereby instantiate even "physical law". As Deely put it to me once in the lounge of the William Penn Hotel in Pittsburgh (2011), semiotics is the only field that studies "the causality of the nonexistent". Such is the real power of the ideal, of potential.

Therefore, we can now complete the "Semioethic-Animal Principle":

THE SEMIOETHIC-ANIMAL PRINCIPLE (continued): CONCERNING HOW THE (ecological) WHOLE OF THE "SEMIOTIC ANIMAL" CALLS OUT ITS (sustainable) PARTS:

(1) Environmental ethics are personal ethics, and that is because **(2) we are in fact ourselves environments for others,** and because **(3) we carry models**

of our environments within us (our DNA), models that represent us as indexical signs of the very environments that we hope will interpret us into our shared future ("the word or sign that man uses is the man himself" [Peirce]), and because **(4) even free will (the basis of ethical choice) is an "environmental" phenomenon,** as the benefit to individuals of an *environmental* advantage over *other* individuals led to an early emergence of a physiological strategy that privileges "behavioral output" over of "sensory input", a privileging that, according to Martin Heisenberg, is the neurological basis of "free will" (2009: 164–165) (as Deely writes, "signs do not fall strictly among the things objectified by perceptions of sense *but act prior to* that perception to enable it to reconstruct the physical environment along objective lines that are meaningful to the species" [2010: 119]).

Indeed, it is only because life has evolved to put *behavioral output* ahead of *sensory input* that "man-signs" are capable of "act[ing] prior to that perception" of the environment that would otherwise fix them in place; man-signs, then, have a predisposition to act prior to our perceptions of environment-signs, this predisposition being the very ontological basis for *responding to* environmental problems: we need to respond to the *idea* of climate change *before* we are fully present to all its effects—by which time it would be too late!

In unleashing Deely's "semiotic animal", we make a semiotic argument for a subjectivity without identity (that is, without the enforced unity of the "Id"—from "identity", itself from the Late Latin identitas < Latin idem, the same < id, it), an argument for an anti-representational view of the self, a view of the self as an abductive structure (which itself is just a refinement of putting "behavioral output" ahead of "sensory input"), a self that can survive precisely because of its excess (its capacity for "infinite semiosis"), of its constitution in its own dividedness *for* (not *against*) itself, of the self as a series of guesses about or enactments of what it might wish to be in the future, versions of the self that that self might in fact one day encounter in its environment, be ignored or rebuked by, respond to, and even incorporate within itself in a kind of psychosymbiogenesis. Paradigmatic here then is not Oedipus's fatal encounter at the crossroads but Case's serendipitous recognition in cyberspace, in William Gibson's *Neuromancer*, of an Other and autonomous version of himself—and of how that recognition of the autonomous other of one's self is always already a resource for the self.

Cary Wolfe, one of the formative figures in critical animal studies, writes about this process of psychosymbiogenesis through the lens of "the animal": "the power and importance of the animal is almost always its pull toward a multiplicity that operates to unseat the singularities and essentialisms of identity that were proper to the subject of humanism" (2003: 88). Deely's own "postmodern definition" of the "semiotic animal" provides a deep historical, philosophical, and semiotic underpinning for Wolfe's characterization, uniting the medieval and the postmodern worlds of discourse in a remarkable manner. Deely writes, "a semiotic animal ... is an animal that lives with the awareness of the action of signs as more fundamental to the constitution of human experience than are either objects or things" (2010: 117). He continues,

> I think the recognition that the boundaries of semiotic reality are never fixed and always shifting is the key realization for this new, this postmodern, humanism, wherein traditional objective 'ethics' is transformed as 'semioethics' by the discovery that human knowledge in the whole of its extent—speculative no less than practical—depends upon the action of signs, an action that is presupposed to every 'world of objects', every Umwelt around the whole planet (or elsewhere in this universe, as the case may be). Things may preexist us in various ways, but only as they are translated into objects can we intelligently deal with them. (123–125)

Here Deely argues that our environments and ourselves are best understood as open, multiple (Wolfe), interpretive structures, as "environ*meants*" and "environ*means*" (Coletta 2014: 316)—terms that define the semioethic premises (places and principles) and properties (place and characteristics) of the world of the "semioethic animal", of the posthuman: the environment is personal; there is no environment "out there"; environments are intentional structures; environmental ethics are necessarily personal ones—but not in the traditional modes of the conservation and preservation of The Environment. Relevant here is Harvard geneticist Richard C. Lewontin's postmodern ecology, the "last rule of which ... is that the very physical nature of the environment as it is relevant to organisms is determined by the organisms themselves" (1991: 91). This is the essence of Jacob von Uexküll's Umwelt theory in biology and the ecological basis of Deely's notion of the "semiotic animal", that we are under the moral imperative, since the personal is the ecological, to construct sustainable selves/worlds; that this imperative and its resultant obligation results from the fact, encoded in the term "semiotic animal," that man is BOTH a "symbol" (an avatar of *goal direction*, himself a/the world) (See Peirce's "It is that the word or sign which man uses is the man himself") AND a conscious "symbol user" (an avatar of *goal intention* [Anttila 1993]); that for the Earth any number of worlds is possible ("infinite semiosis") and "good" as long as they are sustainable—no essentialist ecology here. Indeed, for the semiotic animal, under the sway of Umwelt theory, there is no such thing as the (so-called) Environment—there must be no totalizing ideologies.

Thus, the "semiotic animal", as both world and world maker, must necessarily be a "semioethic" one.

For Deely, the Peircean "habits" that the "semiotic animal" forms AND the "habitat" that those "habits" in fact form (and in which the "semiotic animal" lives) combine to make for a postmodern ethics of sustainability, that is, an ethics of a pragmatic rather than an essential nature. If, then, for the "semiotic animal", signs make the world, what are some of the "Signs upon which the whole of life depends", as Deely writes? If the "semiotic animal" is both a "contextualized" and a contextual*izing* animal, how then does an embracing of that notion of ourselves cause us to re-assign the ethical spaces that we inhabit "in habit" and in "free choice"? Do we invent wholesale new ethics, or are our ethical directives already here and merely in need of a "re-assigning", as Crystal Downing puts it. We side with the latter; therefore, according to the logic of "The Semioethic-Animal Principle",

1. *if* environmental ethics are personal ethics;

2. *if* we are in fact ourselves environments for others;

3. *if* we carry models of our environments within us (our DNA as world maps), models that represent us as indexical signs of the very environments that we hope will interpret us into our shared future; and

4. *if* even free will (the necessary basis of ethical choice) is an environmental phenomenon;

then, the following *eleven semioethic directives* may be thought to have been "called out by" the interpretant force of Deely's "semiotic animal" and Petrilli's "semioethic animal", and so we dedicate them to Professors Deely and Petrilli.

Eleven Semioethic Directives

1. Thou shalt not pollute, in both the intertwined physical and moral sense that the etymological trajectory (final interpretant function) of the word "pollute" prefigured.

2. Thou shalt not steal, either from others today or from future generations.

3. Thou shalt not murder, even indirectly, thus causing people or other nonhuman persons to be harmed from the manageable side effects of your actions.

4. Thou shalt not stereotype, thus making into absolute (i. e., graven) images species, races, or ethnicities, and thereby denying the unique individuality of each being.

5. Thou shalt not consider any life form (species, group, or individual) to be more or less "advanced" than any other.

6. Thou shalt not allow thine own conception of the "next world" (heaven) to lessen the value of the diverse and just sustainable worlds derived from this one, My Creation (remember the Earth Day and keep it holy).

7. Thou shalt not consider thine own views to somehow necessarily represent universal ones (and therefore in effect bear false witness against thy neighbors' views).

8. Thou shalt not consider the fate of humans as separate from that of other living things; thus Genesis bids not only humans to "be fruitful and multiply", but Genesis also bids that birds and fishes be permitted to do so as well: "Be fruitful and multiply and fill the waters in the seas, and let birds multiply on the earth" (Genesis 1:20). (Since one cannot maximize two variables in a single equation, here the Lord creates an ecological aporia that should serve to check anthropocentrism.)

9. Thou shalt not commodify or privatize water or air.

10. Thou shalt not create, patent, and profit from genetic graven images of my Creation (thus committing adulterous acts against that Creation).

11. Thou shalt not interfere with the shepherding of being, that is, with the ushering into creation of a new self or selves—mineral, vegetable, animal, human, or post-human—as long as non-interference is in accord with the other commandments and as long as the beings that are so ushered into being are autonomous.

References

ANTTILA, Raimo.
    1993.   "Change and Metatheory at the Beginning of the 1990; the Primacy of History", in *Historical Linguistics: Problems and Perspectives*, ed. C. Jones (London: Longman Press), 43–73.

COLETTA, W. John.
    2014.   "A Peircean Semiotic Model for Describing the Anti-Oedipal Structure of 'Humanimal' Selves", in *The Semiotics of Animal Representations*, ed. Kadri Tüür and Morten Tønnessen (Amsterdam: Rodopi), 313–341.

DEELY, John.

2005. "Defining the Semiotic Animal," chapter 8 in Deely, Petrilli, and Ponzio 2005.

2010. *Semiotic Animal: A Postmodern Definition of Human Being Transcending Patriarchy and Feminism* (South Bend, IN: St. Augustine's Press).

DEELY, John N., Susan PETRILLI, and Augusto PONZIO.

2005. *The Semiotic Animal* (Toronto: Legas).

DOWNING, Crystal L.

2012. *Changing Signs of Truth: A Christian Introduction to the Semiotics of Communication* (Downers Grove, IL: IVP Academic).

HEISENBERG, Martin.

2009. "Is Free Will an Illusion?" *Nature* 459 (14 May): 164–165.

HIRD, Myra J.

2009. *The Origins of Sociable Life: Evolution After Science Studies* (London and New York: Palgrave Macmillan).

HOFFMEYER, Jesper, and C. EMMECHE.

1991. "Code-Duality and the Semiotics of Nature", in *On Semiotic Modeling*, ed. Myrdene Anderson and Floyd Merrell (Berlin and New York: Mouton de Gruyter).

LEOPOLD, Aldo.

1949. *A Sand County Almanac* (Oxford: Oxford University Press).

LEWONTIN, R. C.

1991. *Biology as Ideology: The Doctrine of DNA* (Concord, Ontario, Canada: Anansi).

MARAN, Timo.

2014. "Biosemiotic Criticism", *Oxford Handbook of Ecocriticism* (Oxford: Oxford University Press), 260–275.

MODIANO, Raimonda.

1985. *Coleridge and the Concept of Nature* (Tallahassee: Florida State University Press).

PEIRCE, Charles Sanders (10 September 1839–1914 April 19).

1866–1913. *The Collected Papers of Charles Sanders Peirce*, Vols. I–VI ed. Charles Hartshorne and Paul Weiss (Cambridge, MA: Harvard University Press, 1931–1935), Vols. VII–VIII ed. Arthur W. Burks (same published, 1958); all eight vols. In electronic form ed. John Deely (Charlottesville, VA: Intelex Corporation, 1994). Dating within the CP is based on the Burks Bibliography at the end of CP8. The abbreviation followed by volume and paragraph numbers with a period between follows the standard CP reference form.

1868. "Some Consequences of the Four Incapacities", *The Essential Peirce* Volume 1 (1867–1893) (Bloomington and Indianapolis: Indiana University Press).

1908. The Prescott Book/MS [R] 277.

PETRILLI, Susan.
2005. "From the Semiotic Animal to the Semioethic Animal", chapter 4 in Deely, Petrilli, and Ponzio 2005.

PETRILLI, Susan, and A. PONZIO.
2005. "Semioethics and Symptomatology of Globalization: Global Communication from the Perspective of Global Semiotics", chapter 5 in Deely, Petrilli, and Ponzio 2005.

SAN JUAN, Jr., E.
2004. "Charles Sanders Peirce's Theory of Signs, Meaning, and Literary Interpretation", *St. John's University Humanities Review* 2.2.

SEBEOK, Thomas A., and Marcel DANESI.
2000. *The Forms of Meaning: Modeling Systems Theory and Semiotic Analysis.* (Berlin and New York: Mouton de Gruyter).

STEIN, Gertrude
1936. *The Geographical History of America; Or the Relations of Human Nature to the Human Mind* (New York: Random House).

TABORSKY, Edwina.
1995. "Subject: Indexicals", Online posting, 16 June 1995.

WOLFE, Cary
2003. *Animal Rites: American Culture, the Discourse of Species, and Posthumanist Theory.* (Chicago: University of Chicago Press).

The Semiotic Species:
Deelying with Animals in Philosophy

Silver Rattasepp and Kalevi Kull
University of Tartu, Estonia

Abstract: Animals are treated in philosophy dominantly as opposed to humans, without revealing their independent semiotic richness. This is a direct consequence of the common way of defining the uniqueness of humans. We analyze the concept of 'semiotic animal', proposed by John Deely as a definition of human specificity, according to which humans are semiotic (capable of understanding signs as signs), unlike other species, who are semiosic (capable of sign use). We compare and contrast this distinction to the more standard ways of drawing the distinction between humans and animals.

Keywords: John Deely, semiotic animal, philosophy of biology, biosemiotics, *conditio humana*

> [T]he first thing that postmodernity accomplishes is to restore to the
> human animal its animality, together with the realization that all
> thought, all perception, is in signs.
> —John Deely (2009: 216)

Introduction

Much like the numerous other concepts, properties, and defining traits that have been proposed to draw the distinction between humans and animals, the concept of *semiotic species* attempts the same in properly semiotic terms. While such an attempt may be dubious to begin with (cf. Rattasepp 2014 for a general critique), John Deely's particular conception moves away from the standard ways of drawing the distinction and toward more interesting conclusions, which are more suitable for the biosemiotic perspective.

In addition to elaborating the semiotic specificity of human beings, the concept of semiotic species shows a way toward a more precise and better

ISSN 0277-7126

doi: 10.5840/ajs2016112316

Online First: November 24, 2016

The American Journal of Semiotics 32.1–4 (2016), 35–48.

founded understanding of the semiosic nature of nonhuman animal life, and as such lays the foundation for an improved philosophical discourse on the semiosic, albeit non-semiotic aspects of epistemology and ontology of non-human life. For while the more traditional ways of defining human uniqueness portray "man" as separate and divided from nonhuman life by postulating a binary opposition between humans and animals, the semiotic definition is, or at least should be, non-hierarchical and multi-dimensional. Moreover, such a distinction eschews the folk-definition of "animal" as opposed to the "human", and instead allows for an analysis of the myriad forms of sign use in all of life's diverse forms. As one of us has put it, "What philosophy lacks is not discussion of animals, but rather discussions of animals where they would appear as living representatives of nonhuman modes of being, of alterity, of a life that is not human" (Rattasepp 2016). It is this that the biosemiotic understanding of nonhuman life would help to rectify.

In the pages that follow, we will take as the object of study and the target of some brief remarks John Deely's book *Semiotic Animal* (2010), in order to examine his particular answer to the age-old question of "what is man?", and how does "he" relate to other living beings. In the course of these few pages we will come to the conclusion that Deely, ever the reluctant philosopher but a great celebrant of semiotics, begins from what appears to be a very typical, historically commonplace and philosophically untenable position, but ends up providing unique insights that are all his own. But before commencing on a brief analysis of Deely's text, we will first provide some remarks on the concept of semiotic animal itself, and then proceed to a brief description of what the role and function of animals has been in philosophy proper, and why it should be considered problematic.

Traditionally, philosophy has lacked, with few notable exceptions and up until the recent surge of animal studies and related fields in the past few decades, any kind of sophisticated treatment of animals from a philosophical perspective. This is not to say that philosophers do not talk about animals. It is to say that they commonly lack any interest in animals as creatures worth knowing in their own right, as nonhuman modes of being and subjects that represent umwelten that differ from that of humans. Animals can be symbols, exemplars, metaphors, ciphers, zoomorphic classifiers, the entire purpose of which is nevertheless to reveal something about humans: Jean Buridan, in his famous fable of the ass who dies of thirst and hunger for his lack of capacity for choosing, was not at all interested in actual donkeys.[1]

---

[1] For further discussion on the absence of animals in philosophical thought, see Rattasepp 2014.

As a result, for the philosophical discussion of the *conditio humana*,[2] animals are systematically represented as those creatures who are collectively *lacking* some human characteristic. The goal for such an analysis then is to find a singular dividing line that would place all animals in their totality to one side of the line, and all humans as completely unique and exceptional on the other, resulting in a binary opposition in which both sides are defined in direct opposition to the other. In the *Semiotic Animal*, Deely remarks on this, as when he describes critically the traditional conception of humans as rational animals, according to which they are in possession of a "feature that set it *above* the rest of animal nature, and *apart* from material nature as a whole" (Deely 2010: 103, emphasis in the original). Despite this declaration, below we will see whether Deely, in this particular book, fares well on the philosophical, or on the biosemiotic side.

On the Concept of Semiotic Animal

It is interesting to note that the concept "semiotic animal"—as *semiotisches Thier*—was first used already in 1897 by a founder of mathematical topology, Felix Hausdorff:[3]

> Der Mensch ist ein semiotisches Thier; seine Menschheit besteht darin, daß er statt des natürlichen Ausdrucks seiner Bedürfnisse und Befriedigungen sich eine conventionelle, symbolische, nur mittelbar verständliche Zeichensprache angeeignet hat. (Mongré 1897: 7–8)

> [Man is a semiotic animal; his humanity lies in the fact that, instead of naturally expressing his needs and wants, he has developed a language of signs which is conventional, symbolic, and only indirectly understandable.]

This was well known, for instance, to Max Bense (Bense 1992), who was interested in mathematical aspects of semiotics.

Yet as often happens, the one and the same concept can be coined independently numerous times, for concepts too, much like words in everyday language, are often polyphyletic. Rossi-Landi (1978) made use of the concept (a wholly semiotic animal), as quite frequently did Petrilli and Ponzio (2010).[4] For John Deely, however, the interest in the question of what constitutes the human in relation to other animals goes back to his pre-semiotic works. In his paper "Animal Intelligence and Concept-formation" (Deely 1971), written

---

[2] See Plessner 1976. Of course, as a prerequisite for understanding the *conditio humana*, one should understand the *conditio vitae*.

[3] Paul Magré was F. Hausdorff's pseudonym which he used for his philosophical works.

[4] An additional distinction has been drawn by Petrilli and Ponzio (2010: 158): "if each human being is a semiotic animal, a ... semiotician is a *metasemiotical animal*".

under the influence of a book by Mortimer Adler (Adler 1967), who was his mentor at the time, Deely already remarked:

> That distinction depends on seeing that there are things and aspects of real-ity independent of one's ambit of interest and activity, just what the brute animal in principle cannot and in fact does not see. (Deely 2009 [1971]: 127)

For both Adler and Deely, this is "a defense of humans as different in kind (rather than in degree) from animals" (Cobley 2009: 7), a strict formulation which he would later relax and elaborate, while not entirely abandoning it. Notably, Deely (1971) also already by that time refers to the works of Jakob von Uexküll (Deely 2009 [1971]: 127). Another of Deely's papers on this theme, published in a book from 1980 titled *Signifying Animal*, edited by Rauch and Carr, deals with the same question from a different aspect, namely on the relations of linguistics (which deals with the human sign system) and semiotics (which covers semiosis of all kinds) (Deely 1980).

In his *Basics of Semiotics*, the expression 'semiotic animal' appears twice (Deely 1990: 1, 124) but is not, as yet, thought of as a concept proper (it is not included in the index). At the time Deely was unaware of the earlier usages of this expression (see Pelkey 2016: 447–448), although the basic insight that he would later develop more fully is already present, as when he discusses "the reflective experience of linguistic animals" (Deely 1990: 13), and narrative, which is argued to be absent in nonhuman animals (Deely 1990: 2–3). In a further indication toward his later thinking, Deely writes with a reference to Jacques Maritain: "Animals make use of signs without knowing that there are signs" (Deely 1990: 36). This claim would remain the cornerstone of his conception of the human-animal difference, although in a much more developed form, as we see in its further elaboration in his magnum opus, the *Four Ages of Understanding*. In the very last paragraph of the book (right before the Resumé), in a subchapter titled "The Semeiotic Animal" (Deely 2001: 736–737), he writes:

> [T]he human animal, as the only animal that, besides making and making use of signs, knows that there are signs, is properly called *animal semeioti-cum*, the *semiotic animal*. Even as Descartes' definition of the human as a *res cogitans* served to mark the transition from ancient and medieval thought (inasmuch as the Greeks and Latins alike concerned in defining the human being as the "rational animal", *animal rationale*) to rationalistic an empiricist modern thought, so this definition will serve to mark for future generations the transition from modern to postmodern thought. (Deely 2001: 736)

Soon after, the concept of semiotic animal becomes the theme of a longer treatise. In the *John Deely Reader*, the bibliography of Deely's works (Cobley 2009: 410–411) lists three versions of the paper "The Semiotic Animal" as the first systematic draft (Deely 2003), the humanist version (Deely 2003a), and the definitional version (Deely 2005b). In 2005, Deely published it as a paper (Deely 2005; 2005b) and also as a longer treatise on the topic (Deely 2005a), plus his chapters in a book together with Susan Petrilli and Augusto Ponzio (Deely, Petrilli, and Ponzio 2005). In 2010, he published the earlier text (of Deely 2005a) expanded into a book (Deely 2010).[5]

The core of Deely's conception is as follows (Deely 2003a: 10):

> Of all living things we can say that they are semiosic creatures, creatures which grow and develop through the manipulation of sign-vehicles and the involvement in sign-processes, semiosis. What distinguishes the human being among the animals is quite simple .... Every animal of necessity makes use of signs, yet signs themselves consist in relations, and every relation (real or unreal as such) is invisible to sense and can be understood in its difference from related objects or things but never perceived as such. What distinguishes the human being from the other animals is that only human animals come to realize that there are signs distinct from and superordinate to every particular thing that serves to constitute an individual in its distinctness from its surroundings.
>
> Such an animal, capable of coming to know that there are signs as well as of using signs to hunt and fish and find its way through the surroundings, is generically semiosic but specifically semiotic, the only animal capable of knowing that there are signs to be studied as well as made use of to more "practical" ends.

This difference in awareness about signness has numerous implications—in particular, it gives rise to both ethicality and true violence, and thereby leading to the understanding of semioethics appropriate for the sign-aware semiotic animal (Petrilli and Ponzio 2010). The concept grows (Deely 2013).

We will now turn to a brief analysis of what we can conclude from Deely's discussion, which almost entirely deals with humans as the semiotic species, to that often neglected but necessary mirror counterpart, the nonhuman animals: in attempting to define human specificity, what becomes of nonhumans in Deely's treatment of man?

Dealing with Animals in Philosophy: Some Aspects in John Deely's Approach

There are several characteristic ways that animals are commonly discussed in philosophical literature, and they constitute a set of interlinked lines of thinking, the unfortunate consequence of which is the expulsion of animals from philosophy and the reassurance of human uniqueness at the face of the

---

[5] The three versions of the text were recently reviewed by Seif 2016; Mladenov and Iankova 2016; Pelkey 2016.

rest of nature.[6] We will now briefly summarize some of these dimensions of discourse, and see how Deely fares with respect to them.

First, in asking the question of human uniqueness, in asking "what distinguishes humans from animals", the emphasis is placed squarely on the "human" side of the question, and not on the "animal" side. Ethological knowledge of nonhuman animals seldom enters philosophical discussions on the nature of the human animal (one notable exception: Merleau-Ponty 2003). Taking the example of language, Lippitt notes that in a sense such a search for the properly human is tautological: "only human beings are capable of speech, which, in turn, founds the human subject. Animals enter that tautology as a phantasmatic counterpoint to human language" (Lippitt 2000: 15). This is Deely's starting point as well, for despite being called a study on the semiotic *animal*, the very few references to actual nonhuman animals all merely note briefly a simplistic behaviour of an animal before immediately moving on to the analysis of human capacities (e.g., "cat stalking its prey", Deely 2010: 59, "howl of the wolf", ibid., 62).

Second, the way in which the distinction between different species of nonhuman animals is drawn is markedly different from the way in which the distinction is drawn between animals and humans. Animals *differ*, humans are *unique*. While one nonhuman species is distinct from another on the basis of its particular species-specific traits, humans, to the contrary, are described as sharing a base animal nature with the rest of the living world, but with a certain addition on top, such as reason, language, consciousness, etc. As Tim Ingold puts it,

> We like to picture ourselves as animals *plus*. ... According to this view of humans as animals plus, we are constitutionally divided creatures, split between the physical condition of animality and the moral condition of humanity. ... In short, the human being is represented not as a specific manifestation of animality, but as the manifestation of a specific human essence superimposed upon a generalised animal substrate. (Ingold 1990: 210)

It is here that we see Deely moving away from philosophy proper, and into a more biosemiotically sensible position. Indeed, Deely's repeated insistence that semiosic capacities are always only species-specific rather than transcendent (indeed, the book's index contains references to 28 separate instances of various forms of species-specific in its scant 125 pages of text), lends a certain modesty to Deely's position, conceiving as it does that that which is "uniquely human" is in fact just a narrow capacity to make use of one particular means

---

[6] For an extended discussion of this, and for one semiotic possibility for the return of animals to theoretical thought, see Rattasepp 2016.

of meaning-making. As such, it eschews the possibility of hierarchization entailed in the "animal plus" conception, according to which only humans have somehow transcended the animal base and are therefore set above and beyond all other animals.

Third, the purported property that marks human uniqueness is invariably mental (e.g., language, cognition, reason), or becomes relevant by its relation to some supposed mental capacity. Such is the case of tool-making, which gains its importance from allowing for the reshaping of matter based on human mental conceptions. Non-mental, merely biological traits are of no interest for philosophy. At first blush, Deely's conception of the semiotic animal seems to follow along the same lines, for his entire discussion seems to be cast in the light of meaning-making, of the understanding and comprehension of the things in the world. A closer look reveals, however, that this is mistaken, as for example when he remarks that "the study of the action of signs finds precisely a path beyond the representative contents of consciousness" and that signs are "rooted in the being of triadic relations which transcend the divisions between nature and culture, inner and outer" (Deely 2010: 97). More broadly, it is the contention of biosemiotics, to which Deely would himself most likely subscribe, that semiosis appears whenever habits or codes are formed in a manner that is irreducible to their material basis. As such, biosemiosis cannot in any way be reduced to any supposedly mental capacity (Kull et al. 2009).

Fourth, nonhuman animals are discussed in the singular, rather than as a plenitude of species covering all of life's endless diversity. For most philosophers, uninterested as they are in actual living forms, the concept "animal" in the singular usually suffices. The function of this singular locution "animal" is to form a background from which human uniqueness is supposed to stand out. As Marchesini puts it, such a conception "creates a horizon of the non-human that is characterized by universality, which is considered to be neither a multiplicity not a bearer of individual characteristics, as opposed to the category of humanity which is intrinsically pluralistic" (Marchesini 2010: 93). It is difficult to judge how this point relates to Deely's thought. On the one hand, *Semiotic Animal* includes very few references to actual nonhuman animals, and even less to their behaviour beyond common-sense stereotypes, as already noted above. Yet his insistence on the limited, species-specific nature of human semiotics as opposed to the semiosis of all life—the distinction which, for Deely, ultimately marks human uniqueness—would at least make any further analysis based on his conception of the nature of semiosis amenable to a detailed, typological, non-hierarchical approach to studying nonhuman semiosis. This is discussed further below.

At this juncture we have, however, come to a point of contention, the solution to which is yet to be found, and will not be attempted to provide here. The issue lies in the fact that while Deely, starting from a general critique of the classical debate between rationalists and idealists, tries to find a semiotic third way out of the impasse, nevertheless remains, to a considerable extent, stuck within the framework established by the earlier debate. For traditionally, humans as rational, reasoning beings are portrayed as engaged in inner contemplation of the external world, yet it is a world which is there merely as a set of things that serve as fodder for thought. In this view, the semiosic activity of the one who apprehends the external things provides the *entirety* of the interpretation. As such, the cognitive activity, the meaning making, is entirely on the side of the one who interprets, and no attention is paid to the distinct forms that the external world can take and thereby provide different kinds of feedback. Most importantly for the present discussion, there is the classic distinction in semiotics between the living and the nonliving, the moving and the immobile, the beings endowed with their own semiosic capabilities, and the things without. Throughout the book, Deely presents his semiotic theory of the human condition as a set of relations linking the interpreter to objects, things, the physical world, etc. (e.g., Deely 2010: 56, 60–62). The unsolved issue here is that, since semiosis is arguably coextensive with life, whether the engagement with and description of the living, as opposed to the nonliving, is a cognitively different phenomenon, since what is alive is apprehended in a different manner from the non-living as a result of the semiosic capacities of the other living being. As it stands, in Deely's analysis of semiosic relations, everything in the world is represented, much like in traditional philosophical discourse, as *objects* of apprehension, with the semiosic capacities of nonhuman animals, for example, needing no separate, distinct description.

Finally, some remarks on the importance and usefulness of Deely's conception of the semiotic animal for philosophically oriented biosemiotics. This is the upshot of what we can conclude from Deely's discussion of the age-old question of *conditio humana*. Semiosis permeates all life, and is arguably coextensive with life. The various living beings are capable of making use of various different types of sign, based on their physiology, sensory and cognitive capacities: "Of all living things we can say that they are semiosic creatures, creatures which grow and develop through the manipulation of sign-vehicles and the involvement in sign-processes, semiosis" (Deely 2010: 99). And these capacities for meaning-making are at first often merely potentialities, and are realized and function only in specific, contextual situations.

Furthermore, no living being is capable of using just one single type of sign. This calls for a typology of signs, which would be non-hierarchical, and for a description of the meaning-making capacities of various organisms that is multi-dimensional and context-bound.[7] The capacity for the use of symbols does not extinguish the capacity for the use of indices, nor is a creature who is capable of making distinctions and of drawing indexical relations from that distinction more part of "nature" than the symbol user. Peirce's nine-fold typology is a classic example of such a conception of sign types, which, however, may need fine-tuning in more biosemiotics terms. There are, of course, numerous others (cf., e.g., Maran 2009 on the semiotization of John Maynard Smith), and moreover, the differences in the capacity for the use of different signs are not limited to the level of the species, but also appear on the level of individuals, groups, groups in different ecological contexts, and in different moments in time (Hendlin 2016).

And then and at last, within this myriad life-forms with their numerous semiosic capabilities, there may indeed be found one species that can be characterized by the capacity to use one particular, perhaps indeed one unique way of understanding: that of semiotics as Deely describes it, that is, "*only human animals* come to realize that *there are* signs", that the human being is "the only animal capable of knowing that there are signs to be studied as well as made use of to more "practical" ends" (Deely 2010: 100–101, emphasis in the original). We are left, then, with the conclusion that is best summarized by Deely himself, and worth quoting in full:

> "Semiotic animal" ... underlies the continuity whereby, in semiosis, all lifeforms, including humans, "live and move and have their being". *What distinguishes the semiotic animal is the awareness of what ties its being in with the whole of nature*, what makes it a part of the unfolding cosmic whole. (Deely 2010: 103, emphasis in the original)

Conditio humana as a Semiotic Problem

How is it possible to be aware of signs? Although this question has not been directly analysed by Deely, we can be rest assured that he would agree that this is a relevant semiotic problem. Let us, then, briefly outline the major types of approaches (types of solutions) to this problem.

(1) One can assume that all differences in semiotic capabilities are, in the end, just differences in degree. This would be the standard nominalist position according to which typologies are a matter of convention, and as such they

---

[7] For some thoughts on non-hierarchical "flat ontology" for general semiotic theory, cf. Rattasepp 2013

would not describe the ways in which semiotic systems themselves build their own boundaries. Or alternatively, that the systems we are describing all have certain intermediate forms of semiosis which would not allow us to delineate any straightforward distinctions as actually present in the semiotic systems themselves.

(2) One can assume that there exist different mechanisms which are responsible for qualitative differences between semiotic systems—differences in kind.

(2.1) The major differences between semiotic systems are described as semiotic thresholds, which can be settled unidimensionally. Any fuzzy boundaries are described as threshold zones.

(2.1.1) The boundary between human and non-human semiosis represents the lower semiotic threshold—between semiosis and non-semiosis.

(2.1.2) The boundary between human and non-human semiosis is not the lowest but an intermediate semiotic threshold.

(2.1.2.1) Such a boundary lies between true signs and meanings without categorized signs (cf. Sonesson 2010).

(2.1.2.2) It would be a boundary between sign types: e.g., symbols *vs* other (pre-symbolic) types of sign. A distinctive feature of humans would then be our ability to use a particular, specific type of sign of which nonhuman animals would not be capable of using (e.g., *animal symbolicum* by Cassirer 1944; symbolic species, Deacon 1997).

(2.1.2.3) Alternatively one could argue, as for instance Bickerton (1990) does, that the difference is primarily not in sign types, but in a new relationship between signs which then enables the appearance of a complex syntax. This has been the major position of biolinguistics, such as developed by Noam Chomsky and his colleagues.

(2.1.2.4) The boundary is described neither on the basis of sign types nor sign relations, but on the basis of a different type of interpretation, such as, in particular, as a difference between interpretation and metainterpretation (as in Deely's own distinction between the semiosic and the semiotic).

(2.1.2.5) The positions (2.1.2.2, 2.1.2.3, and 2.1.2.4) were synthesized by Thomas A. Sebeok in a specific manner. The kernel of his view is the claim that one can observe the appearance of new types of sign that together make proper syntax possible, including those responsible for syntax as such, and thus of human language, which would then allow for a new level of interpretation. In other words, the specificity of the human mind is related to sign types, and the signs that appear as novel in human language are syntactic signs. These are the signs that do not refer to anything other than a type of relationship between different signs. For example, words such as 'and', or 'or', cannot be found in the lexicon of non-human animals. It is these signs that make narration and metadescription possible.

(2.2) The major differences between semiotic systems form a set of thresholds that are settled polydimensionally. Fuzzy boundaries are described as threshold zones. All species partake in a multitude of sign types simultaneously and/or contextually. In this case no unique lower–higher axis can exist. In addition, a relation of negation is not sufficient to describe the difference.[8] This may include a combination of various types of boundaries as described by (2.1.2). To emphasise this plurality, the term 'semiotic species' (instead of 'semiotic animal') may be used.

This last type of approach (2.2) is the one that can serve as a basis for a richer analysis of animals in philosophy.

Acknowledgements

We are most thankful to John Deely for his inspiring work and friendship. Our work is related to IUT2-44.

References

ADLER, Mortimer J.
    1967. *The Difference of Man and the Difference it Makes* (New York: Holt, Rinehart and Winston).

BENSE, Max.
    1992. *Die Eigenrealität der Zeichen: Aus dem Nachlaß herausgegeben von Elisabeth Walther.* Kybernetik und Information 17 (Baden-Baden: Agis Verlag).

BICKERTON, Derek.
    1990. *Language and Species* (Chicago: The University of Chicago Press).

CASSIRER, Ernst.
    1944. *An Essay on Man: An Introduction to a Philosophy of Human Culture* (New Haven: Yale University Press).

COBLEY, Paul, Editor.
    2009. *Realism for the 21st Century: A John Deely Reader* (Scranton: Scranton University Press). [Reprinting of Deely 1971 at 91–139.]

---

[8] Belonging to a species can be based on recognition instead of negation or opposition. Cf. the biosemiotic concept of species (Kull 2016).

DEACON, Terrence.

1997. *The Symbolic Species: The Co-evolution of Language and the Brain* (New York: W.W. Norton & Company).

DEELY, John.

1971. "Animal Intelligence and Concept-formation", *The Thomist* 35.1, 43–93. [Reprinted in Deely 2009.]

1980. "The Nonverbal Inlay in Linguistic Communication", in *The Signifying Animal: The Grammar of Language and Experience*, ed. Irmengard Rauch and Gerald F. Carr (Bloomington: The Indiana University Press), 201–217.

1990. *Basics of Semiotics* (Bloomington: Indiana University Press). [See also Deely 2009.]

2001. *Four Ages of Understanding: The First Postmodern Survey of Philosophy from Ancient Times to the Turn of the Twenty-First Century.* Toronto Studies in Semiotics and Communication. (Toronto: University of Toronto Press). [See Kull 2016a on its reviews.]

2003. "The Semiotic Animal", in *Logica, dialogica, ideologica: I segni tra funzionalità ed eccedenza*, ed. Susan Petrilli, and Patrizia Calefato. Itinerari filosofici. (Milan: Mimesis), 201–219. [First systematic draft, as mentioned in Cobley 2009: 410.]

2003a. "The Semiotic Animal: A Postmodern Definition of Human Being Superseding the Modern Definition 'res cogitans'". Presented Sept. 22, 2003, in Rome: *Congresso Tomista Internazionale L'umanesimo Cristiano Nel Iii Millenio: Prospettiva Di Tommaso D'aquino Roma, 21–25 settembre 2003.* Pontificia Accademia di San Tommaso—Società Internazionale Tommaso d'Aquino. Manuscript 13 pages (online: http://e-aquinas.net/pdf/deely.pdf). [Humanist version, as mentioned in Cobley 2009: 411.]

2005. "Defining the Semiotic Animal: A Postmodern Definition of Human Being Superseding the Modern Definition 'res cogitans'", *American Catholic Philosophical Quarterly* 79.3, 461–481. doi: https://doi.org/10.5840/acpq200579329

2005a. "Defining the Semiotic Animal: A Postmodern Definition of 'Human Being' to Supersede the Modern Definition as 'res cogitans'" (Sofia: Southeast European Center for Semiotic Studies, New Bulgarian University). [See a review in Seif 2016.]

2005b. "The Semiotic Animal", in *Semiotics 2003: "Semiotics and National Identity"*, ed. Rodney Williamson, Leonard Sbrocchi, and John Deely (New York, Ottawa, Toronto: Legas), 111–126. [Definitional version, as mentioned in Cobley 2009: 411.]

2009. *Basics of Semiotics.* 5th ed. Tartu Semiotics Library 4.2. (Tartu: Tartu University Press).

2010. *Semiotic Animal: A Postmodern Definition of Human Being Transcending Patriarchy and Feminism to Supersede the Ancient and Medieval 'Animal*

Rationale' along with the Modern 'res cogitans' (South Bend: St. Augustine's Press). [Updated new printing of Deely 2005a. See a review in Pelkey 2016.]

2013. "Dire quasi la stessa cosa: To Say Not Quite the Same Thing", in *Writing, Voice, Undertaking*, ed. Susan Petrilli. Language, Media & Education Studies Series, vol. 56. (New York: Legas), 129–136.

DEELY, John N., Susan PETRILLI, and Augusto PONZIO.

2005. *The Semiotic Animal* (New York: Legas). [See a review in Mladenov and Iankova 2016.]

HENDLIN, Yogi Halle.

2016. "Multiplicity and Welt", *Sign Systems Studies* 44.1–2, 94–110.

INGOLD, Tim.

1990. "An Anthropologist Looks at Biology", *Man, New Series* 25.2, 208–229.

KULL, Kalevi.

2016. "The Biosemiotic Concept of the Species", *Biosemiotics* 9.1, 61–71. doi: https://doi.org/10.1007/s12304-016-9259-2

2016a. "Opus magnum: Semiotics Uncovers an Order in the History of Philosophy", *Chinese Semiotic Studies* 12.3, 341–349. [A review of Deely 2001.]

KULL, Kalevi, Terrence DEACON, Claus EMMECHE, Jesper HOFFMEYER, and Frederik STJERNFELT.

2009. "Theses on Biosemiotics: Prolegomena to a Theoretical Biology", *Biological Theory: Integrating Development, Evolution, and Cognition* 4.2, 167–173. doi: https://doi.org/10.1162/biot.2009.4.2.167

LIPPITT, Akira Mizuta.

2000. *Electric Animal: Toward a Rhetoric of Wildlife* (Minneapolis: University of Minnesota Press).

MARAN, Timo.

2009. "John Maynard Smith's Typology of Animal Signals: A View from Semiotics", *Sign Systems Studies* 37.3–4, 477–497.

MARCHESINI, Roberto.

2010. "Alterity and the Non-human", *Humanimalia: A Journal of Human/ Animal Interface Studies* 1.2, 91–96.

MERLEAU-PONTY, Maurice

2003. *Nature: Course Notes from the Collège de France* (Evanston: Northwestern University Press).

MLADENOV, Ivan, and Reni IANKOVA.

2016. "Semiotic Anima(l)", *Chinese Semiotic Studies* 12.3, 407–413. [A review of Deely, Petrilli, and Ponzio 2005.]

MONGRÉ, Paul.
    1897.   *Sant' Ilario: Gedanken aus der Landschaft Zarathustras* (Leipzig: C.G. Naumann).

PELKEY, Jamin.
    2016.   "Semiotic Animal: Waking Up to Reciprocity", *Chinese Semiotic Studies* 12.3, 445–454. [A review of Deely 2010.]

PETRILLI, Susan, and Augusto PONZIO.
    2010.   "Semioethics", in *The Routledge Companion to Semiotics*, ed. Paul Cobley (London: Routledge), 150–162.

PLESSNER, Helmuth.
    1976.   *Die Frage nach der Conditio Humana: Aufsätze zur philosophischen Anthropologie* (Frankfurt: Suhrkampf).

RATTASEPP, Silver.
    2013.   "A Metaphysic for Semiotics", *Chinese Semiotic Studies* 9.1, 254–263.
    2014.   "The Anthropological Machine and the Absence of Animals", in *Non-Humans in Social Science: Ontologies, Theories and Case Studies*, ed. Karolina Pauknerova, Marco Stella, and Petr Gibas (Prague: Pavel Mervart), 29–45.
    2016.   "The Philosophical Discourse on Animals, and the Philosophical Animals Themselves", in Timo Maran, Morten Tønnessen, Kristin Armstrong Oma, Laura Kiiroja, Riin Magnus, Nelly Mäekivi, Silver Rattasepp, Paul Thibault, and Kadri Tüür, *Animal Umwelten in the Changing World: Zoosemiotic Perspectives*. Tartu Semiotics Library 18. (Tartu: University of Tartu Press, in press), 51–65.

ROSSI-LANDI, Ferruccio.
    1978.   *Ideologia* (Milan: Mondadori).

SEIF, Farouk Y.
    2016.   "A Prelude to Wholophilia", *Chinese Semiotic Studies* 12.3, 395–406. [A review of Deely 2005a.]

SONESSON, Göran.
    2010.   "Here Comes the Semiotic Species: Reflections on the Semiotic Turn in the Cognitive Sciences", in *Symbolic Transformations: The Mind in Movement Through Culture and Society*, ed. Brady Wagoner (London: Routledge), 38–58.

Analogy and the Semiotic Animal: Reading Marshall McLuhan with John Deely

Christopher S. Morrissey
Trinity Western University

Abstract: Thanks to a helpful tetradic diagram found in the expanded fifth edition of John Deely's *Basics of Semiotics*, in which the context and circumstances of a sign's utterance (in addition to the sign-vehicle itself and the immediate object of the sign) is distinguished from all that is explicit in the sign itself *apart from* the context and circumstances of its utterance, it is possible to bring Deely's insights to bear upon the semiotically suggestive work of Marshall McLuhan. McLuhan's implicitly semiotic understanding of analogy is structurally present in his efforts to visually articulate the "laws of media" with his own "tetrad" diagrams. Deely's discussion of the irreducible triadicity of signs therefore illuminates McLuhan's attempt to understand how analogical thought actually works on the most fundamental structural level in the cognition of the semiotic animal. There is a unique cognitive syntax to analogy, which is operative in the animal that Deely has most appropriately identified as "the semiotic animal". This article discusses McLuhan's understanding of analogy in terms of its figure/ground structure, by using the example of the thermometer from Deely's *Basics of Semiotics*. In relating this example to McLuhan's tetrad, it is shown how McLuhan's implicitly semiotic analysis can also increase our semiotic understanding of other technological tools, such as Skype videoconferencing.

Keywords: analogy, tetrad, interpretant, object, sign-vehicle, nature, culture

ISSN 0277-7126

doi: 10.5840/ajs2016112315

Online First: November 24, 2016

The American Journal of Semiotics 32.1–4 (2016), 49–78.

Twenty-five hundred years of rational culture are in the process of dissolution. Age-old habits of conceptualization will not serve to train observation on the effects of the new man-made forms of energy. Since Plato, philosophers and scientists have attributed constant forms and patterns of action only to the world of "Nature." Both Plato and Aristotle, and their followers, as well as all the other schools of philosophy, have refused to recognize any patterns of energy arising from man-made technologies. Having invented "Nature" as a world of rigorous order and repetition, they studied and observed only "natural" forms as having power to shape and influence psyche and society. The world of man's artifacts was considered neutral until the electric age. As the electric environment increasingly engulfed the old Greek "Nature," it became apparent that "Nature" was a figure abstracted from a ground of existence that was far from "natural."[1]

—Marshall McLuhan

McLuhan on Figure and Ground: Logic within Semiotics

McLuhan's understanding of human experience is founded on this key idea: *we shape our environment, and it shapes us.* Human experience thus consists of an interaction of two realities: the mind-independent *and* the mind-dependent. In other words, there is always an interwoven interaction between what we usually call "nature" and "culture". Now, a Thomist "realism" aims to understand how intellectual cognition is always initially rooted in sensory reality. But what McLuhan brings to this endeavor, and here his innovation comes to the fore, is an effort to recognize how not only *nature* is found at the roots of sensory cognition. What the new technologies make clear, even though it was mostly obscure in the past, is that there is always an undeniable root sensory experience of *culture* that determines human thought as well. For example, if rather than looking out the window to check the weather, you look at an app on your smartphone instead, then clearly, while your intellectual experience may theoretically begin with either nature or culture, in practice you are choosing increasingly to root it more deeply in culture. The ultimate data source of the app, of course, looks out the window at nature somewhere; but it probably does so with robotic eyes, even if they are ones designed by a human, and it certainly gazes at a natural landscape transformed by human culture.

More importantly, within this semiotic web of nature and culture, we tend not to notice how "the medium is the message." As McLuhan also put it, "the user becomes the content." While most people have difficulty grasping what McLuhan means by this, since his mode of expression is paradoxical, deliberately challenging us to make the effort to see what we usually don't

---

[1] McLuhan and Nevitt 1972: 7.

see, the point is an elementary one that expresses the most basic action of signification. Signs are irreducibly triadic in structure. Although while we can readily appreciate the difference between form and content (for example, between the television set, and the program shown on the television screen), we find it more difficult to understand how there is a third node involved in the process: namely, the viewer, who is, yes, in a way being somewhat determined by the content being viewed, but who is also being even more profoundly determined by the *form* of the content. It is this latter part of the process to which McLuhan is drawing our attention. Such determination usually resides outside of awareness. We are preoccupied with the figure (the technological form delivering its content: for example, the figure displayed on a television screen). But there is also the hidden ground of the whole process involving a third element: namely, the user of the technology who is, at the same time, being determined and transformed by the whole process.

This irreducibly triadic structure is what semiotics describes. McLuhan's insights into it can be more readily grasped once we realize that the triadic structure of signification (sign-vehicle, object signified, and interpretant) is what he is in fact talking about. What is most illuminating to realize is that what he means by "ground" is the relatively more hidden node of the triadic structure, namely, the interpretant, whereas "figure" refers the relatively more visible part of the triadic structure: either the sign-vehicle or the object signified or both. Semiosis is the technical term for the dynamic action of signs that this triadic structure enables, and John Deely summarizes the crucial semiotic insight that can help us to understand McLuhan better: "Whether a given interpretant be an idea or not, what is essential to it as interpretant is that it be the ground upon which the sign is seen to be related to something else as signified, which signified in turn becomes a sign relative to other elements in the experience of the interpreter, setting in motion the chain of interpretants on which semiosis as a process feeds."[2]

Thus, when McLuhan makes constant recourse to the distinction between figure and ground, he is doing so in order to bring into awareness the interpretant involved in all semiosis. The reason this is so important to be aware of is because without a semiotic understanding of the triadic structure of signification, there is no way to be able to comprehend, along with McLuhan,

---

[2] Deely 1990, in Chapter 3: "Semiosis: The Subject Matter of Semiotic Inquiry", 26–27. Technically speaking, as Deely explains, a "sign" is the triadic relation itself connecting the three nodes, although we usually call the mediating sign-vehicle at one of the three nodes the "sign". For convenience of expression, I will use this more colloquial term "sign" when speaking in what follows below, although more technically it should really be termed "sign-vehicle". See Figures 1 and 2 (page 72 below), and also Table 1 (pages 70–71 below).

how technologies mediate between nature and culture. Once we can under-stand how the interpretant functions, however, we will appreciate how signs are indifferent to nature and culture and move freely between both. Objects signified may be mind-independently real, or mind-dependently unreal; as far as the process of signification is concerned, the ontological status of whatever resides at one of its three nodes is a matter of indifference. Semiotics, rather, is concerned with helping us understand how the whole process unfolds in its unlimited scope. Only later on can we then inquire into the various as-pects of nature and culture involved in any semiosic process, if we wish. As Deely has observed: "An interpretant in general is the ground on which an object functions as a sign. Interpretants exist, consequently, at those points in semiosis where objects are transformed into signs or signs are transformed into other signs. Ideas are interpretants, but not all interpretants are ideas: interpretants as such are indifferently physical or even mental. They define the points of innovation in semiosis at the level of objective representation. Logical interpretants define the points of innovation in intellectual semiosis, that is, developing understanding. In logic, of course, the ultimate interpretant is also an interpreter, namely, the one understanding the logical point at issue. But as such the interpreter is obviously dependent on a whole network of signs, objects, and interpretants, dynamically suspending the interpreter as a given moment in the development of understanding. In other words, to be a sign is to be involved in a process whereby the web of sign relationships is constantly changing and, in general, growing".[3]

McLuhan's insight that technologies are not static or neutral, but rather they have transformative environmental effects, is fundamentally a semiotic insight. As Deely puts it: "Symbols do not just exist; they also grow."[4] The symbolic world that McLuhan wanted to understand with the trivium's re-sources of grammar and rhetoric, since logic alone was not enough in order to move *beyond nature* to a wider grasp of *culture in relation to nature*, is opened up by his semiotic analyses of figure and ground. While the two terms can be misleading, in that the two terms suggest a dualistic process is at work, it is nevertheless of the utmost importance to realize that McLuhan, with his appeals to the hidden "ground" of any cultural process, is unveiling a triadic structure to us. The ground is the interpretant, i.e., the third element involved in semiosis. Once we move beyond dualisms, into this triadic way of thinking, we transcend the static dualism of nature in eternal opposition to culture. Instead, we can move on to appreciate the dynamic movement that

---

[3] Deely 1992: 27–28.
[4] Deely 1990: 23.

signification, especially technologically-enhanced signification, makes possible as a constant interweaving of nature and culture continually changing.

Signification shuttles back and forth between nature and culture, a fact that, as McLuhan sensed, makes the dualism of "nature" and "culture" practically useless for trying to understand how technological tools transform their users in the process unleashed by the effects of signification. Deely describes the transcendence of the dualism thus: "A sign, in the context of cognitive life, is strictly defined as anything that makes present in cognition something besides itself, or something which it itself is not. There are three essential points within this definition. First, the sign as such—every sign—consists in a relationship. Second, accordingly (i.e., by virtue of consisting in a relationship ontologically, or 'according to its proper being'), the sign exists as a kind of membrane or interface equally permeable to the influence of nature or culture, of cognitive life and physical being. Third, this relationship constitutive of the sign is, as we shall see, an irreducibly triadic one (in contrast to bare relationships of physical interaction as brute force)."[5]

McLuhan's own transcendence of a merely scientific logic of nature is clarified when we ourselves come to understand better how semiosis works. As Deely makes clear, "Semiosis as a type of activity is distinctive in that it always involves three elements, but it is even more distinctive in that one of these three elements need not be an actual existent thing. In all other types of action, the actors are correlative, and, hence, the action between them, however many there may be, is essentially dyadic and dynamical. For it to occur, both terms must exist. A car cannot hit a tree unless the tree is there to be hit, but a sign can signify an upcoming bridge that is no longer there."[6] This dynamic conception of signification is what McLuhan grasps in his understanding of media. McLuhan has moved, with his semiotic insights, beyond the dyadic world of merely physical interactions between mind-independent natural units. He positions us to grasp the triadic interplay involved in our cultural tools, which function semiotically not in opposition to, but as extensions of nature. The key point to grasp is that this extensionality may be natural in some aspects, or it may be cultural in other aspects: "It may be physical, or it may be psychological. In either case, the action takes place between two subjects of physical existence and is, in a terminology we shall be obliged to both clarify and insist upon along our way, always and irreducibly a subjective interaction. Subjective interactions, whether psychical or physical, are always involved in the action of signs, but they surround the semiosis as its context

---

[5] Deely 1992: 25.
[6] Deely 1990: 23.

and condition, while always falling short of the action of signs proper. In other words, while the action of signs always involves dynamical interactions, dynamical interactions need not always involve the action of signs."[7]

To illustrate the whole process, Deely takes an example from Charles S. Peirce. He asks us to consider "the rise of the mercury in a thermometer, which is brought about 'in a purely brute and dyadic way' by the increase of ambient warmth, but which, on being perceived by someone familiar with thermometers, also produces the idea of increasing warmth in the environment. This idea as a mental event belongs entirely to the order of subjective and physical existence, no more and no less than does the rising mercury and the ambient temperature of the thermometer's environs. It is, as Peirce puts it, the 'immediate object' of the thermometer taken as a certain type of sign, namely, one indexical of an environmental condition."[8] This is an excellent example we can now use to further our understanding of McLuhan. Because it uses a technological tool as the sign-vehicle to be considered, it supplies us with a paradigmatic case of how our perception of the environment unavoidably changes whenever we engage in semiosis with that instrument.

Deely describes the process of semiosis involved when we read a thermometer. However, his account is relatively brief and raises too many additional questions. But let us first consider his presentation of the basic triadic structure involved in semiosis, and then afterwards we will supplement his presentation with a further description of our own about how signs, objects, and interpretants change places in ongoing semiosis. First, then, here is Deely's description of the sign-vehicle (or "sign" for short), the object, and the interpretant involved when reading a thermometer; and keep in mind that he is describing the process McLuhan noticed about the user becoming used by the medium whenever semiosis occurs: "The object of the thermometer as a sign is the relative warmth of the surroundings. The object of the idea of the thermometer as a sign is no different. The thermometer, however, prior to being read is involved only in dynamical interactions. On being read a third factor enters in, the factor of interpretation. The thermometer on being seen may not be recognized as a thermometer: in that case, besides being a subject of physical interactions, that is to say, a thing, it becomes also a cognized or known thing, an element of experience or object. But, if it is both seen and recognized as a thermometer, it is not only a thing become object but also an object become sign. As a thing it merely exists, a node of sustenance for a network of physical relations and actions. As an object it also exists for someone

---

[7] Deely 1990: 23.
[8] Deely 1990: 23–24.

as an element of experience, differentiating a perceptual field in definite ways related to its being as a thing among other elements of the environment."[9]

This transformation of the perceptual field is obviously what McLuhan noticed about the process of semiosis involved in technological extensions of perception. Notice that the perceptual objects, however, also function as signs. A thermometer can be recognized as an object; "But as a sign it stands not only for itself within experience and in the environment but also for something else as well, something besides itself. It not only exists (thing), it not only stands to someone (object), it also stands to someone for something else (sign). And this 'something else' may or may not be real in the physical sense: what it indicates may be misleading, if, for example, the thermometer is defective."[10] The possibility of a defective reading introduces a fourth element, which I will take up in the next section of this monograph, where I consider McLuhan's tetrad in light of the triadic structure of signification. But for the moment, let us stay with the example and assume that the reading is correct, in order to elucidate first the simply triadic structure involved.

What happens when the thermometer offers a correct reading of the ambient room temperature? "The idea of surrounding temperature produced by the thermometer as sign represents to the interpreter of the thermometer something that itself is neither the idea nor the thermometer, namely, the presumed condition of the environment indexically represented by the thermometer. The idea as a mental representation, that is to say, a psychological reality, belongs to the order of subjective existence and is the immediate object of the thermometer as sign. But, within that order, the idea also functions to found a relation to something other than itself, namely, a condition of the environment surrounding the thermometer, which condition is both objective (known) and physical (something existent besides being known), presuming the thermometer accurate; or merely objective but deviant from the physical situation rather than coincident with it, presuming the thermometer defective. As founding this relation, in every case objective, in some cases coincidentally physical as well, the idea itself produced by the thermometer has in turn produced 'the proper significate outcome' of the thermometer as sign. This Peirce calls the interpretant, a unique and important notion, the key to understanding the action of signs as a process, a form of becoming, as well as a kind of being, over and above the unique essential structure that makes signification possible in the first place."[11]

---

[9] Deely 1990: 24.
[10] Deely 1990: 24.
[11] Deely 1990: 25.

To make all this clearer, consider now the progression of semiosis as it would happen when we first learn about thermometers. Consider what occupies each of the three nodes of the sign relation as the process of semiosis unfolds. First, imagine you are a young child. Someone shows you a picture of what is going to be your new home. You have not been there yet. But the picture communicates to you what it looks like. Before you first walk thorough this new home, you see a picture of one of the rooms in which you will be living. On the wall of the room in the picture, you see some kind of apparatus. You don't know what it is, but you see that it involves plastic and a thin glass pipe. In this first scenario, the *sign* is the picture (which consists of colored pixels printed on a page of paper) and the *object* is the room of the house in which you will soon be living. The *interpretant* is the idea that the picture brings into your awareness, which in this instance includes your puzzlement over the apparatus on the wall. You don't know what the thing on the wall is yet, so the *interpretant* includes your awareness of something unknown, something whose concept could be characterized as an idea of you-know-not-what. The object on the wall is unknown, and so you simply characterize this state of unknowing as either positive, negative, or indifferent. If you are curious about what the thing on the wall is, you would consider it negative that you do not yet know what it is. If you are not curious about what it is, then that would be registered in the generation of the interpretant as having an aspect of the unknown, towards which you are indifferent.

Second, imagine you now arrive at your new home and you enter the room that you had previously known only by way of the sign of the picture. When you point to the physical apparatus on the wall made of glass and plastic, it is an *object* designated by the *sign* consisting of your pointing index finger, or consisting of the words you use to ask what it is. Again, the *interpretant* here is your idea of something unknown, ranked as negative; that is, ranked as something about which you are unhappy to leave unknown and about which are thus curious to learn more.

Third, imagine that your interlocutor replies, naming the object on the wall: "thermometer." This word, whether spoken or written, is now the *sign* that designates the *object* on the wall consisting of a physical apparatus of glass and plastic. The *interpretant* now becomes the idea that you have of "thermometer" as being the name for this object on the wall. Moreover, as your conversation continues, your idea of the object indicated by the sign, your idea acting as the interpretant, will grow and expand as you learn more about the object. Your concept of "thermometer" will progress beyond being a mere name to being a concept that understands how a thermometer works.

To be precise, what will happen is that the *sign* "thermometer" will then become an *object* for other signs (e.g., the word symbols: "a device measuring temperature") that generate further interpretants explaining the meaning of the first interpretant that was generated (i.e., your bare idea of "thermometer" as being the name designating the object) initially in response to you learning the name of the object.

The network of linguistic interpretants generated in the course of your conversation, in which you learn what a thermometer is and how a thermometer works, follows a certain logic. It is the logic that the traditional study of logic has focused on, namely, as a tool describing how discourse makes sense of networks of ideas, as they are inferred through a process of mediate inference of thinking and speaking, by making use of linguistic communication's symbolic signs. But what McLuhan has noticed is that this kind of purely rational logic is only a small part of the purely objective activity of the action of signs, i.e., any kinds of semioses by which things are brought into our awareness, or even those semiosic processes by which things are simply being *prepared* to be brought into our awareness, but about which we are not even yet conscious, let alone rationally conscious in logical reflection.

For example, during the course of your conversation about the physical apparatus on the wall made of glass and plastic, you may notice for the first time that there is mercury inside the glass tube. Your interlocutor may initially bring it to your attention, using words as *signs* ("mercury") to indicate an *object* (mercury) for you to look for. Your sensory powers then bring it into your direct awareness (an *interpretant* consisting of the idea of what you were looking for) of the *object* (the mercury) that the physical icons impressed upon your senses are taken to present (as *signs*). You are then able to enfold the idea that "a rise in the level of the mercury is made in correlation with an increase in ambient room temperature" into the *interpretant* which is generated by the name "thermometer", since this name acts as the primary *sign* designating the physical *object* that consists of the plastic apparatus attached to the wall containing mercury in a thin glass pipe. Again, the *interpretant* is the concept of a thermometer, i.e., as something that measures the ambient temperature of a room, that is generated in this third scenario, in which you learn the name of the thing and develop, through a conversation about it, a concept associated with it of how it works.

Fourth, you can enter another room somewhere in some other house. Imagine you spot, on the wall, a similar type of object, and recognize it to be a thermometer. What is the semiotic logic of what happens here? In this scenario, the physical apparatus on the wall is no longer the *object* of a sign naming it, nor of the other signs used to develop the idea of what it is (a measure of temperature) and how it works (by correlating to a scale the rise or fall of the mercury). Instead, the physical apparatus itself now becomes a *sign* that evokes the idea (previously developed in an earlier conversation) of the thermometer as an *object*. For example, even if the physical apparatus looks a little bit different, once you recognize the mercury in the glass tube, you will take that mercury in the glass as the *sign* that this whole apparatus, perhaps manufactured with a plastic differently colored and shaped, is a thermometer that you can inspect more closely, to read the scale and find out the temperature. When you make use of the tool in this way, you lose consciousness of the physical apparatus itself relative to the gained consciousness of using it as a sign. This is precisely what McLuhan knew was happening with all the tools that humans use. His greatness lies in recognizing how ubiquitous and profound this transformation of consciousness had become in the "electric age".

Semiotically, we can understand the "logic" of what occurs in the process of semiosis, but only by expanding our consideration of the action of signs, beyond what traditional logic treats in its more restricted analysis of discourse. In this fourth scenario, to fully understand it, what happens is we have to develop an understanding, analogous to logic, which embraces the wider semiosic process unfolding. In this understanding, what happens is that we grasp: The *sign* is the physical apparatus itself now simply recognized as a thermometer, namely, as presenting itself simply as the tool that it is. However, the *object* of this sign is our concept of a thermometer, i.e., the idea we have developed of this tool as an instrument having certain capabilities; namely, as something which is a *measure* of temperature. By contrast, the *interpretant* generated is something distinct: namely, our idea of the ambient room temperature as *being measured*. In other words, the interpretant is *the reading* we make of the temperature (e.g., "twenty degrees Celsius"), by reading it off the thermometer, but the object is our concept of the thermometer as *a tool for measuring*. In other words, the *interpretant* is the ambient temperature *as measured*. But the *object* is our concept of the instrument *as the measure*.

Note that the sign in this scenario is directly perceived with the senses, but because it functions as a sign, it recedes from consciousness. Highlighted instead are the two concepts at either end of the triadic relation: the object and the interpretant, which are purely objective, i.e., totally mind-dependent. We assume that the reading on the thermometer is correct, but if it is not, we will need to develop a semiotic of understanding of why it is not. Such an understanding involves a grasp of the process of reversal in McLuhan's tetrad, so I will defer discussion of this scenario for the moment, saving it for the next section of this monograph. For the moment, we should simply pause and consider that what I have described in semiotic terms here is precisely what McLuhan was aware of. Namely, that with technological tools and instruments, the semiosic activity of objects and interpretants increasingly constructs a purely mind-dependent experience, even if the process relies on the use of signs by the senses. Because signs taken as signs fall out of awareness, because they function to bring other objects into our awareness, they greatly impact our world of experience whenever they grow more extensive, as is the case with technologies whose impact is global in scope. Further, the situation is even more serious when we consider how the interpretants generated in this experience are elaborate mind-dependent constructions that may stand in a highly problematic relation to anything mind-independently real or natural. The problem presented by an incorrectly functioning thermometer is multiplied on a grander scale by technologies used even more frequently and relied upon with even less effort.

Before we go on to consider McLuhan's tetrad as a semiotic resource for self-reflectively understanding how the activity of signs bridges nature and culture, let us summarize the import of what we have considered in this section. In his analysis of media effects, McLuhan's discussions of figure and ground point to a profoundly semiotic awareness of how interpretants function as ground of an irreducibly triadic process. In this process, "the interpreter is obviously dependent on a whole network of signs, objects, and interpretants, dynamically suspending the interpreter as a given moment in the development of understanding," as John Deely puts it. "Of themselves, the signs produce nothing directly; but their perception is an occasion which triggers actions that do produce changes in the world."[12]

The movement between figure and ground is part of this semiotic spiral, which McLuhan came to recognize with increasing awareness. McLuhan notes in his introduction to *Images from the Film Spiral*: "The structural theme of *Spiral* presents the oscillation of two simultaneously and complementary cones or spirals, constituting the synchronic worlds of birth and death. Spiral is not a diachronic or lineal structure but synchronic and contrapuntal interplay in a resonating structure whose centre is everywhere and circumference nowhere". McLuhan adds: "[Sorel] Etrog comes from a rich audile-tactile background and tradition in iconic art. His imagery is always of stark confrontation and his work is always multi-levelled and multi-sensuous in ways that are not easily

---

[12] Deely 1992: 29.

described in conventional literary terminology."[13] It is thus the analogically attuned artist who can help increase our awareness of this dizzying feature of our technological culture. McLuhan counsels us to move "from the habit of data classification" to the analogical habit involving "the mode of pattern recognition", because "instant communication insures that all factors of the environment and of experience co-exist in a state of active interplay", and only a semiotic approach to understanding the spiral of meaning can hope to unravel its analogical patterns.[14]

While Plato may have attacked the mimetic method of "a collective psyche and mind",[15] this sort of purely rational approach is insufficient to understand the new technologies that are creating a technologically constructed collective mind. Drawing upon the successful resources of the classical trivium, McLuhan situates logic within a wider arsenal of resources for understanding the new technological sensorium. That is, he situates logic within semiotics. His constant recourse to the key idea of the hidden ground involved in the semiosic processes unleashed by these technologies is best understood as an expression of a profoundly semiotic consciousness.

The humanistic purpose behind McLuhan's efforts to locate logic within semiotics may be gleaned from his fondness for retelling the story of Edgar Allen Poe's "A Descent into the Maelström": "Poe imagines the situation in which a sailor, who has gone out on a fishing expedition, finds himself caught in a huge maelstrom or whirlpool. He sees that his boat will be sucked down into this thing. He begins to study the action of the *ström*, and observes that some things disappear and some things reappear. By studying those things that reappear and attaching himself to one of them, he saves himself. Pattern recognition in the midst of a huge, overwhelming, destructive force is the way out of the maelstrom. The huge vortices of energy created by our media present us with similar possibilities of evasion of consequences of destruction. By studying the patterns of the effects of this huge vortex of energy in which we are involved, it may be possible to program a strategy of evasion and survival. … The artist's insights or perceptions seem to have been given to mankind as a providential means of bridging the gap between evolution and technology. The artist is able to program, or reprogram, the sensory life in a manner which gives a navigational chart to get out of the maelstrom created by our own ingenuity. The role of the artist in regard to man and the media is simply survival."[16]

---

[13] McLuhan and Etrog 1987: 125.
[14] McLuhan, Fiore, and Agel 1967: 63.
[15] Ibid.: 113–114.
[16] McLuhan and Staines 2003: 285.

Now that we have highlighted the necessity of semiotics for survival amidst the semiosic maelstrom unleashed by technology, let us move on to consider how the action of signs can be viewed in a tetradic structure. It is the structure of the tetrad that can be seen as embracing the type of situation in which the thermometer reading, for example, is defective. The great achievement of McLuhan's tetrad, then, is that it provides us with a semiotic resource for understanding the maelstrom, because it provides us with the framework with which we must think in order to recognize the dysfunctional or deleterious effects of technology's enhanced significations. In this regard, the key to understanding the tetrad as an empowering comprehension of semiosis is, as we shall see, this remark of McLuhan: "All metaphors are figure/ground in relation to figure/ground."[17]

McLuhan's Tetrad: A Semiotic Bridge between Nature and Culture

What happens when the thermometer offers an incorrect reading of the ambient room temperature? "In this case, its immediate object, the idea it produces as sign, becomes in its turn a node of sustenance for a network of relations presumed to be physical but that in fact, because of the defective nature of the thermometer being observed, is merely objective."[18] In other words, the *interpretant* from the fourth scenario discussed in the previous section above, i.e., the objective representation of the ambient room temperature *as measured*, now comes to be understood as not actually corresponding with the actual ambient room temperature *as the actual temperature*. What we must therefore consider now is this fifth scenario, in which a fourth element (the actual ambient room temperature of the physical environment) must be placed somewhere on a node in a triadic relation. In the Fifth Edition of *Basics of Semiotics*, John Deely added an "Addendum to Chapter 3" that provided additional discussion to clarify this very example and he also offered a tetradic diagram to illustrate the process.[19] Because Deely's semiotic tetrad may illuminate what McLuhan's tetrad has caught sight of, it is worth making sure we understand, clearly and in detail, the semiosis at work in this final example.

In the fourth scenario, the *sign* was the physical apparatus of the tool taken as an indication of its objective function. That is, the *object* of this sign is the

---

[17] Ibid.: 289.

[18] Deely 1990: 24.

[19] Deely 2009: 38–50. The diagram is Figure 2 at 41. It is reproduced as Figure 2 accompanying this monograph.

concept of the thermometer as a *measure* of temperature. In other words, we do not see the tool as an object; we see instead what it can do for us, looking past its merely physical appearance, at least when we grasp its objective function. We see it as signifying a measure. Further, the *interpretant* in this scenario, in which we assume the thermometer is functioning effectively without error, is the concept we have of the ambient room temperature as *measured*, i.e., as it being presented to us by the tool in an objective representation. In other words, the interpretant is *the reading* that the thermometer allows us to make; e.g., "twenty degrees Celsius". In sum, the *sign* is the physical apparatus of the thermometer, taken as presenting the idea of a thermometer as an *object* (something that can measure the ambient room temperature), which therefore generates the effect of an *interpretant*, namely, its significance for us as furnishing an objective representation of the ambient temperature as *measured*, which is what we can thus immediately read off of it.

In the fifth scenario now under consideration, something else will have to be taken as a sign that the thermometer is not functioning correctly, despite the fact that the thermometer reading is still twenty degrees Celsius. The *interpretant* generated will thus be the idea that the thermometer reading is incorrect. The *sign* of this could be the very cold chill we feel upon entering the room, or also our seeing the room's windows as having been left open, with snow observed falling outside. The *object* that any of these signs present to us is thus the *actual* ambient room temperature of the physical environment, i.e., the context and the circumstances in which the sign was previously assumed to be properly functioning, but which was left out of the triadic structure in the previous scenario, because the objective representation of the temperature as measured can only be taken as such when the temperature is read and understood and *interpreted* as being objective, i.e., as something known and understood apart from the context (the physical environment of the room) and the circumstances (whether it is accurate or not, or whether it is broken or not) of the thermometer taken as a sign. This very distinction (between context and circumstances, and the interpretant's objective signification apart from the same context and circumstances) is absolutely crucial, because it is what McLuhan implicitly relies on in order to tetradically arrange his analysis of media effects. It is worth quoting at length how Deely describes it:

> Peirce suggests (c.1906: 5.473) that 'it is very easy to see what the interpretant of a sign is: it is all that is explicit in the sign itself apart from its context and circumstances of utterance'. In the case at hand: the sign is the thermometer; the context and circumstances of its utterance are the ambient warmth producing a certain level of the mercury correlated—accurately or inaccurately, as we have seen—with a scale, the whole of which apparatus is seen and

recognized as a temperature measuring device; and what is explicit in the sign itself apart from this context and these circumstances is representation of something other than the thermometer, namely, the ambient temperature, as being presumably at what the thermometer indicates it to be, although this may be wrong due to defect in the mechanism. In other words, all that is explicit in the sign itself apart from its context and circumstances of utterance is 'its proper significate outcome', the objective element of the situation as involving representation of one by another, irreducible to the dynamical interactions involved, and establishing channels and expectations along which some of the interactions will be diverted in ongoing exchanges.

In our example, the idea of the thermometer enabling the thermometer to function as a sign was in the first instance a mental representation. The interpretant of a sign, however—and this is a very important point—'need not be a mental mode of being', nor, as we have seen, is it as mental mode of being that the idea produced by the thermometer functions as interpretant. Whether a given interpretant be an idea or not, what is essential to it as interpretant is that it be the ground upon which the sign is seen to be related to something else as signified, which signified in turn becomes a sign relative to other elements in the experience of the interpreter, setting in motion the chain of interpretants on which semiosis as a process feeds. In other words, what is essential to the interpretant is that it mediate the difference between objective and physical being, a difference that knows no fixed line. This is the reason why, at the same time, the triadic production of the interpretant is essential to a sign, and the interpretant need not be a mental mode of being, although, considered as founding a determinate relation of signification for some animal, it will be.

We see now with greater clarity the difference between the action of signs and the action of things. The action of signs is purely objective, always at once involving and exceeding the action of things as such, while the action of things as such is purely subjective or, what comes to the same thing, physical or psychic and restricted to the order of what exists here and now.[20]

Because this can be somewhat confusing to follow, a diagram helps, which Deely supplied in the Fifth Edition of his text (see Figure 2, p. 72), and which McLuhan also created with his tetrad (see Figure 1, p. 72). The semiotic function of the tetrad is that it enables "exploration of the 'grammar and syntax' of each artefact, a dynamic tool to describe 'situations that are in process.'"[21] McLuhan uses it to bring the wisdom of the wider approach of the classical trivium to bear upon the problems of media analysis.

---

[20] Deely 1990: 26–27.

[21] Library and Archives Canada, "Old Messengers, New Media: The Legacy of Innis and McLuhan": <http://www.collectionscanada.gc.ca/innis-mcluhan/030003-2030-e.html>.

The way the tetrad works is that enhancement and reversal are relatively visible figures, which McLuhan places at the top left and top right of his tetrad, respectively. Below them, he places retrieval and obsolescence in the respective bottom left and bottom right positions. It is a visual stacking of figures, placed upon their hidden grounds, in order to unveil the analogical relationships, which transcend mere logic by virtue of their semiotic dynamism.

In the case of the thermometer, the visible figure on the thermometer of the temperature *as measured* is the *interpretant*. This temperature readout is a technological *enhancement* that we can place at the top left of McLuhan's tetrad.

Below it is its hidden ground, namely, the objective idea of the thermometer *as measure* that the user of this tool has. It is placed at the bottom left of McLuhan's tetrad because it influences cognition by presenting it with a new *immediate object* that pulls along with it aspects of the environment that concomitantly assume greater prominence. For example, it will encourage us to use the tool to take control over the surrounding environment, perhaps by using the measurement of temperature to regulate the production of heat in the room. Then we will have to place a thermometer in every room. The eventual effect will be the retrieval of a uniformly pleasant summertime environment, no matter what the actual season and outside temperature is. The thermometer thus retrieves use of light clothing, which usually only occurs in particular seasonal weather, or else it retrieves the dwelling space and communal habits of a home not centered around a fireplace. In any case, whatever is connected with our idea of a thermometer, including the full range of its possible uses, becomes the hidden ground with respect to our ability to use it and to make temperature readings.

At the bottom right of McLuhan's tetrad we can place the *sign* of thermometer. That is, when we understand the significance of the tool (i.e., as measure and as measured; i.e., as connected triadically to both the idea of what it is used for, and the idea it supplies to us when it is being used), then what was previously taken merely as a physical object as part of environment, now assumes, by being taken as a sign, the ability to generate new grounds of immediate experience rather than older grounds. For example, when we consult the thermometer on the wall (by looking at the mercury in the glass against the affixed scale of measurement), the thermometer as a physical apparatus slips out of our awareness, because in order to consult it as a sign, we have to become aware of its immediate object, i.e., of the thermometer as a measure of ambient temperature. It is this *obsolescence* of the sign itself in its most obvious physical aspects, whenever it supplies to cognition its immediate object, that subsequently most impacts the environment's semiotic landscape. We begin to look at rooms and ask: does this room have a thermometer? And then, rooms without thermometers eventually become obsolete features of the physical environment.

At the top right of McLuhan's tetrad, unlike the relatively invisible hidden ground beneath it of the sign functioning as a sign (which concomitantly influences, over time, the surrounding landscape by obsolescing certain aspects of it), we can place the relatively more visible figure of the *actual* ambient room temperature of the physical environment. This is what comes into our awareness when a *reversal* happens, i.e., when what we previously understood as the objective representation of the temperature as measured (i.e., the interpretant) ceases to be an enhancement to the environment, because it can now no longer be understood *apart* from the context and circumstances of the actual environment. Instead, the measured temperature is held in contrast with the real ambient temperature of the room, i.e., the actual context and circumstances in which the thermometer is found. Thus, what was the *interpretant* when the thermometer was previously read as a correctly functioning environmental enhancement (i.e., the temperature reading on the thermometer understood as a correct representation of the environmental situation), now becomes overthrown by the *object* of the current semiosis (in which the *interpretant* of a cold chill presents the actual subjective ambient room temperature as *no longer* signified *objectively*), when a *new immediate object* is generated (from the old interpretant, which now becomes an object): namely, the idea that the thermometer is broken. In other words, the current semiosis distinguishes between the reading on the thermometer as incorrect (by moving it from the *interpretant* node of the triadic relation to the "immediate object signified" node) and the actual subjective physical state of the ambient temperature (which a correct objective reading would have to correspond to), by taking the actual temperature now at the *interpretant* end of the triadic relation—and this could either be a conscious interpretive inference that the thermometer is broken, or (because an interpretant need not be mental) it could simply be the cold chill one feels on one's skin even before entertaining the thought that the thermometer is broken.

The *sign* that functions to distinguish between these two things (the idea of the thermometer reading as incorrect and thus purely objective, and the actual physical temperature) is whatever generates in us the interpretant supplying such a semiotic distinction. For example, a cold chill will compel us to think that what we took as an interpretant (the temperature reading) corresponding objectively to the thing (the actual physical temperature) is now simply to be taken as objectively malfunctioning. The chill is the new interpretant, which can then also be taken as a sign pointing to the actual contrasting physical state. This physical state can be an object signified by the chilly sign. But it can also be pointed to by the new immediate object of semiosis, the idea that the thermometer is broken, if that object is then taken as a sign of something else, i.e., of that state of physical affairs of which the thermometer can no longer objectively represent.

In the earlier semiosis, however, when the *sign* (the thermometer recognized as such) taken as a measure (the thermometer understood as an *objective* tool) generated the effect of the measured (its temperature reading) as the *interpretant*, the state of the actual physical environment was taken to be the same as its objective representation. The temperature reading was taken as a reliable technological interpretation of the ambient environment. It was understandable precisely on the basis of the fact that we understand a thermometer, due to the technological intent of its design, to function in objectively the same way in *any* environment (i.e., it is to be read the *same* way, *apart* from any context or circumstances of its use). Only when the context and circumstances of the use of the tool diverges from its ostensible objective function does that environment re-enter our awareness. Until then, the tool *is* our environment. Or as McLuhan put it, until such a reversal happens, it is the tool that uses *us*.

Notice that the analogical structure of the tetrad thereby consists of its ability to bridge mind-independent nature and mind-dependent culture. On the left side of the thermometer tetrad we have two *mind-dependent* aspects. The temperature reading as the objectively understood *enhancement* is the interpretant *figure* on the top. The *ground* on the bottom is the concept of the thermometer determining its objective use in the environment as a technological object that *retrieves* certain potentialities latent in that surrounding environment.

On the right side of the tetrad, however, we have two *mind-independent* aspects. At the top is the *reversal* of figures, namely, of the *interpretant* of the temperature reading now reversing into the *object* of the real ambient room temperature (i.e., into an *objective* idea that the temperature reading is not correct). At the bottom is the hidden *ground* of the thermometer itself taken as a *sign*, which whenever it is functioning smoothly recedes out of immediate awareness and thus *obsolesces* its visibility in the surrounding environment, and which also obsolesces other features of the environment in its ongoing transformation of the field of semiosic perception. When looking for rooms to live in, for example, we may perhaps stop noticing other features, and instead are focused on whether or not every room has a thermometer. (If the example seems ridiculous, then change up the technology: surely wireless Internet access is an essential real estate selling feature, whereas absence of Internet access would be a real estate deal-killer.)

McLuhan pursued a wider semiotic orientation for logic within the classical trivium.[22] He was thus able to recognize the dynamism of the semiotic interpretants at play in the interplay of figure and ground for any technology understood as a cultural extension of human nature. Following the deeper logic of metaphor, he was thereby able to bridge nature and culture with the analogical tool of his tetrad. With the example of the thermometer, we have seen how the fundamental structure of the tetrad is semiotic in its visual placement of a figure and ground in analogical relationship to another figure and ground. Because of McLuhan's famous contrast between the visual and the acoustic, the visual nature of the tetrad also itself suggests an intended harmonization with the logical aspirations of that one essential part of the trivium, in which logic focuses on the analysis of pure intelligibility in the linguistic symbolization of discourse, with all of sign-action.

We conclude, therefore, by using the tetrad to consider another example, Skype video-conferencing, in the same way we have considered the thermometer. The salient features of Skype have been noticed by media ecologists: Skype "enhances communication at a distance"; it "retrieves personal contact and direct verbal communications as the means of making decisions"; it "renders obsolete written orders, memos, requests and thank-you letters"; and it "reverses into bullying (the loudest voice wins); confusion (who has the right to talk?); indecision (the talking never stops); [and] misunderstanding (individual memories replace written minutes)."[23]

In this example, the mental *figure* generated by Skype is the enhancement it serves up as its interpretant. This interpretant is the person as seen as at a distance. Because we do not understand the person we are talking to over Skype as being present in the room with us, we are semiotically understanding our computer screen to be serving up the signs (pixels on a screen) that generate this interpretant. Our ability to interpret Skype on our screen this way is shown by the fact that we do *not* think Skype is some kind of magic that conjures the person into being in the room with us, as a technologically illiterate person might. Because we understand Skype as a technological tool, we are able to distinguish the interpretant: i.e., we are able to understand the person on the screen as still being at a distance.

---

[22] Cf. McLuhan 1943.

[23] Owen Kelly, "McLuhan's tetrads: what they are and how they work": <http://www.owenkelly.net/984/mcluhans-tetrads/>.

The mental *ground* of this experience, then, is the idea we have of Skype as Skype. While the *interpretant* is our idea of the person on the screen as being still at a distance and not really present, the *immediate object* of the signs (the pixels on the screen, the audio sent via speakers and microphones) is the representation achieved by those very signs of the person as if they were indeed physically present, making us experience personal communication through direct visual and verbal contact, despite the fact that the person is still at a distance. In short, the semiosic *object* is the idea of Skype in its technological function as simulating a person *as presented*, whereas the interpretant is the semiotic idea by which we simultaneously distinguish Skype *as presenting* a person at a distance. Because our technological experience is one of a person in this way being present and yet not being present, only a triadic relation is capable of describing and distinguishing the sign action on Skype screens.

Both the figure and ground just mentioned (the *interpretant* of seeing Skype as a tool and not as magic, and its *object* as our idea of this tool, i.e., an idea by which we grasp its objective function as the hidden ground, according to which we also assess when it is or is not functioning smoothly: e.g., is the screen image and speaker sound adequately objectively representing our friend), both are *mind-dependent* experiences.

But technologies also have a *mind-independent*, physical impact on the *environment* as well.[24] Skype as a sign rises into prominence when it becomes a manifest physical feature; for example, we may notice that it comes to be used everywhere. (Even our parents are using it!) Not only can the sign then pass out of immediate physical awareness (as when everyone is using Skype, and so we come to think nothing of it), it *obsolesces* not only itself as a visible physical object when it assumes ubiquity as a universally functioning sign, but it also obsolesces other signs that used to be more prominent features of the physical environment. For example, phone calls and phone booths and merely verbal communications fade out of the environment as Skype habits take root instead.

All these hidden *grounds*, as they play themselves out in the wider environment that is now being marked by the enhancements of Skype, can thus effectively function to *reverse* the *figure* of video conferencing: i.e., from something first seen as an *enhancement*, to something seen as more environmentally problematic. In short, the new figures that result from the hidden grounds will eventually register, via the causality of semiosis, the wider environmental impact of the new Skype technology as it plays itself out. For

---

[24] "Extrinsic formal causality" is the very useful Scholastic term for naming the registration of the impact of the technology's *enhancement* on the rest of the environment. Cf. Deely 1990: 22–31.

example, nobody looks directly at another anymore; they look instead at the screen in the palm of their hand.

Conclusion

McLuhan's tetrad is thus the culmination of what in retrospect may be viewed as an implicitly semiotic approach to understanding the problems generated by the new technologies in our time. Historically, the classical trivium demonstrated that, beyond logic, a kind of analogical thinking was required to understand the action of signs. McLuhan recognized the irreducibly triadic nature of sign action by distinguishing the ground as the interpretant inextricably implicated in the signifying action of any figure. As the culmination of his efforts, his tetrad achieved a visual summation of the analogical structure of the wider logic by which semiotics is able to bridge both nature and culture, i.e., the mind-independent and the mind-dependent. Spiraling clockwise from the bottom right of the tetrad, we start with the mind-independent physical features of signs operating as signs in our environment, proceeding up on the left, from the immediate objects that we understand as the functions of these technological signs, up to the interpretants they generate in a process that transforms our own semiotic consciousness. As semiotic animals, any reversals that happen in this process are not just occasions on which we should call tech support; they ought also to become opportunities for reflection and meditation, for what was previously an interpretant, taken for granted, can now be interrogated as itself a sign of something. An interrogation of the action of signs as the action of formal causality can in fact yield knowledge of those signs as objects, immediate objects which need no longer determine us unawares. By making the analogy of McLuhan—that is, by holding the tetrad's four nodes together in consciousness, in one act of meditatively analogical thinking—we can grow in semiotic awareness and thereby become able to comprehend the inner logic of the maelstrom's patterns. In so doing, we realize our debt to McLuhan for his pioneering application of the basic semiotic operations that Deely has identified within the cognitive life of the semiotic animal.

Table 1: Expanded consideration of the example of a thermometer

Scenario	Sign (*Representamen*)	Immediate Object	Interpretant
1. Someone shows you a picture of what is going to be your new home.	The **picture** (which consists of colored pixels printed on a page of paper)	The **room** of the house in which you will soon be living	The idea that the picture brings into your awareness (+), which in this instance includes your puzzlement over the apparatus on the wall (−); your awareness of **something unknown**: an idea of you-know-not-what (0)
2. You enter the room that you had previously known only by way of the sign of the picture, and you point to the physical apparatus on the wall made of glass and plastic	Your pointing index finger, or the **words** you use to ask what it is	The **physical apparatus** on the wall made of glass and plastic	Your idea of **something unknown**, ranked as negative (−); that is, ranked as something about which you are unhappy (−) to leave unknown (0) and about which you are curious to learn more (+)
3a. Your interlocutor replies, naming the object on the wall: "thermometer"	**"Thermometer"** (spoken or written)	A **physical apparatus** of glass and plastic	Your bare idea of "thermometer" as being **the name for designating this type of object**
3b. As your conversation continues, your idea of the object indicated by the sign, your idea acting as the interpretant, will grow and expand as you learn more about the object	Further word symbols, e.g., **"a device measuring temperature"**	**"Thermometer"** (spoken or written)	Concept of "thermometer" beyond being a mere name; a **concept that understands how a thermometer works**, i.e., as something that measures the ambient temperature of a room

4. You can enter another room somewhere in some other house. You spot, on the wall, a certain type of object, and recognize it to be a thermometer.	The **physical apparatus** itself now becomes a *sign* that evokes the idea previously developed in an earlier conversation; the physical apparatus itself now simply recognized as a thermometer, namely, as presenting itself simply as the tool that it is.	The concept of a thermometer as a measure of ambient room temperature; our concept of a thermometer, i.e., the idea we have developed of this tool as an instrument having certain capabilities; namely, as something which is a *measure* of temperature; our concept of the thermometer as *a tool for measuring*.	Our idea of **the ambient room temperature as being measured**; i.e., **the reading** we make of the temperature (e.g., "twenty degrees Celsius"), by reading it off the thermometer. The ambient temperature *as measured*; i.e., the **objective** representation of the ambient room temperature *as measured*; e.g., for "the idea of increasing warmth in the environment".
5. The thermometer is broken, because the actual *subjective* ambient room temperature of the physical environment is not *objectively* represented by the thermometer. So, a fourth element (the actual ambient room temperature of the physical environment) must be placed somewhere on a node in a triadic relation.	The **physical apparatus** taken as a *sign*; the physical apparatus itself recognized as an **alleged** thermometer, namely, as presenting itself as the tool that allegedly functions as such a tool.	The **idea that the thermometer reading is incorrect**; e.g., "It's getting cold in here, so the thermometer must be broken." That is, our idea that **the tool is broken**, i.e., that **the ambient room temperature as not being objectively measured**. That is, the reading is now *interpreted* as being only objective, i.e., as something known and understood apart from the context (the physical environment of the room) and the circumstances (whether it is accurate or not, or whether it is broken or not) of the thermometer taken as a sign. The *subjective* context and circumstances is here recognized as other than the thermometer's *defective* objective representation.	The *actual* **ambient room temperature of the physical environment,** i.e., the *subjective* context and the circumstances in which the sign was previously assumed to be properly functioning, but which was left out of the triadic structure in the previous scenario, because the *objective* representation of the temperature as measured can only be taken *as such* when the temperature is *interpreted* as being objective. Example: The very **cold chill** we feel upon entering the room, or also our seeing the room's windows as having been left open, with snow observed falling outside suggests the reading is incorrect; i.e., whatever generates an idea of tool as not working.

ENHANCEMENT	REVERSAL
= Immediate Interpretant	= new Immediate Object
• Objective ambient temperature of environment being measured (the reading on the thermometer) • Person you are talking to is understood as being at a distance	• Subjective ambient temperature of environment being measured (vs. the reading on the broken tool) • Bullying, indecision, confusion, misunderstanding: vs. real presence
RETRIEVAL	**OBSOLESENCE**
= Immediate Object	= Sign-Vehicle
• Thermometer seen as a tool for measuring (the concept of a thermometer) • Person being experienced on screen as if being present	• The physical apparatus of the thermometer (plastic, glass, mercury, scale, etc.) • Physical presence in environment of Skype, FaceTime, etc.

Figure 1: McLuhan's Tetrad Applied to Thermometers and Video Calls

SEMIOSIS: THE SUBJECT MATTER OF SEMIOTIC INQUIRY

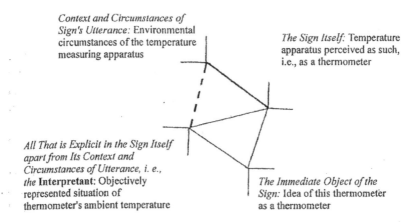

Context and Circumstances of Sign's Utterance: Environmental circumstances of the temperature measuring apparatus

The Sign Itself: Temperature apparatus perceived as such, i.e., as a thermometer

All That is Explicit in the Sign Itself apart from Its Context and Circumstances of Utterance, i. e., the **Interpretant:** Objectively represented situation of thermometer's ambient temperature

The Immediate Object of the Sign: Idea of this thermometer as a thermometer

FIGURE 2. The Irreducibility of the Action of Signs

Figure 2—Source: John Deely, "Addendum to Chapter 3", in *Basics of Semiotics: Expanded Fifth Edition* [bilingual Estonian/English edition] (Tartu: Tartu University Press, 2009), pp. 38–50. The diagram above is Figure 2 at page 41.

References

ANTON, Corey, Editor.

2010.   *Valuation and Media Ecology: Ethics, Morals, and Laws* (Cresskill, New Jersey: Hampton Press).

CHRYSTALL, Andrew Brian.

2007.   "The New American Vortex: Explorations of McLuhan", Ph.D. dissertation (Massey University, Palmerston North, Aoteraroa/New Zealand).

DANESI, Marcel.

2008.   "The Medium is the Sign: Was McLuhan a Semiotician?", *Media Tropes* 1, 113–126.

DEELY, John.

1990.   *Basics of Semiotics* (Bloomington: Indiana University Press).

1992.   *Logic as a Liberal Art*, [Loras College] Student Edition, Fall 1992 (Dubuque, IA: Letterheads to Books).

2009.   *Basics of Semiotics: Expanded Fifth Edition* [bilingual Estonian/English edition] (Tartu: Tartu University Press).

DUGGAN, Joseph P.

2009.   "Marshall McLuhan: Postmodern Grammarian", *The University Bookman* (May 18, 2009): <http://www.kirkcenter.org/index.php/bookman/article/marshall-mcluhan-postmodern-grammarian/>.

2011.   "McLuhan's Centennial", <http://spectator.org/archives/2011/07/21/mcluhans-centennial>.

ELSON, Brigid.

1994.   "In Defence of the Human Person: The Christian Humanism of Marshall McLuhan", *Canadian Catholic Review* (May).

GOERING, Joseph, and Francesco GUARDIANI, Editors.

2000.   *Medievalism: The Future of the Past*, a St. Michael's College Symposium, April 30th–May 1st, 1999 (Ottawa: Legas). Contains Eric McLuhan 2000 at 67–83.

GUIDI, Sylvia.

2011.   "McLuhan, much cited, but little known", *L'Osservatore Romano* (July 27).

HAVERS, Grant.

2011.   Radio interview with Alan Saunders, "The Conservative Marshall McLuhan", *The Philosopher's Zone* (July 16, 2011): <http://www.abc.net.au/radionational/programs/philosopherszone/the-conservative-marshall-mcluhan/2923342>.

INNIS, Harold Adams (1894–1952).

1951.   *The Bias of Communication* (University of Toronto Press). Introduction by Marshall McLuhan.

McDONALD, Hugh James Francis.
  1999. "McLuhan as a Thomist—some notes"; First posted on August 10, 1999 as a work in progress. Last updated August 24, 1999: <http://www.hyoomik.com/philo/mcluhan-aquinas.html>.

McLUHAN, Eric (b. 1941).
  2000. "St. Thomas Aquinas's Theory of Communication", *McLuhan Studies* 6: <http://projects.chass.utoronto.ca/mcluhan-studies/v1_iss6/1_6art2.htm>. Reprinted in McLuhan and McLuhan 2011a, to which page numbers are keyed. Also published in Goering and Guardiani, eds. 2000: 67–83.
  2005. "On Formal Cause", *Explorations in Media Ecology* 4.3–4. Reprinted in McLuhan and McLuhan 2011, 83–139.
  2010. "Concerning Media Ecology", in Anton, ed. 2010, 75–88.

McLUHAN, Eric, and W. Terrence GORDON, Editors.
  2005. *Marshall McLuhan: Unbound* (Corte Madera, CA: Gingko Press).

McLUHAN, Eric, Kathryn HUTCHON, and Marshall McLUHAN.
  1977. *City As Classroom: Understanding Language and Media*, with (Agincourt, Ontario: Book Society of Canada).

McLUHAN, Eric, William KUHNS, and Mo COHEN, Editors.
  2003. *The Book of Probes*, with art direction by David Carson (Corte Madera, CA: Gingko Press). Paperback edition 2011.

McLUHAN, Eric, and Marshall McLUHAN.
  1988. *Laws of Media: The New Science* (University of Toronto Press, 1992).
  2011. *Media and Formal Cause* (Houston, TX: NeoPoiesis Press). Reprinted as 4 individual chapters: McLuhan 1967a, McLuhan and Nevitt 1973, McLuhan 1976, and Eric McLuhan 2005.
  2011a. *Theories of Communication* (New York, NY: Peter Lang).

McLUHAN, Eric, and Jacek SZLAREK, Editors.
  2003. *The Medium and the Light: Reflections on Religion* (Corte Madera, CA: Ginkgo Press).

McLUHAN, Marshall (21 July 1911–1980 December 31).
  1934. "George Meredith as a Poet and Dramatic Parodist". M.A. thesis, University of Manitoba.
  1936. "G. K. Chesterton: A Practical Mystic", *Dalhousie Review* 15.4 (January), 455–464.
  1943. *The Classical Trivium: The Place of Thomas Nashe in the Learning of His Time* (Corte Madera, CA: Gingko Press, 2006).
  1944. "Edgar Poe's Tradition", *Sewanee Review* 52.1, 24–33.
  1945. "The Analogical Mirrors", in *Gerald Manley Hopkins*, 15–27, Kenyon Critics Edition (Norfolk, CT: New Directions Books). Reprinted 1969

in *The Interior Landscape: The Literary Criticism of Marshall McLuhan 1943–1962*, ed. Eugene McNamara (Toronto: McGraw0Hill), 63–74.

1947. "Introduction" to Hugh Kenner, *Paradox in Chesterton* (New York: Sheed & Ward). Also in McLuhan and McLuhan 2011a.

1948. "Henry IV, A Mirror for Magistrates", *University of Toronto Quarterly* 17.2, 152–160. doi: https://doi.org/10.3138/utq.17.2.152

1949. "Mr. Eliot's Historical Decorum", *Renascence* 2.1 (Autumn), 9–15.

1951. "Joyce, Aquinas, and the Poetic Process", *Renascence* 4.1 (Autumn), 3–18.

1951a. "Introduction" to Innis 1951.

1951b. *The Mechanical Bride: Folklore of Industrial Man* (New York: The Vanguard Press; reissued by Gingko Press, 2002).

1952. "Defrosting Canadian Culture", *American Mercury* 74.339 (March), 91–97.

1953. "Maritain on Art", *Renascence* 6.3 (Autumn), 40–44.

1954. *Counterblast: 1954 Facsimile* (Corte Madera, CA: Gingko Press, 2011).

1955. "A Historical Approach to the Media", *Teachers College Record* 57.2 (November), 104–110.

1956. "Educational Effects of Mass-Media of Communication", *Teachers College Review* 20.4, 566–575.

1957. "Verbi-Voco-Visual", *Explorations* vol. 8 (Autumn). (Reprint New York: Something Else Press, 1967).

1958. "Media Alchemy in Art and Society", *Journal of Communication* 8.2 (Summer), 63–67.

1959. "Myth and Mass Media", *Daedalus* 88.2 (Spring), 339–348. Reprinted in *In Myth and Mythmaking*, ed. Henry A. Murray (New York: Braziller, 1960).

1960. *Explorations in Communication*, edited with Edmund Snow Carpenter (Boston: Beacon Press).

1960a. "Report on Project in Understanding New Media"; National Association of Educational Broadcasters, U.S. Dept. of Health, Education and Welfare. <http://blogs.ubc.ca/nfriesen/files/2014/11/McLuhanRoPi-UNM.pdf>.

1962. *The Gutenberg Galaxy: The Making of Typographic Man* (University of Toronto Press.) Reissued with new essays by W. Terrence Gordon, Elena Lamberti and Dominique Scheffel-Dunand (Routledge & Kegan Paul, 2011).

1964. *Understanding Media: The Extensions of Man* (New York: McGraw Hill, 1964). 30th anniversary edition with a new introduction by Lewis H. Lapham (MIT Press, 1994). *Critical Edition*, ed. W. Terrence Gordon (Corte Madera, CA: Gingko Press, 2003).

1965. "Art as Anti-Environment", *Arts News Annual* 31 (February), 55–57.

1966. "Invisible Environment", *Canadian Architect* 11 (May–June), 71–74, 73–59.

1967. *The Medium is the Massage: An Inventory of Effects*, with Quentin Fiore, produced by Jerome Agel (Random House; reissued by Gingko Press, 2001).

1967a. "The Relation of Environment and Anti-Environment", in *The Human Dialogue: Perspectives on Communication*, ed. Floyd W. Matson and Ashley Montagu (New York: New York Free Press), 39–47. Reprinted in McLuhan 2005 as #4. Also reprinted in McLuhan 2011, 11–25, to which references are keyed.

1967b. "Technology and Environment", *Arts Canada* 105.24 (February), 5–7.

1967c. *Verbi-Voco-Visual Explorations* (New York: Something Else Press).

1968. *War and Peace in the Global Village* design/layout by Quentin Fiore, produced by Jerome Agel (Bantam, NY; reissued by Gingko Press, 2001).

1969. *The Interior Landscape: The Literary Criticism of Marshall McLuhan 1943–1962*, selected, compiled, and edited by Eugene McNamara (New York: McGraw-Hill).

1969a. Playboy interview: <http://www.digitallantern.net/mcluhan/mcluhanplayboy.htm>. Cf. Theall 2001 on how this was assembled from other sources than the interview itself.

1976. "Formal Causality in Chesterton", *The Chesterton Review* 2.2 (Spring–Summer), 253–259. Also in McLuhan and McLuhan 2011. doi: https://doi.org/10.5840/chesterton19762224

1976a. "Inside on the Outside, or the Spaced-Out American", *Journal of Communication* 26 (Autumn), 54–60.

1977. "Laws of Media", *Et Cetera* 34.2 (June), 173–179. Also published in *English Journal* 67.8, 92–94. Reprinted as #19 in McLuhan 2005, to which references are keyed.

1987. *Letters of Marshall McLuhan* (Oxford University Press, 1987).

2003. *The Book of Probes*, with art direction by David Carson, an anthology edited by Eric McLuhan and William Kuhns (Gingko Press, 2011).

2003a. *The Medium and the Light: Reflections on Religion*, ed. Eric McLuhan and Jacek Szlarek (Ginkgo Press).

2005. *Marshall McLuhan: Unbound* (Gingko Press).

2011. *Media and Formal Cause*, with Eric McLuhan (NeoPoiesis Press).

2011a. *Theories of Communication*, with Eric McLuhan (Peter Lang, 2011).

McLUHAN, Marshall, and Sorel ETROG.

1987. *Images from the Film 'Spiral'* (Toronto: Exile Editions).

McLUHAN, Marshall, Quentin FIORE, and Jerome AGEL.

1967. *The Medium is the Massage: An Inventory of Effects* (New York, London, Toronto: Bantam Books). Reissued by Gingko Press, 2001. Words by

Marshall McLuhan, design and layout by Quentin Fiore, produced and coordinated by Jerome Agel.

1967a. *The Medium is the Massage; with Marshall McLuhan.* Long-Playing Record. Produced and composed by John Simon. Conceived and co-ordinated by Jerome Agel. Written by Marshall McLuhan, Quentin Fiore, and Jerome Agel. Recorded 1967 in New York City on April 24, May 9–11, and 23. Released as Columbia CS 9501 (in 1967), and CL2701. Reissed on CD in 2011 by Sony Music. Archived online in two MP3 files: <http://www.ubu.com/sound/mcluhan.html#massage>.

1968. *War and Peace in the Global Village* (New York: Bantam; reissued by Gingko Press, 2001). Words by Marshall McLuhan, design and layout by Quentin Fiore, produced and coordinated by Jerome Agel.

McLUHAN, Marshall, and Barrington NEVITT.

1970. *Culture is Our Business* (New York: McGraw Hill/Ballantine).

1972. *Take Today: The Executive As Dropout* (Don Mills, Ontario: Longman Canada Limited).

1973. "Causality in the Electric World", *Technology and Culture: Symposium* 14.1, 1–18. Reprinted in McLuhan 2005 as #3. Also reprinted with responses by Joseph Owens and Frederick D. Wilhelmsen in McLuhan 2011, 27–72, to which references are keyed.

McLUHAN, Marshall, and Harley PARKER.

1968. *Through the Vanishing Point: Space in Poetry and Painting* (New York: Harper & Row, 1969).

1969. *Counterblast* (Toronto: McClelland and Steward).

McLUHAN, Marshall and Bruce R. POWERS.

1989. *The Global Village: Transformations in World Life and Media in the 21st Century*, with Bruce R. Powers (Oxford University Press).

McLUHAN, Marshall, and Wilfred WATSON.

1970. *From Cliché to Archetype* (New York: Viking Press, 1970; New York: Pocket Books, 1971, to which references are keyed).

McLUHAN, Stephanie, and David STAINES, Editors

2003. *Understanding Me: Lectures and Interviews* (The MIT Press). Foreword by Tom Wolfe.

McMAHON, Kevin, director.

2002. *McLuhan's Wake*, National Film Board of Canada, 94 min. documentary film. Written by David Sobelman. Packaging with Teaching Guide: <http://onf-nfb.gc.ca/sg/100064.pdf>. Online video: <http://vimeo.com/23890132>.

THEALL, Donald F.

2001. *The Virtual Marshall McLuhan* (Montreal: McGill-Queen's).

2005.   Review of McLuhan and Staines, eds. 2003, in *Canadian Journal of Communication* 30.4: <http://www.cjc-online.ca/index.php/journal/article/view/1719/1838>.

Analogy Reframed:
Markedness, Body Asymmetry,
and the Semiotic Animal

Jamin Pelkey

Ryerson University

Abstract: The evolution of arm-leg relationships presents something of a problem for embodied cognitive science. The affordances of habitual bipedalism and upright posture make our two sets of appendages and their interrelationships distinctively human, but these relations are largely neglected in evolutionary accounts of embodied cognition. Using a mixture of methods from historical linguistics, Cognitive Linguistics and linguistic anthropology to analyze data from languages around the world, this paper identifies a robust, dynamic set of part-whole relations that emerge across the human waistline between upper and lower appendage sets cross-culturally. The general pattern—identified as "arm-leg syncretism"—provides a plausible primary source for the uniquely human penchant for creative analogy, or "double-scope conceptual blending", said to underlie the human language faculty (Fauconnier and Turner 2002, 2008; Deely 2002; Anttila 2003; Bybee 2010). This account not only addresses a conspicuous gap in the literature but also enables us to better understand what it means to be human—including how we came to be unique among other species and how we are still vitally interrelated with other species. Deely (2010) blends both sides of this tension into a single phrase: "the semiotic animal". The paper further develops this distinction by drawing attention to one of the roles upright posture played in the emergence of semiotic consciousness.

Keywords: embodied cognition, anthropology of language, antisymmetry, conceptual Blending, universal grammar, body memory, phenomenology of movement, semiotic consciousness

ISSN 0277-7126

doi: 10.5840/ajs2016101113

Online First: October 12, 2016

The American Journal of Semiotics 32.1–4 (2016), 79–126.

The Semiotic Animal

Many claim that human uniqueness is rooted in a species-specific capacity for language (see esp. Chomsky 1966). Others insist that this is an inadequate account (see esp. Deely 2010): language must be situated within a broader semiotic capacity—our species' unique ability to recognize, theorize and thematize sign relations whether linguistic or extralinguistic. But there is more to the story. To ask what sets human beings apart from other animal species is to assume, in keeping with the findings of evolutionary biology, that human beings are also a species of animal. If the human animal is semiotic, and if one wishes to know how this semiotic capacity developed, it becomes necessary to ask about the embodied evolution of the semiotic animal. Failure to do so has sweeping consequences, as Deely describes: "Enlightenment thinking refused to see that if the experience that semiotic animals acquire simply by virtue of having the bodies that they do has no independent validity, then neither could the specialized knowledges developed by [embodied humans] have any validity either" (Deely 2009: 4). This paper draws attention to the neglected role of arm-leg specialization afforded by upright posture, arguing that the functionally distinct but diagrammatically unified part-whole relations shared between arms and legs across the transverse anatomical plane (i.e., the human waistline) is at least partially responsible for the evolution of semiotic consciousness—with a special focus on the development of creative analogy, or "double-scope conceptual blending" (Fauconnier and Turner 2002), said to underlie the human language faculty (Fauconnier and Turner 2002, 2008; Deely 2002; Anttila 2003; Bybee 2010). In short the paper makes a case for "primary blends" that underlie both the emergence of language and the prior emergence of the semiotic animal.

The inaugural English coinage of the term "semiotic animal" occurs in the first edition of Deely's *Basics of Semiotics* (1990). Previous coinages in German ("*semiotisches Thier*", Felix Hausdorff 1897) and Italian ("*animale semiotico*", Ferucio Rossi-Landi 1978) were unknown at the time; and in neither of the other two cases, was the concept developed thematically or systematically beyond passing mention (Deely 2010: 29–31). The distinction itself and the task of its development are important for numerous reasons, prominently including logical and conceptual clarity and the implications these hold for the responsible development of philosophical presuppositions. All animals are able to recognize, employ and exploit sign relations to their own advantage; but while this capacity is "generally semiosic", the human capacity is also "specifically semiotic". This is true since humans are "the only animal capable of knowing that there are signs to be studied as well as made use of to more 'practical' ends" (Deely 2010: 100–101). Because of this, it will not do to refer to humans as "signifying animals", "symbolic animals", "linguistic animals" or even "*Homo semioticus*". Although such titles also cast a wide net for the description of human uniqueness, the first two are yet too wide, the third is still too narrow, and the fourth denies our animal heritage.

"Signifying animal" is too wide simply because the same is true of every animal: the term identifies nothing unique about humans. "Symbolic animal" works only if symbols are artificially restricted to linguistic applications (i.e., as linguistic symbols); otherwise, as Deely argues, "while human beings are the only animals capable of thematizing signs, they are far from the only animals that employ symbols" (2010: 47). As for "linguistic animal" (or related proposals like *Homo loquax* or *Homo loquens*) such designations not only sell ourselves short but also cut ourselves off—both from the animal kingdom and from the broader material world. To be a "linguistic animal" is akin to being a "rational animal" in this regard. The latter term is a well-known designation that singles out human beings for possession of *res cogitans*—Cartesian mental substance. This, in turn (along with alternative titles like *Homo semioticus*), serves to elevate humans above all other animals, establishing a "false hierarchy" in the process.

Humans situated in such a hierarchy are suspiciously (mis)construed as beings analogous to the angels once presumed to transcend the earth and govern the celestial spheres (Deely 2010: 103). Because of such dynamics, the *res cogitans* model serves to alienate us not only from other animals but also from the "material interactions of things" (2010: 103). In short, to assume that language is the sum of human being is to neglect extralinguistic semiotic consciousness and to fall prey to the same illusions of angelic transcendence and ethereal aloofness that are implicit throughout modernist worldviews (with devestating interpersonal and ecological consequences).

Notably, then, a label like "*Homo semioticus*" would also be misguided since this too would imply that we are cut off from the material world in general and the animal kingdom in particular when we make use of our semiotic and linguistic capabilities. This is why the semiotic *animal* distinction is so important. As Deely notes, the distinction affirms at once our animality and our "uniqueness *among* the animals" (2010: 52). In contrast to historical views that idolize (and alienate) humans as *res cogitans* or *animal rationale*, the semiotic animal "*shows that what sets us apart is an awareness of the very process that ties us into nature as a whole*" (2010: 103, emphasis in the original). There is, then, as I have noted elsewhere, "an elegant simultaneity in this proposal—a kind of robust interdependence that resists reduction to either-or binaries—identifying our uniqueness in the most general way possible while simultaneously affirming our vital link to the here-and-now of planet earth and the raw-and-ready of animal behavior" (Pelkey 2016). It is precisely within the context these distinctions afford that we are prepared to more carefully examine the nature, origins and evolution of language and analogy.

Language, Conceptual Integration, and Creative Analogy

One oft-cited feature of our linguistic capacity is its "metalinguistic" or "reflexive" affordance—the ability language grants us to reflect on, and comment on, language. Notably, though, humans are are also able to use signs-in-general (both linguistic and extralinguistic) to reflect on signs-in-general (whether linguistic or otherwise). This, in a word, is "semiotics" or "metasemiosis" (Deely 2010: 48–52) and may also be referred to as "semiotic consciousness". One remarkable tool that is made available to semiotic consciousness is creative analogy—now widely claimed to be the bedrock that underlies language, as noted above. I say "creative analogy" deliberately since many who make sweeping claims about analogy in general do not appear to consider the possibility that non-creative modes of analogy may actually be capacities we share in common with other animal species. Deely himself (2002) neglects to consider this possibility; but he is in good company.

In Raimo Anttila's view (2003: 428, 438), "It can be said that the faculty to analogize is innate, and language faculty falls under this imperative." Furthermore, "Analogy gives the best and only agent for universal grammar." In the words of Joan Bybee, [analogy is] the process by which a speaker comes to use a novel item in a construction … [usually] based on semantic or phonological similarity with existing forms", and "analogical processing is the basis of the human ability to create novel utterances" (2010: 58, 59, 75). Deely's own perspective on the matter broadens the scope of the phenomenon to a more general semiotic capacity that underlies the emergence of language:

> In fact, analogy names not so much a category of terms but a process whereby one term modifies the meaning of another term. Analogy, in short, is a quintessential part of the human use of signs, so much so, we may say, that it needs to be understood as naming the most distinctive aspect of species-specifically human communication through linguistic signs. Analogy […] is but a name for the most distinctive aspect of the action of signs ("semiosis," as that action has come to be called) at play in human language. (2002: 522)

Although linguistic sign systems and creative analogy appear to be unique to human beings, they are also vitally dependent on, and situated within, more general modes of analogy as Fauconnier and Turner (2002) describe in their theory of conceptual blending. According to Fauconnier and Turner (hereafter F&T, 2002), human thought and meaning construal are permeated with conceptual blends. Conceptual blends are networks of compressed relationships rooted in memories (see also crucially Bouissac 2007 and Fuchs 2012 in this connection) that are formed and shared between patterned clusters of experience called 'frames' or 'mental spaces'. F&T identify four blending network types (2002: 119–135), listed here in order of increasing sophistication: 1) simplex, 2) mirror, 3) single-scope and 4) double-scope. I touch on each of these blending types briefly below, with a special interest in double-scope networks. Not only are the latter claimed to underly the human language faculty—thus emerging late in the course of human evolution—but as F&T argue, they also grow out of types 1–3. Since types 1–3 are claimed to have slowly developed over the course of human (and necessarily pre-human) evolution (2002: 171–187; 2008), conceptual blending theory provides a more gradient evolutionary account of the emergence of aspects of semiotic awareness, rooted in more primitive modes of analogic consciousness. This point is important not only for a more adequate evolutionary account of analogy, but also for a more rigorously integrated approach to the semiotic animal.

It is important to note that many non-human animals, such as dogs, cats, bonobos and dolphins, rely on non-creative varieties of analogy on a daily, if not hourly, basis. This point is made clear, albeit brief and unsystematic, by Hofstadter and Sander (2013: 178–181) in their rambling tribute to analogy "as the fuel and fire of thinking". A dog who hears the jingling of house keys in the background and goes to fetch its leash is necessarily employing a kind of basic analogical processing. This mode of analogy is also present in more creative analogies, but the latter differ in being able to map on new analogues, often in asymmetrical or disproportionate ways—and often for no immediately apparent purpose. To develop the key-and-leash example, for instance, a human observer of the dog's behaviour might be inspired to write a poem on the reversals and ironies that suggest themselves between house keys and jailor keys, a dog's leash and a prisoner's handcuffs, the dog's master and a prison warden. The dog experiences greater freedom of movement through the restraint of the leash as the keys deadbolt the door behind them; much like a prisoner released from his cell but, restrained by handcuffs, is allowed to have his day in court as the cell door locks behind the warden. If, on these grounds we say that walking one's dog is taking a prisoner to the courthouse, this type of analogy is what F&T refer to as a "double-scope" network.

A more frequently cited example of a double-scope network is the Computer Desktop blend (F&T 2002: 131; Birdsell 2014: 80). Computer "desktops" have become familiar and relateable as the direct result of our ability to integrate certain accessories of an office workspace schema or frame imaginatively with certain analogous features (and/or constraints) of a digital screen. This process results in new, previously unconsidered functional possibilities, enabling the newly integrated frame or "blend space" to be a fluid, selective analogy that might lead us to construe novel relationships onscreen like the placement of a trashcan alongside files and file folders that can then lead to further syncretic analogies. Such blends are reversible and often involve reversals. If one's screen is a desktop with a trashcan, one's trashcan might be relocated to the desktop. This is a possibility that has in some places actually become institutional policy. In 2005 when I was beginning my PhD at La Trobe University, in Melbourne, Australia, the university determined (in an effort to cut waste on campus) that large trashcans should be removed from office spaces and replaced by miniature bins for personal use and personal disposal—one for each desktop. This is creative analogy at work.

How did this capacity emerge? Rooting creative analogy in more basic modes of analogy shared with other animals is a start, but it does not explain the development of the new. To better understand the breadth and depth of this gap and the challenges (and dangers) inherent in attempting to span it, we will first find it necessary to orient the discussion in the Cognitive Linguistics literature and related pathways, with a special focus on embodied cognition.

Conceptual Integration Embodied?

Embodied cognition theory is in grave danger—or so some theorists caution, issuing warnings of a powerful historical undercurrent that threatens to drown recent advances in the depths of formal abstraction. To be sure, the old Cartesian paradigm is weighty. Its conceptual and ideological milieu is also saturated with familiar ideas, scripts and schemas that have a kind of collective "common sense" about them: culturally sanctioned mind-as-machine metaphors; widespread assumptions that the mind is the brain; normative pressure to dismiss feelings as chemical events; presuppositions that cognition can be modeled by mirror-representations in which the world is simply given instead of interpreted; the reduction of movement to motor synapses; and the reduction of persons to neural networks. In all such cases, the body becomes, once again, little more than an epiphenomenon of consciousness. Shaun Gallagher indicts this undertow as "the invasion of the body snatchers" (2015). Violi identifies it as a fatal movement toward "embodiment without the body" (2008: 5). Sheets-Johnstone suggests that it exposes the embodiment enterprise itself as little more than a "lexical bandaid" covering a centuries-old suppurating wound: the Cartesian lesion separating mind and matter (2011: 453).

Mark Johnson, by comparison, is more sanguine. Though he is himself no advocate of the ideologies cited above, he still insists that discourse and inquiry into the neural dimension of embodiment should occupy as much as a full third of the movement's attention. After all, he affirms, "without a brain, there is no meaning." But for Johnson there is much more. He goes on to stress two other necessary dimensions: "Without a living, acting body—no meaning. And without organism-environment interaction—no meaning" (2007: 175). The current paper makes a further contribution to the middle premise of this triad: the meaning of our lived bodies (not li*ving* or lived-*in*, but experienced live, through movement and interaction in space).

If current priorities are shifting toward the "neurocomputational modelling" dimension of embodiment (Rohrer 2007: 355), causing embodiment theorists to be more attentive to brain simulations and neural-motor mechanics than actual bodily feeling, kinaesthesia and proprioception, work in this latter direction is crucial. It is not necessarily crucial for the *refutation* of neural embodiment, but rather for counterbalancing and complementing advances in cognitive neuroscience. On the other hand, as Sheets-Johnstone (2011) points out, movement is developmentally prior to neural organization. Because of this, kinaesthesia, proprioception and the affect they entail are organizing principles around which other dimensions of mind and meaning develop.

With this in mind, the phenomenology of movement should be granted something of an ongoing theoretical and empirical priority—regardless of current trends and trending currents in academic fashion. Accordingly, we would be ill-advised to neglect the dynamics of movement, and the patterned relations they afford for human cognition, when developing embodied accounts of language and culture. And yet this is precisely the current tendency in the development of cognitive models and their application. Conceptual blending theory is prominently implicated in this neglect. But this is not the case for all levels of theory-building in the Cognitive Linguistics enterprise.

For some theoretical mainstays of Cognitive Linguistics, great care has already been taken to discover ways in which our capacities for relatively abstract modeling are grounded in more basic modeling templates or "input spaces" that are themselves directly rooted in bodily movement and body memory. Conceptual metaphor, for instance, is grounded in primary metaphor. Both phenomena are exclusively unidirectional or "asymmetric" mappings; but, while conceptual metaphors like LIFE IS A JOURNEY are culturally conditioned, primary metaphors like IMPORTANT IS BIG, are inherited from the constraints and affordances of bodily experience in early childhood development. As such, primary metaphors are developmentally given and more likely to be universal features of human cognition.

Imagine a crying infant being gently hoisted from her crib day after day. Each time she is held close to her affectionate caregiver, she feels the warmth of the caregiver's body; and each time she stops crying. Slowly, over time, at least two primary metaphors emerge from this interaction: HAPPY IS UP and AFFECTION IS WARMTH. The unwitting affective mappings onto two target domains, happiness and affection, are drawn from two radically sensory-kinaesthetic and proprioceptive source domains—UP and WARMTH, respectively. These mappings, along with many other primary metaphors serve to create a basic cognitive template for more abstract conceptual metaphors to draw on (cf. Grady 2005: 1608–1609). Conceptual metaphors also map asymmetrical relationships, although they are much more abstract—relationships such as TIME IS MONEY (don't waste it) or ARGUMENT IS WAR (a strategic position that can be defended).

These same asymmetric cognitive mappings are brought into the conceptual blending fold by F&T (2002: 127) as "single-scope integration networks"—one of four phases of conceptual integration, as mentioned above. It is then incidental to the theory of conceptual blending that one of its recognized phases is theoretically (and experientially) endowed with embodied grounding in primary metaphor. No comparable grounding layer exists in the literature to date for the three other phases of conceptual blending F&T identify. This theoretical gap is especially problematic in view of the privileged position granted to double-scope conceptual blending in the theory. Double-scope networks are held to be responsible for a distinctively human singularity: the emergence of language (F&T 2002: 171–187; 2008). Indeed, it may even be impossible to make a case for the emergence of conceptual metaphor out of its primary metaphor template without the prior emergence of double-scope integration. As Croft and Cruse (2004: 207–208) note, these latter, more fluid blending activities are necessarily implicated in the early (novel) stages of metaphor formation, "eventually to disappear altogether, as a metaphor becomes established." F&T concur that only through double-scope blending does innovation occur, "which is unique to cognitively modern human beings" (2002: 299).

My claim that primary grounding mechanisms are lacking in theories of conceptual blending should not be read as a suggestion that discussions of embodiment are absent altogether in the conceptual blending literature. F&T address the topic of embodiment implicitly, at least, by noting that blends involve compression or conversion of complex dynamics to "human scale" (2002: 322–324), due to our preference for dealing with "natural and comfortable ranges" (2002: 322) when confronted with ideas or relationships that are too complex to fathom. F&T also discuss "material anchors" or "cultural products" such as money, books and watches that inform our double-scope concepts of "buying, telling time and reading", respectively (2002: 215). Even treated together, the use of "material anchors at human scale" (2002: 216) provides a degree of embodied grounding than can be described as "oblique" or secondary at best—certainly not primary. Primary grounding by contrast would be experientially engaged with lived dynamics of kinaesthesia and proprioception.

Building on F&T's concept of "human scale" compression, Slingerland (2005) discusses "somatic marking" as a motivating factor behind the production of complex conceptual blends. Somatic marking identifies a dimension of conceptual blending that would appear to be more immediately embodied. Slingerland describes the motivating factor in question as the processes of finding out how to feel about a particular issue or idea. In the blend "That surgeon is a butcher", for instance, there is not only a conceptual integration of various butcher features with certain features of a surgeon, there is also a normative dimension making appeals to felt value judgments. If the blend is successful, the interlocutor may be dissuaded from scheduling a surgery with this particular physician, for instance. This helps better explain why we seek to use blends to achieve "human scale". In short the point has more to do with the persuasive rhetoric of conceptual blending than its bodily grounding. In other words, although this insight demonstrates the *relevance* of blending *for* embodied feeling, it does nothing to demonstrate the *origins* of conceptual blending *in* embodied feeling—i.e., felt bodily action and its memory-based organization.

Grady (2005) takes the topic a step further by identifying primary metaphors as a unique input class for the formation of conceptual blends. Indeed, as described above, this helps explain the bodily origins of single-scope integration networks; but it is not necessarily a comprehensive account, and it does nothing to account for the bodily origins of double-scope blends.

In relation to double-scope blending, Grady's (2005) contribution simply serves to expand our knowledge of the range of source material available for input spaces.

Elsewhere, Scott Liddell's (1998) treatment of "grounded blends" may appear to be a promising approach to the topic at hand; but his definition of the term shifts attention away from first-person experiential embodiment to the interplay between one's abstracted imagination and one's immediately surrounding context. This is typified in the "suspension of disbelief" we experience in a well-produced stage play for example. The actors and set become an input space useful for blending with a second imaginative "mental" space of one's own that is integrated into a seamless blend space until the event is interrupted by applause (or by an actor forgetting his lines). Notably, F&T identify Liddell's "grounded" input space as an instance of what they would come to call "material anchors", the obliquely embodied term discussed above. Once again, then, Liddell's distinction is a useful advancement of blending theory (see Dudis 2004 for further applications), but it does little or nothing to address the question of the bodily origins of conceptual blending—much less the origins of double-scope networks.

All of these distinctions provide helpful insight into the nature of conceptual blending. But if this is the extent of conceptual blending's bodily grounding, especially in relation to double-scope integration networks, we are left holding the bag. At present all discussion of embodied double-scope blending assumes the prior presence of a unique ability, the origins of which have not yet been accounted for in primary embodied terms. F&T (2002, 2008) assure us that double-scope conceptual blending evolved out of simpler forms once the human mind "reached a critical level of blending capacity" (2002: 187). But how? What critical level? What constituted the tipping point? How was this capacity reached? Was there a "mental leap"? Did a new Platonic form or Cartesian algorithm emerge unbidden from the ghostly ether of disembodied mind? It would make for an exciting story.

Anyone looking for more than an exciting story might do better to ask a different question. Consider the following: What are the primary experiential sources of double-scope blending? What body-based networks would be unique enough to be exclusively typified in the experience of anatomically modern humans, basic enough for common understanding across the population, and yet experientially rich enough to foster the new class of fluid, analogic cognition F&T propose? In short, is there a more radically grounded explanation for the emergence of the cognitive templates required for double-scope integration networks? I propose that there is; but the solution, partial or not, is sure to seem impossibly simple. Plainly put, the solution I propose is nothing less than *arms and legs*.

Arms, legs and their part-whole relationships are at least one primary embodied source that should be taken seriously as an answer to the enigma of the double-scope singularity. There is at least a substantial (i.e., plausible, elegant and data-empirical) possibility that the human double-scope "singularity" may owe its emergence to the evolution of upright posture and the inherited consequences this affords. Bipedalism gave rise to a slow reconfiguration of the old mammalian anatomical planes that organize our experience relative to the earth. This is discussed by Belgian anthropologist Henri Van Lier as "orthogonality" (2003, c.2009),[1] a default right-angle orientation to the perceived planar surface of the earth. Along with this came the slow reconfiguration of fore-paw, hind-paw relations into arm-leg specialization. This was followed by matching and mapping activities of arm-leg parts and their part-whole relations. By the time these parts and their relations came to be assigned speech labels, the matching and mapping were already formalized experientially. This formalization process played an important role in the creation of a new kind of cognitive template for a new kind of cognitive modeling.

This too may seem like just another story. It is a less dramatic story too, and it may seem to be lacking in dignity. But there are two reasons I prefer this story as an explanation over its more dignified or thrilling (spooky) alternatives: first, because it strikes me as a more plausible hypothesis; second, because of the cross-linguistic evidence supporting the hypothesis. In short, the story is in the data. And better yet, the data is at our fingertips: we don't have to stand on our tiptoes to reach it.

Body Parts Disembodied?

Toetips are toe-parts, and toes are foot-parts—at least as long as we are speaking English. In English it is also safe to say that toes are to feet as fingers are to hands. Both are "digits" at the ends of our "appendages". But to ask whether or not such relations hold true cross-linguistically is to ask a question with a surprisingly tangled answer. Even so, the question must be asked if we wish to explore the semiotics of arm-leg relations with ideological clarity. My task in this section, then, is to present (if not untangle) the answer and its broader context by summarizing the state-of-the art in "body partonomy" research—the study of part-whole relationships between body parts and their cultural and linguistic extensions in world languages.

---

[1] My appreciation goes to Stéphanie Walsh Matthews for introducing me to the work of Van Lier in May 2015.

Recent years have witnessed a flourish of studies exploring body-part taxonomies and body-part mappings in languages around the world, including their potential for fostering a better understanding of the fundamental nature of language, culture and cognition. Prominently included are three book-length collections devoted to the topic, all of which draw on more than a century of work by earlier scholars in the field. These are Enfield et al. (eds., 2006) *Parts of the Body: Cross-Linguistic Categorisation*, Maalej and Yu (eds., 2011) *Embodiment Via Body Parts: Studies from Various Languages and Cultures*, and Brenzinger and Kraska-Szlenk (eds., 2014) *The Body in Language: Comparative Studies of Linguistic Embodiment*.

The latter two volumes emerge from broader questions in the Cognitive Linguistics tradition, especially in their focus on the human body "as the donor domain for conceptual transfers to a wide range of target domains" (Brenzinger and Kraska-Szlenk 2014: 3). More specifically, these two collections develop pathways forged by Bernd Heine (1997) in his modern classic *Cognitive Foundations of Grammar*. The first volume, led by N. J. Enfield, aims to cast doubt not only on the cognitive approach but also on a diametrically opposed paradigm established by Anna Wierzbicka, known as "Natural Semantic Metalanguage" (NSM). True to form, Wierzbicka responds in close succession (2007) with a thoroughgoing rebuttal of Enfield.

In sum, a variety of general conclusions emerge from recent body-part studies, and their respondents—some of which are distinctly at odds with each other. The major disagreements are rooted in theoretical predispositions (and philosophical presuppositions) that ultimately center on the question of human cognitive universals and their cultural-linguistic manifestations (or lack thereof). These can be summarized in three positions regarding the status of the human body:

1. **Conceptual body:** There *are true cross-linguistic universals* that inform body-part taxonomies and body-part mappings across cultures. These are semantic primitives—innate concepts shared across all cultures (Wierzbicka 2007).

2. **Physical body:** There are *no true cross-linguistic universals* that inform body-part taxonomies or body-part mappings across cultures—a conclusion based on lacking evidence to the contrary in concrete vocabulary (Enfield et al., eds. 2006).

3. **Cognitive body:** There are *clear universal tendencies* evident in linguistic constructions through time and space that point to a mutually shared bodily experience across cultures, including general body partonomy (Heine 1997).

Notably, the first two approaches to body partonomy represent opposing poles in the entrenched classical-modern split between mind and matter respectively: nativist rationalism (Wierzbicka) and behaviorist empiricism (Enfield). The two are mutually defining pairs that will not be reconciled. Each engages in deliberate debate with the presuppositions of the other without registering the possibility of a third position in which subject and object are intertwined (as proposed by Maurice Merleau-Ponty 1945, c.1960). Since this basic presuppositional binary is so influential, it will be helpful to consider it more carefully before proceeding with a discussion of arms and legs and their part-whole relationships in a mode more closely aligned with Cognitive Linguistics.

For Enfield et al., human bodies are corpse-like: "physical entities with parts" (2006: 146). Enfield and colleagues recognize that "the body is a physical universal and all languages have terms referring to its parts" (2006: 137); but, since these part-whole relationships do not precisely correspond in "concrete vocabulary of the body" across cultures, Enfield and colleagues conclude that "there are fewer points of convergence across language communities ... than previously imagined" (2006: 146). Some languages of Australia and Papua New Guinea, for instance, make no distinction between 'body' and 'person' or 'hands' and 'arms'; other languages have no word for 'head', others no word for 'eye', others none for 'body'—or even 'part'. Such gaps are said to call into question the validity of any conclusions based on the assumption of part-whole relationships shared by all humans (cf. Enfield 2006: 199).

For Wierzbicka, by contrast, human bodies are abstracted mental states: "the body is, almost certainly, a *conceptual*, rather than 'physical', universal" (2007: 15, emphasis in the original). She casts doubt on the reliability of claims made by Enfield and colleagues that certain cultures fail to distinguish parts from wholes. The key problem, Wierzbicka argues, is that insufficient attention is beng paid to the nature of nuanced and gradient polysemy in the languages researched. She asserts that Enfield and colleagues are attempting to "practice 'cognitive anthropology' in a theoretical vacuum and have no methodology for distinguishing genuine and spurious polysemy" (2006: 17). She further asserts that this neglect results in uncritically exoticizing non-western languages. Her solution to these problems, quite simply, is for everyone to learn to apply her own trademark approach: "systematic semantic analysis in the NSM framework" (2007: 18). NSM is a system in which a minimal set of 60–70 innate concepts accounts for all human meaning construal.

In short, both Enfield et al. (eds., 2006) and Wierzbicka (2007) propose disembodied approaches to the embodiment of body parts. The Cognitive

Linguistic approach (CL), by contrast, differs fundamentally from either of these two dualist positions—foregoing mind/matter and nativism/behaviorism binaries by shifting attention to lived bodily experience and its fluid schematic organization. This is not to say that CL is in complete disagreement with either Wierzbicka or Enfield. CL can agree heartily with Wierzbicka's conclusion, for instance, that "the basic model of the human being is something that we all share" (2006: 18) without validating the premises she offers in support of this conclusion (i.e., the existence of innate concepts). CL can also accept the conclusion of linguistic relativity implied by the apparent variation Enfield and colleagues describe. But this does not necessitate agreement with the assumption that human experiential universals (and the explanatory grounds they supply for language, culture and cognition) are invalidated by lexical gaps. Instead of insisting on the discovery of strict universals in body-part taxonomy and their extensions across languages, CL allows for category gradience or continuity (following Lakoff 1987, cf. Johnson 2007) and pans out to acknowledge universal linguistic *tendencies* across time and space (following Heine 1997; see also Bybee 2009).

According to Bernd Heine, CL assumes the presence of another kind of universal that is at least implied by observing linguistic tendencies across cultures. For Heine, "the major patterns of human conceptualization are universal in nature" since the "human species, irrespective of whether it is located in Siberia or the Khalahari Desert, has essentially the same pool of options for conceptualization" (1997: 14). This is an extension of Lakoff and Johnson's "experientialist synthesis" (1980). Accordingly, athropological linguists following Heine's approach are able to identify general tendencies that coalesce into universal embodied patterns.

Brenzinger and Kraska-Szlenk affirm, for instance, that "The human body in an upright position provides structural templates for expressing spatial regions in all languages of the world" (2014: 3). These spatial regions are then lexicalized or grammaticalized further to represent temporal relations. However, speakers of different languages may construe such relations in ways that are markedly different. In Chinese, for instance, 前 *qián* 'front' is used to refer to the past while 后 *hòu* 'back' is used to refer to the future (compare 前年 *qián nián* 'year before last' with 后年 *hòu nián* 'year after next'). Naturally, English speakers also use front and back for temporal mapping but assume, in contrast to Chinese, that the future is ahead while the past is at one's back (compare "Your best years are still in front of you." with "I'm glad that's behind us."). Even so, competing historical evidence suggests that English spatio-temporal organization was at some point closer to Chinese!

This can be noted in comparing the bound roots found in the lexicalized adverbials 'be*fore*' ('fore' ~ front → past) and '*after*' ('aft' ~ back → future).

In short, the Cognitive Linguistic approach to embodiment, body partonymy and body part extension is integrative and experiential. The approach affirms principles of universal human cognition *and* linguistic relativity. Finally, the CL approach is not only descriptive and comparative but also historical. Practitioners expect that category gradience, functional typology and social communication dynamics will vary in some ways and correspond in others across speaker populations through time and space. These features of the approach are helpful to bear in mind when considering relationships between arms and legs—their parts, partitions and part-whole relations— across cultures.

Primary Blends in Arm-Leg Syncretism

Toes-and-fingers, hands-and-feet, ankles-and-wrists, elbows-and-knees: arm/leg joints and partition sets are curiously parallel—marked at once by salient resemblances and obvious differences. Something about our two sets of extremities and their respective parts invites comparison and contrast. This principle is evident across languages. We not only *see* matching sets and *categorize* our observations, we also *feel* the contrasting paradigms in our bones—radically embodied experiential patterns that we coordinate in concert through an array of daily movements that are widely distinct functionally—being involved in specialized tasks above and below the waistline. The partitions, parts and patterns that we feel and find and name between our limb sets across the transverse plane are far from perfect matches, especially across cultures; but lock-step "isomorphism" is not the point when it comes to creative analogy—much less when considering a candidate for the primary *ground* of creative analogy. And that is my primary concern in this paper.

To think of arms in terms of legs—and legs in terms of arms—is hardly a mechanical exercise. The curious parallels that are evident in the part-whole relationship sets shared between arms and legs correspond in ways that are less precise and hierarchical than syncretic and functional—both within and between languages. Matisoff (1978) discusses this type of parallel categorization as "intrafield semantic association". Intrafield associations shared by human extremities across the waistline consistently emerge as robust experiential paradigms cross-linguistically. These dynamic structures are prime candidates to consider in seeking to account for the missing link identified above. They are a plausible way to explain the origins of double-scope integration via primary blending. The embodied cognitive paradigms, or body memory templates these experiential structures generate would naturally lend themselves to further blend creation. These possibilities can also help explain the ontology of similar theories of creative analogy proposed elsewhere (see e.g., Hofstadter and Sander 2013, Silverman 2015). And yet the importance of parallels and paradigms in arm-leg partonomy is something that comparative body-part studies have yet to recognize, much less embrace.

To better illustrate the dynamics in question, consider Table 1. This dataset juxtaposes English arm-leg partonomy with that of Helpho Phowa, an aboriginal language of southeastern Yunnan Province, China (Tibeto-Burman > Burmic > Ngwi), first classified with preliminary descriptions in Pelkey (2011, 2011a). Both English and Hlepho maintain robust sets of congruent intrafield associations between appendage pairs across the waistline. Language internally, these systematic congruences can be described as matching paradigm sets. On the other hand, neither set is entirely free from aberrant constructions; and cross-linguistic comparison between the two languages suggests widely divergent construals of bodily taxonomy in the domain of appendage relations.

Whereas the English dataset features two internal pairs of congruent hierarchies neatly divided at the wrist above and the ankle below, the Hlepho dataset features no true hierachy at all. The Hlepho model, is far more "egalitarian" than its English counterpart. In fact, Hlepho *lē* and *tshî* can be legitimately glossed 'upper limb' and 'lower limb', respectively. Not only is this confirmed by local consultants, it is also demonstrable in the data itself, which exhibits a high degree of iconicity in morphological construction. With only one exception below the waist (see *tlhâphē* 'thigh'), and no exceptions above, each construction in these matching paradigms is headed by the root lexeme for the transverse field in question (*lē* or *tshî*). Both *lē* and *tshî* are demonstrably polysemous, however; and the general region most typically associated with each term corresponds roughly with English 'hand' and 'foot' respectively. In sum, then, the English intrafield paradigm shows category-congruence in terms of "multiple-recursion"—notably featuring embedded relationships at four removes. The Hlepho system, by contrast, shows congruence in terms of radial categorization relative to a central prototype (*a la* Lakoff 1987)—with all parts in each of the two fields being governed by a single exemplar.

Aside from this level of organization, which is the most general pattern in play, there are plenty of correspondences between the two languages at other levels, including congruent lexical constructions and indices of shared

Table I. Experiential and conceptual paradigms in part-whole extremity categorization across the transverse anatomical plane in English and Hlepho Phowa

English			Hlepho Phowa		
upper limb		lower limb	upper limb		lower limb
arm	:	leg	lɛ̄vùi	:	tsh̩vui̩
upper arm	:	thigh	–		tɬhâphē
elbow	:	knee	lɛ̄n̂	:	tsh̩sɛ̂pēzâ
forearm	:	shin/calf	–		–
wrist	:	ankle	lɛ̄tsi̩	:	tsh̩tsi̩
hand	:	**foot**	lɛ̄	:	**tsh̩**
palm	:	sole	lɛ̄fâ	:	tsh̩thɔ̄
finger	:	toe	lɛ̄tsūzâ	:	tsh̩dzo
fingernail	:	toenail	lɛ̄sɔ̂	:	tsh̩sɔ̂

experience. Speakers of both languages identify identical physiological joints, for example, and (to a lesser degree) similar partitions between these joints. At the morphological level, both use similar compound constructions for 'fingernail' and 'toenail' (though *sɔ̂* can also mean 'claw' in Hlepho). A full partition from shoulder to wrist can also be identified in both languages (i.e., English *arm / leg*, Hlepho *lɛ̄vùi / tsh̩vùi*). The Hlepho morpheme *vùi* 'bone' helps explain the lack of differentiation between upper and lower leg-arm divisions (with the exception of 'thigh') in the language. Both upper and lower limbs in Hlepho can be described as a single continuous 'bone' (cf. *ɛ̄-vùi* 'stem; stalk') that is interrupted in each instance by a single joint at the *lɛ̄n̂* 'elbow' above and the *tsh̩sɛ̂pēzâ* 'knee' below.

Lest we miss the larger point, though, let me assert that what is truly remarkable from a comparative perspective is not so much the presence or absence of precise mappings between the two languages but the fact that both languages (and world languages in general) feature conspicuous interfield *classificatory complementarities* between arms and legs across the waistline. My proposed term for this phenomenon is arm-leg syncretism. The phrase "classificatory complementarities" is coined by British Anthropologist Roy Ellen (1977: 367). Until now, Ellen has come closest to capturing the profound (and profoundly neglected) status of intrafield body part networks organized by the anatomical planes of upright posture (as described above).

Ellen demonstrates the importance of considering the role body-part classification schemes play cross-culturally in the development of symbol systems drawn from bodily analogies. Such symbol systems function in the context of more abstract structural relations that must be interpreted against a bodily experiential ground to adequately understand the meanings of cultural rituals, architecture, customs, kinship systems and other dimensions of social construction. He proposes that such bodily semiotic networks provide further validation and further development of structuralist anthropology, with special reference to the work of Claude Lévi-Strauss (1962) and Victor Turner (1966). He also issues a cogent complaint that is still relevant today: "There has been a tendency to stress the function of individual [body] parts rather than the relationships between them, either anatomically or functionally" (1977: 364). Little has changed in the intervening decades.

Old habits die hard, but integrated bodily paradigms persist (whether or not they are recognized). In a clarion discussion of "the parallelism of extremities"—one that is, again, as fresh and untapped today as it was in 1977—Ellen notes that in languages around the world "there is generally a recognition of similarity between the upper and lower parts of the body, reflected in identifiable structural and terminological correspondences between upper and lower limbs" (1977: 349). He goes on to argue that "relationships between parts are often more important than individual features" (1977: 367). If so, we cannot afford to overlook these relations—neither in Cognitive Anthropology nor in Cognitive Linguistics; but this is precisely what has happened in both disciplines.

In a quest to discover—or discredit—universal patterns of hierarchy and partition in body part systems, researchers have neglected to identify and theorize systemic parallels across the waistline. Narrow searches for universal taxonomies and isomorphic mappings between languages distract attention from a strong universal signal of an altogether alternative type: the syncretic experiential paradigms indexed by arm-leg partonomy. For a specific example of these dynamics, consider Savosavo, a Papuan language of the Solomon Islands. In researching the partonomy and taxonomy of the body in Savosavo, Claudia Wegener finds it "difficult to structure the body part terminology hierarchically, because there is no linguistic evidence for part-whole relations between body parts" (2006: 344). This analysis, in turn, is used to support Enfield et al.'s (2006) claim that body partonomy does little to establish the embodied cognitive approach to grammar and meaning; instead, as discussed above, the apparent gaps are used as evidence that "there are fewer points of convergence across language communities [in these regards] than previously imagined" (2006: 146).

Revisiting Wegener's Savosavo data, however, reveals numerous terminological and structural correspondences that are shared system-internally between upper and lower limbs. Terminologically, there are synthetic lexemes for 'digits' (*ririkina*) and 'nails' (*kelekelemuzi*). Structurally, the language lexicalizes terms for both 'knee' (*tuturinga*) and 'elbow' (*bulikaku*); and, similar to the Hlepho pattern introduced in Table 1, the Savosavo terms for both 'leg' (*nato*) and 'arm' (*kakau*) "are semantically general in that they cover the whole extent of the limb, including hands, feet, fingers and toes" (2006: 348). Taken together, these six lexemes map onto eight specific arm-leg locations and partitions—forming a primary blend complete with three syncretic, experiential mappings across the transverse plane. In short, there is an unmistakable paradigm-of-paradigms in Savosavo arm-leg partonomy. The fact that Wegener neglects this transverse pattern and its implications is not so much a discredit to her own analysis as it is further symptomatic of a far more general situation of neglect described above.

From the perspective of an English mother-tongue speaker, the undifferentiated arm-hand and leg-foot continua featured in languages like Hlepho and Savosavo may seem unusual; but this feature is actually commonplace elsewhere in the world. Witkowski and Brown (1985) find the general pattern to be predominant in equatorial regions, where they discuss cultural and environmental reasons for understanding why "limb parts are less salient and limb polysemy is more common" (1985: 207). The feature is also common across entire language families, such Bantu and Burmic, whose speakers extend far beyond equatorial zones. This is not to suggest, however, that typologically unusual patterns do not exist elsewhere. Drawing on years of study in Kewa, a language spoken in the southern highlands of Papua New Guinea, Karl Franklin (1963) describes a number of partonomic mappings between upper and lower extremities that are unusual from a typological-comparative perspective.

Given the discussion above, it comes as no surprise that Kewa speakers consider 'arm' (*kii*) to map onto 'leg' (*aa*) or 'forearm' (*pígípígí*) to map onto 'calf' (*roaape*); but, as can be noted in Table 2, many other transverse mappings in the language are far from common. The Kewa lexeme *rŭmu* 'knee', for instance, functions as the inverse parallel of *pasaa* 'shoulder'—a fact that is further supported by a complementary correspondence between *átóraa* 'arm pit' and *kólóbo* 'space behind the knee'. A marked *non*-correspondence between *komaa* 'upper arm' and *pálaa* 'thigh' is also notable. Neither partition is considered by Kewa speakers to have a match across waistline. Furthermore, Kewa speakers maintain a unique array of synthetic classifications in the hand-foot domain, with particularly fine-grained attention being paid to gradient correspondences between the 'heel-and-ankle' domain below the waist and its correlative pairings in the 'elbow' domain above. Kewa features no fewer than six lexemes that qualify as "synthetic partonyms" for classifying transverse relations between arms and legs. These are shaded gray in Table 2. This evidence adds substantially to the richness of the primary blend.

Table 2. Parallels and correlations in extremity categorization across the transverse plane in the Kewa language of Papua New Guinea (adapted from Franklin 1963)

Lower Limb		Upper Limb	
aa	'leg; foot' :	'arm; hand'	*kíi*
pálaa	'thigh'	–	–
rúmu	'knee' :	'shoulder'	*pasaa*
kólóbo	'behind knee' :	'arm pit'	*átóraa*
–	–	'upper arm'	*komaa*
roaape	'calf' :	'forearm'	*pígípígí*
kíbu	'shin' :	'lower forearm'	*noe*
kéréop	'wrist'	–	–
kákálo	'ankle joint' :	'elbow joint'	*kákálo*
káláló	'ankle bone' :	'elbow bone'	*káláló*
kínyálú	'heel' :	'elbow'	*kínyálú*
wáraa	'sole' :	'palm'	*wáraa*
kilikili	'toe' :	'finger'	*kilikili*
kídípaa	'toenail' :	'fingernail'	*kídípaa*

Contrary to ongoing trends in body partonomy that find arm-leg syncretism either unremarkable (due to earlier priorities) or theoretically damning (due to non-universal correspondences), the thesis I am exploring in this paper embraces such evidence and places it center-stage. The phenomenon is a prime (though by no means exclusive) candidate for a more grounded explanation of the evolution of creative analogy. Any search for grounding "mechanisms" for double-scope integration in embodied cognitive experience might naturally expect to find richly variegated instances of primary double-scope blending at work in experiential source itself. The primary process would work in ways that naturally fostered the discovery and generation of both similarity and difference in patterned, functional sets. This principle would hold true not only within the primary candidate domain in question but also between mappings across cultures. In other words, any primary source robust enough to generate body-memory templates or "scaffolding" for the more general creative analogic ability in question (i.e., "double-scope" conceptual integration) would itself naturally function in a congruent mode. My basic term for the primary blending candidate considered in this paper is "arm-leg syncretism". Framed negatively, my basic proposal is that without arm-leg syncretism (and related phenomena), double-scope integration may never have evolved.

Toe-Counts and Finger-Tracks

Further evidence of the cognitive indispensiblity of arm-leg syncretism can be drawn from cognitive linguistic research on the origins of numeral systems. Although many hold mathematics and numerals to be the ultimate example of arbitrariness or pure abstraction, Bernd Heine (1997) begs to differ. Numeral systems are ultimately motivated and iconic since "in seeking terms for numerals, speakers across the world tend to rely on their bodily extremities for linguistic expression" (Heine 2014: 25). Heine asserts that "the body-part model" is ubiquitous in the creation of numeral systems (Heine 1997: 21), just as it is in other domains of grammatical construction. The body-part model Heine reconstructs, however, favors a "top-down" orientation. Although this reconstruction cannot account for the evolution of creative analogy, it certainly makes sense as an account of the origins of counting.

Independent empirical studies continue to demonstrate the indispensible role fingers play in the foundations of mathematics (Penner-Wilger et al. 2007, Berteletti and Booth 2015). In addition to the cognitive insights such findings provide, they also serve to discredit long-entrenched biases against the use of finger-counting in mathematical education. This principle is echoed and explained with reference to the lexical residue of an experiential principle whose origins lie at the core of the embodied foundations of mathematics. In Zulu, *isithupha* 'thumb' and *isikhombisa* 'index finger' double as the numerals '6' and '7', respectively (Heine 2014: 24; Doke 1927: 326); the Kewa term for 'four' *kii* is polysemous with 'arm; hand' or 'hand bones' (Franklin 1963: 63); but beyond individual numbers, the most common basic body parts for organizing numeral sets among world languages are hands and feet.

In a recent survey of counting systems in 196 world languages, Bernard Comrie (2011) determines that 63 percent are either "decimal" systems, based on the number 10, or "quinary" systems based on the number 5. This fact points to the profound importance of fingers and hands in establishing mathematical concepts. Another 21 percent of world languages are either based the number 20 ("vigesimal") or some hybrid of 20 and 10. This latter fact points to the intrafield relations of hands *and* feet.

A single 'hand' is the most common source of the numeral '5'; and the most common source for '10' is 'two-hands'. Beyond 10 it is most common for numeral systems to move on to foot-based derivations, up to '20'—at which point the most common lexical source is either 'hands and feet' or 'whole-person' (Heine 1997: 21; Stampe 1976: 596). In the Api language of Vanuatu, for instance, '5' is derived from *luna* 'hand' and *lua luna* 'two hands' is used for the numeral '10' (Heine 1997: 21; Dantzig 1940: 25). In Mamvu, a Nilo-Saharan language of central Africa, the word for '10' is derived from a phrase meaning "all hands", while '11' is derived from a construction meaning "the foot seizes one". Once the feet have seized nine—resulting in the numeral '19'—the next numeral is derived from a construction meaning 'one whole person', i.e., '20' (Heine 1997: 20, Vorbichler 1965: 94–96).

Since fingers are unmarked for dexterity relative to toes; and since fingers are also unmarked for ease of viewing, they are naturally more suited to counting and a more salient testing ground for launching numeral systems. Heine makes little of such dynamics, opting rather to identify finger-counting as a key token of a more general type: his "top-down" principle governing bodily organization (and grammatical constructs based on such systems). This, it should be noted, is itself a rather top-down approach to theory building. Heine assumes that since the upper half of the body is "more differentiated and more salient for perceptual and communicative purposes", all intrafield mapping must proceed "from upper to lower parts of the human body—that is the lower half tends to be conceptualized in terms of the upper half" (1997: 134). In short this hypothesized asymmetrical mapping is also assumed to be exclusively unidirectional—i.e., from upper parts, locations and functions to lower parts, locations and functions. In seeking to identify embodied sources of conceptual blending, then, it is worth noting that, although this might help account for single-scope conceptual integration, it would seriously restrict possibilities for identifying bodily sources for double-scope integration networks across the transverse plane.

Approached as a universal *tendency* relevant to the specific domains and relations Heine selects for discussion, his observations may be valid; but extended to other relations and domains, the tendency itself breaks down. In support of this critique, I wish to suggest that Heine's bid to generalize the proposition in question to the status of a restrictive universal neglects six important points:

1. The conspicuous proliferation of piecemeal evidence to the contrary.

2. Synthetic classifications of body partonomy across the transverse plane.

3. Other parallels in intrafield categorization across the waistline that cannot be reduced to a top-down model.

4. Integrative patterns of intrafield semantic shift (e.g., ambidirectional and unified shifts).

5. Unified interfield mappings of transverse embodied paradigms to material and organic culture.

6. The functional (vs. anatomical) nature of transverse markedness.

Points 4–6 are explored further in the next three sections. Point 3 is explored in the previous section. Points 1 and 2 are alluded to above, but it will be helpful to expand on both a bit more here before moving on.

Regarding the first point, Heine himself spends several pages (see esp. 1997: 134–136) attempting to swat away a swarm of counterexamples that contradict his supposed universal claim of top-down unidirectionality in body-part mapping. First he dismisses German *Handschuh* ('hand shoe') 'glove' by saying that gloves are not body parts themselves but merely a covering and that protecting the feet is more common than protecting the hands. Then he dismisses Hausa 'knee of arm' by suggesting that this is better analyzed as a shift from back to front since elbows face backward while knees face frontwards (1997: 135). He dismisses the many world languages in which there is genuine synthetic polysemy between 'fingers' and 'toes' by doing little more than hoping no language will ever be found in which the polysemous term originally meant 'toe' instead of 'finger'.

This final phenomenon is the focus of my second critique in the list above. The point is illustrated in the previous section with numerous examples. It is widespread and is by no means restricted to fingers and toes as evidence cited in the previous section from Hlepho to Kewa to Savosavo to English bears witness. Considering English alone—in addition to the synthetic term 'digits' (which genuinely originates with fingers to Heine's credit)—we find 'nails', 'limbs' and 'appendages' as clear examples of arm-leg syncretism. In the former three cases, at least, the top-down claim is simply a moot point. Something else is "afoot"; and it might be "handy" not to be bound "hand-and-foot" by a theory that prohibits its recognition. Such prohibitions tend be quite costly in the long run. In this case they might even cost "an arm-and-a-leg". In other words, the mappings are ambidirectional and simultaneous—certainly not top-down and unidirectional. Similarly, we might explore synthetic morphological constructions like 'pinkie toe' and 'pinkie finger', which have corrollaries in many other languages as 'child toe' and 'child finger' relative to a 'mother toe' and 'mother finger' (see Matisoff 1992; Pelkey 2013; Wilkins 1996; Heine 1997: 132).

These items fly in the face of a strict top-down ideology. Aside from the fact that such an agenda misses the larger point of structural relationships that hold between upper and lower extremities, and misunderstands the functional status of markedness across the transverse plane, counterexamples will continue to surface that demonstrate the lower extremities' potency to serve as source domain for corresponding body parts above the waistline.

In the Phola language of south-central Yunnan Province (Tibeto-Burman < Burmic < Ngwi, Pelkey 2011, 2011a), the lexicalized construction for 'arm' (segmented from shoulder to wrist)' is a compound of *lā* 'hand / arm', *ɣùu* 'bone' and *pɔ̄* 'thigh':

> *lāɣùupɔ̄*
>
> lā   +ɣùu   +pɔ̄
>
> hand.arm   +bone   +thigh
>
> 'arm' (shoulder to wrist)

The final morpheme in this construction is clearly cognate with Proto-Ngwi etymon #121B *(ʃ)-boŋ² 'thigh' (Bradley 1979: 304). Unfortunately for Heine, this mapping cannot (and should not) be explained away. The direction of the mapping is bottom-up.

Consider also the Dene Sųłiné word for 'fingerprint(s)' *dene-lá-ké* (Rice 2014: 90). Dene Sųłiné is an Athabaskan language spoken by Chipewyan aboriginals of northwestern Canada. The term in question is glossed, 'person-hand-foot':

> *deneláké*
>
> dene-   lá-   ké
>
> person-   hand-   foot
>
> 'fingerprints'

This lexicalization strategy only makes sense by recognizing that *ké* foot has been extended in the language to denote 'footprints'. Thus, the lexicalization involves an intrafield primary blend of hand/finger prints and toe/foot prints. It may be true enough that the mapping is unidirectional; but it is certainly not "top-down". In fact, as Sally Rice's earlier work on the language demonstrates, the lower half of the body is unmarked as a source domain for upper-body references, and even basic motion verbs are organized relative to the transverse plane (Rice 2002).

These examples are offered not as a comprehensive survey, but as a reminder that an incessant stream of counterexamples will continue to be found by anyone willing to look—counterexamples that beset Heine's universal claim relative to the transverse plane. In short, it may well be the case that Heine (1997) is so intent on establishing "what appears to be a universal strategy to conceptualize the lower half of the body in terms of the upper half" (1997:

47) as a unidirectional top-down mapping that he ignores the broader picture of paradigmatic relations. Among other things, these relations shift in concert through time and reveal themselves as ambidirectional mappings in everything from German gloves and Hausa elbows to the pinkie children of Sino-Tibetan and the footprinted fingertips of Dene Sųłiné. Even the contemporary "toe-shoe" phenomenon, discussed further below (cf. Pelkey 2015) is problematic for Heine's top-down unidirectional assertion. Yes, it is true enough that toes are fingers in the blend; but fingers are also toes.

As David Wilkins establishes in his landmark historical linguistic project exploring universal trends of semantic shift in body part terms, these overlooked principles can also be readily observed in ambidirectional semantic shifts across the transverse plane. Wilkins consults extensive comparative data from seven major language families: Austronesian, Bantu, Dravidian, Indo-European, Papuan, Tibeto-Burman and various Native American languages. One of his discoveries is a systematic, syncretic relationship between the 'upper' and 'lower' appendages and their analogous membership. He finds, in language families around the world, that it is commonplace, to find a word that once meant "toenail" having shifted to mean "fingernail" and vice-versa. Furthermore, upper and lower appendages show directly analogous patterns of metonymic semantic shift from part to whole such that words which once meant "palm" may gradually shift to mean "hand" and, likewise below the waist, words that once meant "heel" may gradually shift to mean "foot". Although Wilkin's study is much cited, the reflexive embodied paradigms implicit in his analysis have received very little attention in the literature. The next section seeks to correct this situation.

Limb-From-Limb: Semantic Shifts

A general hypothesis that guides the present study, and the larger project to which it belongs, is that the inverse specialization of our human extremities—organized relative to the transverse plane—may hold untapped potential for developing a more robust evo devo account of human cognition. Some of the most compelling evidence for reevaluating the importance of our extremities in this regard emerges from the field of historical and comparative linguistics. All words are informed by networks of relations whose origins we can retrace to discover the idiosyncrasies of their adventures through time. It is the etymologist's job to reconstruct these adventure stories. Polysemy, synonymy and semantic shift are among the most familiar side-plots. Sometimes history repeats itself, making for stories that are remarkably similar across languages and language families. When this happens historical linguists refer to the change as a "natural tendency".

Diachronic research on natural tendencies of semantic shift reveals that arms and legs, hands and feet (and the internal part-whole relationships they entail) not only share implicit, analogous sets or paradigms but also tend to subsist and shift in lexical concert through time and across languages, via layered mappings that are directly parallel—unified, blended, inversely (a) symmetrical and multiply paradigmatic. But these remarkable bodily diagrams shared cross-culturally across the transverse plane receive scant attention in the literature. Even sources that present the most compelling evidence for their salience do so without registering broader implications. This is an oversight the present section works to correct.

As described above, Wilkin's (1996) project on natural tendencies of semantic shift in body part terms identifies both ambidirectional and uni-directional semantic shifts that provide evidence of transverse mapping between upper and lower limb metonymy across language families. Here I consider each in turn beginning with ambidirectional semantic shifts across the transverse plane, something Wilkins identifies as one of five natural ten-dencies in body-part oriented semantic shifts across language families. In his own words, "Where the waist provides a midline, it is a natural tendency for terms referring to parts of the upper body to shift to refer to parts of the lower body and vice versa (e.g., 'elbow' ⇔ 'knee'; 'uvula'→ 'clitoris'; 'anus' → 'mouth')" (1996: 273–274). His findings suggest, notably, that the primary blending principle in question is not exclusive to arm-leg networks. It also extends to face-groin analogies. Indeed, the face-groin domain provides another potential experiential space for primary blending. This is an important point that has also received little attention (cf. Paul 1973; Matisoff 1978), unfortunately, it opens up questions so large that they warrant a research project of their own. For now we have further "legwork" to do on the topic at "hand".

As mentioned above, Wilkins, following Matisoff (1978), discusses these semantic shifts as "intrafield metonymic changes". This is a groundbreaking insight, but given the patterns that emerge between semantic fields in the data, this narrow focus needs to be expanded. What Wilkins and many others working in this vein overlook is the existence of profound category paradigmaticity that exists between intrafield sets. This is understandable. Historical linguists are typically more concerned with distinguishing between innovations that are useful for subgrouping language relationships geneti-cally and diachronically and those that are not. The former are discussed as "non-natural changes", the latter as "natural changes". Since natural changes are not useful for subgrouping, their explanation becomes fodder for other disciplines—such as psycholinguistics and dialectology. In other words the discipline-specific focus on discovering the naturalness and non-naturalness of person-part semantic shifts, has led to the neglect of other important patterns inherent in the data.

Wilkins's proposes a 75-item wordlist "centered on the most commonly attested semantic changes within the domain of person-parts" across language families (1996: 283–284). No fewer than nine of these terms participate in semantic shifts that actually belong to higher-order sets. These higher-order sets involve tacit relationships shared between the extremities in inverse patterns relative to the waistline. The superordinate pattern in question has not, to my knowledge, been indentified (much less explained) in the literature to-date. The nine terms in question are involved in three ambidirectional shifts as summarized in the following list:

1. 'elbow' ⇔ 'knee'

2a. 'claw' → 'fingernail'

2b. 'claw' → 'toenail'

3a. 'calf/shin' → 'thigh'

3b. 'forearm' → 'upper arm'

Set 1 provides the clearest example of an intra-field, ambidirectional shift across the waistline. It is common, in other words, for the word glossed 'knee' in a given language to have shifted from a more archaic term that was originally glossed 'elbow'. The inverse is also true: it is common for the word glossed 'elbow' in a given language to have shifted from a more archaic term that was originally glossed 'knee'. This pattern on its own is interesting enough; it suggests a kind of embodied chiasmus at work diachronically and cross-linguistically. It also suggests a very basic instance of primary embodied blending. Thinking of elbows as knees and knees as elbows involves proprioceptive and kinesthetic body memories that come to be blended conceptually through processes of semantic extension, polysemy and shift.

Considered in relation to the other two sets in this list, Set 1 is the most prototypical instance of ambidirectional shift across the transverse plane. Set 2 is also ambidirectional but only via an external mapping. Whereas the elbow-knee blend pattern is an intrafield mapping, the fingernail-toenail blend is an *inter*field mapping. It is also inter*specific*. Non-human animal claws are a common source for both toenail and fingernail lexemes cross-linguistically. In the Phupa language of China (Mengzi County, Yunnan), for instance, $sə^{33}$ means '[animal]claw'; and the Phupa terms for 'fingernail' and 'toenail' are $la^{55}s\partial^{33}$ (hand/arm + claw) and $t\varepsilon^h i^{21}s\partial^{33}$ (foot/leg + claw), respectively. This is not merely evidence for a natural semantic extension, however. It is also evidence of our capacity and tendency to think of fingernails as toenails and toenails as fingernails via reference to a third. In other words, it gives us evidence for identifying basic modes of primary blending.

As discussed above, conceptual blends are classified by Fauconnier and Turner (2002) along a continuum of complexity ranging respectively from simplex and mirror networks to single-scope and double-scope networks. Applying these categories, the blend in Set 1 above can be analyzed as a "mirror network". Even though both are pointy joints, elbows and knees are quite different. The former are small and open forward (toward the anterior half of the coronal plane) while the latter are larger and open backward (toward the posterior half of the coronal plane). But the two pointy joints share a common frame: in addition to both being pointy joints, both are also located midway along their respective limbs. Because of this, and due to the cross-linguistic naturalness of the ambidirectional shift, they qualify as an instance of primary grounding for more abstract mirror networks. The blend in Set 2, in turn, can be analyzed as two "single-scope networks" (involving source-target mappings between claws and nails) lexicalizing as a unified "mirror network" (in which fingernails and toenails come to be perceptually and conceptually organized according to a common frame).

The blend in Set 3 is more complex. It involves an ambidirectional shift only in a relatively oblique sense. This sense, however, is perhaps the most crucial to grasp since understanding its significance is key for unlocking one of the most radically embodied paradigms of nested bodily paradigms. This network of networks informs (and reveals) our capacity for what I am referring to in this paper as "primary blending", only it amps up this capacity to a more advanced level: that of the double-scope network. Double-scope networks "have two different organizing frames and parts of both of them are used in the blend as well as in a new emergent structure" (Birdsell 2014: 80). The cross-linguistic naturalness of 'calf' → 'thigh' shifts is directly analogous to the cross-linguistic naturalness of 'forearm' → 'upper arm' shifts. This tendency points to a potential source of primary grounding for double-scope networks. Both linguistically and experientially, humans are prone to think of legs and arms ("two different organizing frames") analogously such that their partitions are used in blended shifts semantically "as well as in a new emergent structure" (2014: 80). The new emergent structure in this case may actually be as old as the evolution of double-scope conceptual blending itself.

The tendency to shift semantics from calf to thigh below the waist and from forearm to upper arm above the waist is a single embedded instance of a primary double-scope network functioning tacitly in a much larger network of networks that emerges cross-linguistically. Treated in isolation each of these shifts could only be called unidirectional semantic mappings. This sense is captured in each individual arrow listed in Figure 1. This figure constitutes a major reorganization of Wilkin's own individual mappings for these schemas. Until now, no development of this pathbreaking research has drawn attention to the unified analogy implicit in the data above and below the waistline.

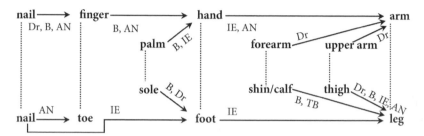

Figure 1. Reframing Wilkins's (1996: 276) diagram of "Attested semantic changes involving visible parts and visible wholes" as a pattern of inverse multiple-paradigmaticity. Language family abbreviations: AN=Austronesian, B=Bantu, Dr=Dravidian, IE=Indo-European, TB=Tibeto-Burman

It is important to keep in mind in pondering this diagram that the mere absence of a shift in a given language family is not proof that this aspect of the macro-network is only weakly supported. First of all, Wilkin's dataset is limited—such relations may still be discovered in futher treatments. Second, as mentioned above, some distinctions in the chart are usually realized as semantic composites in various language families (hand-arm and foot-leg tend to be unified lexemes in Bantu and Burmic languages for instance). Third, simply because a pattern is not lexically realized does not mean it is not experientially realized. On the contrary, the strength of this analogous pattern cross-linguistically suggests that the full paradigm is at least a tacit universal for human perception and cognition. Fourth, and most importantly, the overall pattern is the point. Human languages across the millenia provide conceptual categorical evidence of an underlying universal experience of our extremities, patterned in nested sets of analogous relations above and below the waistline. This provides empirical, evolutionary evidence of a primary source for double-scope conceptual blending. Further empirical evidence comes from linguistic anthropology and cultural mapping processes known as embodied meronymy.

Feet for Roots: Meronymic Mapping

In the Greek myth of Daphne and Apollo, Apollo the son of Zeus care-lessly hurls an insult at Cupid the god of love. Cupid promptly retaliates, striking Apollo in the heart with a golden arrow. This causes Apollo to fall in love with Daphne, a local wood nymph. To round out his revenge, Cupid then strikes Daphne with an arrow of lead causing her to resist Apollo's ad-vances. As Apollo pursues her, she flees deep into the forest. When at long last he catches up to her, and reaches toward her verklempt with longing, Daphne reacts with an abrupt surprise. On the spot she transforms herself into a laurel tree—ensuring that she will never be forced to marry Apollo. This moment of woodland magic is made intelligible by a spell of linguistic magic—a radically embodied rhetorical spell. According to Ovid, *in ramos bracchia crescunt, pes modo tam velox pigris radicibus haeret*: "her arms grow into branches, sluggish roots adhere to feet that were so recently so swift" (8CE[2005]: 37).

This is a classical Latin instance of embodied meronymic mapping, one that is easily intelligible cross-linguistically. Body parts are mapped onto tree parts (arms/hands → branches; feet/legs → roots); and even though these body parts actually *become* the tree parts, the tree parts are still in some sense body parts. In short, what results is a complex primary blend with a paradigmatic *corporeal* anchor for input space 1 and a paradigmatic *material* anchor for input space 2. Extrusions above and below the waistline blend with analogous extrusions above and below the tree trunk. The person is now a tree, but the tree is also a person. Whereas most of the mappings in the previous section can be identified as intrafield embodied meronymy, Ovid's classical Latin example is an instance of *inter*field embodied meronymy.

Through the centuries many painters and sculptors have attempted to capture this moment of transformation. In most instances Daphne is depicted with arms raised and hands sprouting branches as her parted feet succumb to roots. This is vividly illustrated in the Figure 2 reproduction of a late-13th-century painting by Italian artist Antonio del Pollaiolo. Daphne's posture in the painting incorporates the spread-eagle pose; and the visual rendering of the primary blend draws attention to a cross-linguistic lexical phenomenon as well.

In a "stratified probability sample" of body-part mapping strategies across world languages, Hilpert (2007: 82, 85) finds that a full 15 percent maintain lexical extensions from bodily 'arms' to tree limbs. Although this may seem unimpressive, it occurs in languages from widely diverse families. This gives us reasons to assume not only that the individual lexical mappings

Figure 2. *Apollo and Daphne* by Antonio del Pollaiolo, c.1475

emerged independently but also that they are a feature of our shared human experience—a universally available concept rooted in tacit, embodied cognition situated in similar environments. The fact that English speakers lexicalize an inverse mapping—from tree 'limbs' to bodily arms (and legs)—suggests that the primary blend in question is a mirror network at the level of tacit cognition. At the level of lexical mapping in any given language, it should be identified as a single-scope network (mapping from source domain to target domain). In other words, at the level of pre-linguistic, tacit cognition the meronymic mapping in question can function in both directions—much like our understanding of Daphne's arms. Even when they shift into branches, we still know the branches as Daphne's arms. Once the primary mirror blend becomes lexicalized, a default unidirectional mapping is established.

Although they are not represented in Hilbert's sample, the Phula languages of Yunnan, China (Tibeto-Burman > Burmic > Ngwi > Southeastern, see Pelkey 2011, 2011a) are among the languages of the world that make the 'hand/arm' → branch mapping lexically explicit. What makes the Phula languages worth mentioning in this context is the fact that many of them round out the blend with a foot/leg → root complement. I wish to suggest that this dual linguistic mapping moves the primary "single scope" network into the domain of primary "double-scope" conceptual blending. The double-scope meronymic blend in question is especially notable among the five Phula languages listed in Table 3.

Morphemes cognate with Alugu ei^{33} are glossed 'wood' and/or 'tree' in these languages; while morphemes cognate with Alugu i^{33}- are noun class prefixes for organic material. Thus the mappings above the transverse plane can all be glossed roughly 'wood hand/arm' while those below the transverse plane can be glossed roughly 'organic foot/leg' or—in the case of Phala— 'wood foot-leg'. These five languages descend from four distinct sub-branches of Southeastern Ngwi diachronically (Pelkey 2011), suggesting that the dual transverse mapping was a feature of the ancestor language. The $lj\varepsilon^{21}{\sim}l\varepsilon^{33}$ variation in Southern Muji 'hand/arm' → branch is due to historical lexicalization processes (see Pelkey 2013). The Phola-Phala pairing represents two closely related sister languages that have only recently diverged. In all four cases, then, an explicit lexical mapping is preserved at the primary blend across the transverse plane.

Table 3. Lexicalized body-part → tree-part mappings in four Phula languages: Inverse parallelism in embodied meronymy across the transverse anatomical plane

Language	Transverse Body Parts			Transverse Tree Parts	
Alugu	hand/arm	la^{52}	→	$ei^{33}la^{52}$	branch
Khlula		$la^{33}pə^{55}$	→	$s\eta^{33}la^{33}$	
Muji, Southern		$lj\varepsilon^{21}$	→	$ei^{33}ka^{21}l\varepsilon^{33}$	
Phola		$la^{33}b\varepsilon^{21}$	→	$si^{31}la^{33}k\underline{a}^{31}$	
Alugu	foot/leg	$ts^ha^{33}tc^hi^{33}$	→	$i^{33}tc^hi^{33}pə^{33}$	root
Khlula		$ts^h\eta^{21}$	→	$i^{33}ts^h\eta^{21}$	
Muji, Southern		tc^hi^{21}	→	$i^{21}tc^hi^{21}$	
Phala		$k^hi^{55}bo^{33}$	→	$ei^{33}k^hi^{55}mi^{21}$	

Another reason it is plausible to posit this primary blend as a universally available concept across cultures is the marked nature of orthogonality that humans share with trees. Both humans and trees share "upright posture": the life lines of both exist at perpindicular angles relative to the earth. Combining this basic experiential analogy with shared slender torsos or trunks, and combining these observations with a spread-eagle frame, trees provide a prime domain for mapping primary blends across the transverse axis. They also provide a plausible mechanism for the formation of one of the first sets of mental space projections capable of functioning at the level of primary double-scope blending.

The salience of upright transversality shared between humans and trees does not prevent us from mapping the primary blend space of our bodily extremities onto other mobile orientations in space, such as the caudal-rostral/dorsal-ventral orientation, even though these experiences are more typical in non-human animal locomotion (and in our experience of four-wheeled vehicles). This point is vividly illustrated in one of the most famous examples of embodied meronymic mapping: the Western Apache analogy for parts of an automobile as recorded by Keith Basso (1990: 13–24). In Western Apache, automobile parts are systematically named according to a detailed and elegant embodied template, such that *bidáá* 'eye' is extended to headlight, *biyedaa'* 'chin/jaw' is extended to front bumper, *bijíí* 'heart' is extended to distributor, and so on. Although the example is frequently cited and has been discussed from numerous angles in the literature, one aspect of the elaborate analogy has gone unnoticed. The data in question are listed in Table 4.

Table 4. Transverse embodied paradigm in Western Apache car part meronymy

Western Apache Term	Body Part		Car Part
bigan	'hand/arm'	→	front wheel
bikee'	'foot'	→	rear wheel
biwos	'shoulder'	→	front fender
bikai'	'hip/butt'	→	rear fender

The paired 'hand' and 'foot' mappings to front and rear wheel, respectively, are analogous to the blended body-tree meronymies among the Phula languages. The blend spaces are doubled in Western Apache, however, making for an even more elaborate paradigm that includes the inversely (a)symmetric relations between analogous body part relations—relations that link up bodily extremities with the torso. hand/arm : shoulder :: hip : leg/foot)—and the immediately adjacent car parts—front wheel : front fender :: rear fender : rear wheel—

respectively. Given the visceral level of embodiment featured in this network, the Apache automobile should also be identified as an instance of primary blend extension. It also helps illustrate how radically embodied relations can be theorized as the wellspring of our capacity for double-scope conceptual blending and abstract paradigms in general. Primary blending across the transverse plane can also help us account for other features that inform human cognition and human language such as markedness relations.

Markedness, Upside-Down

We find in languages and cultures around the world that the inverse lateralization of brains and extremities has evolved physiologically to favor left-brain + right-hand dominance. This explains the normalization of the dextral (right) over the sinistral (left) in these same cultures, thus setting up not only a powerful template for the infinite generation of antithetical binaries in these same cultures but also a scheme by which one member of the binary comes to be privileged, taken for granted, or simply "unmarked". My working hypothesis is that markedness relations in language are deeply rooted in this same experiential, kinesthetic memory-based template. But this asymmetrical left-right template does not account for the full story of the origins of markedness. In fact, the nature of tranversalization sets up markedness relations in quite a different mode. The inverse status of the upper half of the body relative to the lower half creates an integrated field for experimental, but systematic, classification. This, in turn, allows not only for the emergence of lexicalized primary double-scope networks of arm-leg partonymy but also novel primary double-scope networks like the foot-finger integration of upper and lower extremities featured in FiveFingers footwear, as I discuss further below.

With this in mind, let me suggest that lateral relations provide grounding for our analytic capabilities as human beings while transverse relations provide grounding for human-specific modes of analogic modelling. Whereas the markedness of left-right lateral relations is more *a priori* and ideology-oriented (i.e., "analytic"), the markedness of upper-lower transverse relations is more, *a posteriori* and analogy-oriented (a.k.a., "synthetic"). One of the core hypotheses of the larger project from which this study emerges is that these relations—both of which come into their own with upright posture—are crucial primary sources of our penchant for both analytic presupposition and analogic imagination.

Whereas analytic thinking is often humorless and devoid of nuance, with analogy comes humor, irony and paradox. Even if the upper limbs are construed as superior to the lower limbs for their "angelic" ability to reach up high into the sky, toward the very heavens; it takes only a moment's reflection to recall that the "inferior" lower limbs are more in touch—"more rooted" more "down to earth"—and "actually going places". Both sets are dominant for certain correlative tasks, subordinate for others. Emphasize either to the neglect of the other, and the tables are easily turned. Transverality, in short, affords a very different kind of markedness.

As I demonstrate elsewhere (Pelkey forthcoming), schematic mappings that inevitably draw on these transverse body memories construe the upper as the place of universal propositions, the place of normative gender binaries, the place of the ideological given. But these privileged statuses are easily upended across the transverse plane, whether through an upside-down logic like Peirce's existential graphs, upside-down gender differences that call normative binaries into question, or upside-down escape routes from ideological double-binds.

The upside-down effect is a radically embodied feature of human experience. We might well anticipate that it could play some role in the organization and development of our cognitive/affective faculties. We understand someone head-over-heels in love, for instance, with reference to acts as mundane as a somersault or a series of cartwheels. Thinking of arms as legs and legs as arms in a more sustained, experiential way is made possible by veiwing or doing a handstand—or, better, by seeing (or being) someone *walking* on their hands. German athlete Mirko Hanßen even skates on his hands for YouTube audiences of thousands. He specializes in performing stunts while wearing customized inline skates on his hands—jumping ramps and navigating obstacle courses all in sustained handstand position. He calls it (what else?), "Handskating". The captivating spectacle and its intrinsic humor owes itself in large part to what I am describing as "transverse markedness reversal".

Transverse reversals can also play an explicit role in mythical and ritual systems. As African ethnographer John Middleton (1960) reports, the Lugbara people of Uganda and Congo traditionally assumed that cultural outsiders such as Europeans and neighboring tribes such as Logo and Keliko peoples would "walk about upside down" until they were spotted by a Lugbara, at which point they would pretend to walk about on their legs (1960: 234, 241).[2] Similarly, according to Myerhoff (1978, as cited in Norrman 1999), Huichol aboriginals of the Sierra Madre Occidentál in north central Mexico incorporate complex series of reversals into ritual practices. This can happen

---

[2] My appreciation goes to Geoffrey Owens for bringing this source and connection to my attention in October 2014.

in speech, including reversals in terms of reference (calling the old 'young' and the young 'old'), and in gesture, including the subtitution of a foot for a hand in ritual performance.

Markedness emerges with very different characteristics via primary blending across the transverse plane. Semiotically informed analyses of markedness phenomena since Jakobson have insisted that markedness theory is a theory of interpretants (Shapiro 1983: 17; Andrews 1990: 1, 45). If the interpretant is a "living habit" (Savan 1976: 48) that prepares us to interpret events, or anticipate an outcome, or make assumptions in a particular way, the interpretant becomes much more immediately salient in analogic modelling processes. This is vividly apparent in primary blending activities across the transverse plane.

Contrary to Heine's assumptions (1997: 135), we cannot say that the upper body or upper limbs are unmarked; we can only identify the purpose *for which* they are unmarked. Hands are unmarked for object manipulation. This is an activity which, in its unmarked modality, is best accomplished using bare skin. Hence hands are unmarked for digit differentiation. Feet, by contrast are unmarked for things like standing and locomotion. This latter is an activity which, in its unmarked modality, is often best accomplished using protective covering. Since protective coverings are more efficiently produced without digit differentiation, and since toes are marked for purposes of object manipulation for which digit differentiation is useful, the unmarked shoe is manufactured with a singular "toe". As we find in the FiveFingers shoe line manufactured by Vibram footwear (see Pelkey 2015 for further discussion), any of these relations may be upended, often suddenly, and usually in ways we find surprising (if not revolting) and often hillarious. Because of such dynamics, we should consider the possibility that oppositions shared across the waistline—above and below the transverse plane—are of a different experiential/cognitive class than oppositions shared between left and right—the two halves of the sagittal plane.

My term for the transverse phenomenon explored above is "arm-leg syncretism", and my thesis is that the phenomenon is an indispensible source of primary blending—a blend source robust enough to create an analogic base grounded in body memory that would be suitable for the creation of more abstract double-scope integration networks, or creative analogies. Creative analogy, is a feature of human language that sets human cognition and communication apart from all other species. This means it is quite possible that there is something about the mundane (cognitive, embodied) experience of living with arms and legs that is at least partly responsible for the evolution of semiotic consciousness and, eventually, language.

Naturally, this possibility warrants far more attention and critical exploration. For now it is important to stress again that arm-leg syncretism could not have emerged and would not have served as embodied grounding for the evolution of language apart from an organizing frame. Upright posture fostered this frame by reconfiguring our anatomical planes relative to the earth, thereby revolutionizing our bodily experience of symmetry and asymmetry. Notably, this account not only separates us from all other species, but integrates us with other species by reframing analogy as a gradient phenomenon, shared to some degree with other animals. This, in turn, brings us full circle to Deely's "semiotic animal".

Upright Posture, Anatomical Planes, and the Semiotic Animal

Reorganized by a new, habitually orthogonal relationship to the earth, upright posture frees our upper limbs for active reflection. Left-right sagittal relations become more pronounced and more conceptual, yielding positive grounds for the development of oppositional markedness as a cognitive, cultural tool. But this is not all: upper-lower transverse relations draw attention to another mode of markedness—functional markedness between part-whole sets that can be used for proto-analogical reflection, forming a cognitive/conceptual base for extension to other domains. I have not argued that these embodied evolutionary dynamics are the sum of the origins of creative analogy (and thereby the language faculty)—but only that they are likely to be a profoundly important component. Such possibilities are also profoundly neglected.

The neglect of embodied dynamics at the level of primary modeling underlying the emergence of creative analogy is partly due to widespread biases against enactive, embodied approaches in general. Another challenge such accounts face in this instance at least is due to other widespread biases against any value being placed, whether—logically, aesthetically, theoretically or cognitively—on the lower half of the human body. It is, naturally, somewhat embarrassing to admit the lower half of our bodies may be crucial to consider in accounting for the fundamental nature of human cognition. The lower half reminds us most clearly of our animal nature. We are not disembodied spirits or angels hovering above the earth. We are drawn to the earth, padding with our paws from place to place; voiding, rutting, mating and bearing young no differently than the vast branching varieties of our mammalian next-of-kin. It is in this connection that Deely's semiotic animal distinction also comes into its own. We cannot fully account for our humanity unless we also embrace our animality. Attending to issues of bodily symmetry and asymmetry plays an important role in this project.

Our animal heritage is underscored not only by transverse "asymmetries" in which the lower body is perceived to be more animal than the upper but also by sagittal "symmetries" in which the left and right sides of all animal bodies (humans included) are perceived to be far more symmetrical—far more perfectly reversible or "enantiomorphic" than those imagined to hold between upper and lower (or front and back). Thus, when confronted with an unfamiliar Huichol ritual cited in Myerhoff (1978) from north central Mexico's Sierra Madre Occidentál, Norrman (1999) declares that the Huichol ritual practice of substituting a foot for a hand, is a "watered-down enantiomorphism"—a corrupted version of "symmetry-proper" (1999: 66). Norrman has good company in making such assumptions.

Contemporary symmetry theory is founded on bilaterality and (mis) construes bilaterality to be perfectly mirror symmetric or "enantiomorphic". Wherever else in nature this may be true, it is not true of the human body. Even human faces are not truly bilaterally symmetric, except in the ideal. Subtle dissymmetries and asymmetries, such as variant patterns of freckles and differing striations of wrinkles, along with more dramatic antithetical symmetries, such as a twinkling left eye, a scar on one side of the chin, or a mole on one upper lip, are the norm. Likewise, our two hands are not perfectly symmetrical but antithetically symmetrical due to lateralization (or handedness) and reflective function (vs. static reflection). Not only is hand physiology marked and unmarked due to specialization, but hands do not match simply by rotating one 180 degrees (in which case one faces front and the other back). Thus, in human experience opposition is the norm—marked symmetries, not pure symmetries.

The modern fixation with bilaterality, typified in Norrman's obsession with enantiomorphy, cuts two ways: it obscures the oppositional dynamics that structure our experience across the sagittal plane; and it obscures our conceptual awareness of analogical relationships across the transverse plane. This fixation appears to be due to an analytic bias introduced as late as the 18th century (Hon and Goldstein 2008), one that is not only conceptually foreign to ancient civilizations but also to many traditional societies around world in contemporary times (Levinson and Brown 1994; Danziger and Pederson 1998; Danziger 2011). This is not to say that tacit relationships of markedness or "lateralization" across the sagittal plane are foreign in these same cultures, however. On the contrary, at a conceptual level, antisymmetry seems to be more familiar or salient in human cultures than mere symmetry.

A long term goal of such inquiry, however, should be to reveal the interdependence between the two, a project that is derivative of a larger goal in thematizing the semiotic animal, as I have argued elsewhere (Pelkey 2016).

The importance of interdependent dynamics for understanding the semiotic animal as a distinction and for understanding anything as semiotic animals is a theme that surfaces throughout Deely's titular monograph on the topic (2010). The theme is not foregrounded at length in the text however, beyond passing illustrations of interdependent dynamics and a few overt assertions that we need to work at "reconceptualizing the whole matter of interdependency" (2010: 123). When Deely remarks that Peirce's project was "to classify the manner in which mind-dependent being and mind-independent being interpenetrate and reveal themselves objectively through the weave and pattern of human experience" (2010: 7), we are faced with a problem of interdependence. When he muses that the notion of relations necessarily involves "permeability" between mind-dependent and mind-independent realities (2010: 56)—between "the otherwise opposed orders of *ens reale* and *ens rationis*" (2010: 63)—these too are reflections on interdependent dynamics. So too is Deely's reference to Sebeok's (1984) assertion that the mission of semiotics is "to mediate between reality and illusion" in the text, along with his insistence that one consequence of semiotic understanding is the blurring of presumably fixed boundaries, especially in places and between phenomena where we we are most habitually conditioned to expect them— e.g., "between sensory intuition and things-in-themselves or between concepts and noumena" (2010: 124).

As I suggest elsewhere (Pelkey 2013a, 2016a), more adequate exploration, explanation and thematization of this aspect of semiosis will require far more attention. Even drawing interdependent dynamics into our awareness will require much more work. However this might be accomplished broadscale and longterm, though, we can be sure that the task will be radically embodied, requiring us to draw on the intertwining felt dyanmics and consequences of sagittal and transverse relations even as we thematize them. To the degree that we are able to do so, to that degree we might also develop analogical bases and evolutionary accounts robust enough to sustain an understanding of the objects of reality as they really are: actively interrelated and interdependent.

Otherwise, moving "beyond patriarchy and feminism", as Deely advises, is no more likely than moving beyond "a misconceived objectivity and a solipsistic subjectivity" or moving beyond the misconstruals of objectivism and subjectivism that underlie our historically oscillating fixation with realism and idealism (2010: 7–8). In my view, moving beyond ideologies such as these, along with the endless litany of other similar culturally constructed binaries, provides, strong motivation and adequate rationale for placing thematic inquiry into the nature, manifestations and possibilities of (embodied) interdependence center stage. Granting embodied interdependence pride-of-place in our efforts toward theory building and systematizing, is also likely to help us go somewhere (instead of nowhere) with language—avoiding the endless feedback loops of tautology and circularity through which categories and concepts cannibalize other concepts and categories—avoiding the inclination to engage in system building primarily in order to validate the system being built. To embrace the embodied dynamics of the semiotic animal as the core of human being would be to embrace not only the interdependence between oppositional contrasts and antagonistic binaries, but also the interdependence between ourselves and everything else.

Coda

In order to model the "the psychic unity of mankind" (Boas 1938) and its vital integration with "animal-kind", it will eventually be necessary to account for the organizing influence of the anatomical planes of the bipedal person— basic experiential realities shared by humankind that also serve to integrate our lived experience with that of other animal species. The visceral origins of markedness in language range both wider and deeper than the experiential knowledge of lateralization. Left and right are important tacit experiences for the cultural organization of logical and semantic relations that underly social constructions, but upper-lower dynamics are equally important for ensuring that such systems can be called into question, re-framed, disrupted and kept fluid. This role is modeled at a visceral level by arm-leg relations as discussed above.

As a vital component of our shared human experience, arm-leg relations are not merely semantic but analogic and dialogic, involving something more than an experience of difference or contrast—something Roman Jakobson discusses as markedness (marked oppositions being subordinate, unmarked being dominant, relative to some end)—thus opening up more functional, complementary relations and paving the way for broader creative analogies between parts and wholes. Applied to theories of analogy and problems in Cognitive Linguistics, these findings suggest that transverse part-whole relationships shared between arms and legs may provide a more adequate account of the origins and development of creative analogy or "double-scope conceptual blending".

Acknowledgements

This research was supported by the Social Sciences and Humanities Research Council of Canada: SSHRC-IDG #430-2015-01226 "Steps to a Grammar of Embodied Symmetry."

References

ANDREWS, Edna.
    1990.   *Markedness Theory: The Union of Asymmetry and Semiosis in Language* (Durham: Duke University Press).

ANTTILA, Raimo.
    2003.   "Analogy: The Warp and Woof of Cognition", in *The Handbook of Historical Linguistics*, ed. Brian D. Joseph and Richard D. Janda (London: Blackwell), 425–440.

BASSO, Keith H.
    1990.   *Western Apache Language and Culture: Essays in Linguistic Anthropology* (University of Arizona Press: Tucson).

BERTELETTI, Ilaria, and James R. BOOTH.
    2015.   "Perceiving Fingers in Single-digit Arithmetic Problems", *Frontiers in Psychology* 6.226, 1–10.

BIRDSELL, Brian J.
    2014.   "Fauconnier's Theory of Mental Spaces and Conceptual Blending", in *The Bloomsbury Companion to Cognitive Linguistics*, ed. Jeannette Littlemore and John R. Taylor (London: Bloomsbury Academic), 72–90.

BOAS, Franz (1858–1942).
    1938.   *The Mind of Primitive Man* (2nd ed., New York: Macmillian).

BOUISSAC, Paul.
    2007.   "Semiotics as the Science of Memory", *Sign Systems Studies* 35.1, 71–87.

BRADLEY, David.
    1979.   *Proto-Loloish* (Scandinavian Institute of Asian Studies Monograph 39, London: Curzon Press).

BRENZINGER, Matthias, and Iwona KRASKA-SZLENK, Editors.
    2014.   *The Body in Language: Comparative Studies of Linguistic Embodiment* (Leiden: Brill).

BYBEE, Joan.
    2009.   "Language Universals and Usage-Based Theory", in *Language Universals*, ed. M. H. Christiansen, C. Collins, and S. Edelman (Oxford: Oxford University Press), 17–39.

2010.   *Language, Usage and Cognition* (Cambridge: Cambridge University Press).

CHOMSKY, Noam.

1966.   *Cartesian Linguistics* (New York: Harper & Row).

COMRIE, Bernard.

2011.   "Numeral Bases", in *The World Atlas of Language Structures*, ed. Martin Haspelmath, Matthew Dryer, David Gil, and Bernard Comrie (Oxford: Oxford University Press), 530–533.

CROFT, William, and D. Alan CRUSE.

2004.   *Cognitive Linguistics* (Cambridge: Cambridge University Press).

DANTZIG, Tobias.

1940.   *Number: The Language of Science* (London: George Allen and Unwin).

DANZIGER, Eve.

2011.   "Distinguishing Three-dimensional Forms From Their Mirror-images: Whorfian Results From Users of Intrinsic Frames of Linguistic Reference", *Language Sciences* 33.6, 853–867.
           doi: https://doi.org/10.1016/j.langsci.2011.06.008

DANZIGER, Eve, and Eric PEDERSON.

1998.   "Through the Looking Glass: Literacy, Writing Systems and Mirror-image Discrimination", *Written Language and Literacy* 1.2, 153–169.
           doi: https://doi.org/10.1075/wll.1.2.02dan

DEELY, John.

1990.   *Basics of Semiotics* (Advances in Semiotics, Bloomington: Indiana University Press).

2002.   "The Absence of Analogy", *The Review of Metaphysics* 55.3, 521–550.

2009.   *Purely Objective Reality*. Semiotics, Communication and Cognition, 4 (Berlin: Mouton de Gruyter).

2010.   *Semiotic Animal: A Postmodern Definition of Human Being Transcending Patriarchy and Feminism* (South Bend: St. Augustine's Press).

DOKE, Clement M. (1893–1980).

1927.   *Textbook of Zulu Grammar* (6th ed., Cape Town: Maskew Miller Longman, 1988).

DUDIS, Paul G.

2004.   "Body-Partitioning and Real-Space Blends", *Cognitive Linguistics* 15.2, 223–238.

ELLEN, Roy F.

1977.   "Anatomical Classification and the Semiotics of the Body", in *The Anthropology of the Body*, ed. John Blacking (New York: Academic Press), 343–373.

ENFIELD, Nick J.
    2006.   "Lao Body Part Terms", *Language Sciences* 28.2–3, 181–200.
                doi: https://doi.org/10.1016/j.langsci.2005.11.011

ENFIELD, Nick J., Asifa MAJID, and Miriam VAN STADEN.
    2006.   "Cross-linguistic Categorisation of the Body: Introduction", *Language Sciences* 28.2–3, 137–147.
                doi: https://doi.org/10.1016/j.langsci.2005.11.001

ENFIELD, Nick J., Asifa MAJID, and Miriam VAN STADEN, Editors.
    2006.   *Parts of the Body: Cross-Linguistic Categorisation*. Special double issue of *Language Sciences* 28.2–3 (Amsterdam: Elsevier).

FAUCONNIER, Gilles, and Mark TURNER.
    2002.   *The Way We Think: Conceptual Blending and the Mind's Hidden Complexities* (New York: Basic Books).
    2008.   "The Origin of Language as a Product of the Evolution of Double-Scope Blending", *Behavioral and Brain Sciences* 31.5, 520–521.

FRANKLIN, Karl J.
    1963.   "Kewa Ethnolinguistic Concepts of Body Parts", *Southwestern Journal of Anthropology* 19.1, 54–63.
                doi: https://doi.org/10.1086/soutjanth.19.1.3628922

FUCHS, Thomas.
    2012.   "The Phenomenology of Body Memory", in *Body Memory, Metaphor and Movement*, ed. Sabine C. Koch, Thomas Fuchs, Michela Summa, and Cornelia Müller. Advances in Consciousness Research, 84 (Amsterdam: John Benjamins), 9–22.

GALLAGHER, Shaun.
    2015.   "Invasion of the Body Snatchers: How Embodied Cognition is Being Disembodied", *The Philosopher's Magazine* (April), 96–102.

GRADY, Joseph.
    2005.   "Primary Metaphors as Inputs to Conceptual Integration", *Journal of Pragmatics* 37.1, 1595–1614.
                doi: https://doi.org/10.1016/j.pragma.2004.03.012

HAUSDORFF, Felix (1868–1942): *see* MONGRÉ, Paul (the psuedonym under which Hausdorff introduced the expression "*semiotisches Thier*").

HEINE, Bernd.
    1997.   *Cognitive Foundations of Grammar* (Oxford: Oxford University Press).
    2014.   "The Body in Language: Observations from Grammaticalization", in *The Body in Language: Comparative Studies of Linguistic Embodiment*, ed. Matthias Brenzinger and Iwona Kraska-Szlenk (Leiden: Brill), 13–32.

HILPERT, Martin.
 2007.   "Chained Metonymies in Lexicon and Grammar: A Cross-linguistic
          Perspective on Body-part Terms", in *Aspects of Meaning Construction*,
          ed. Günter Radden, Klaus-Michael Köpcke, Thomas Berg, and Peter
          Sigmund (Amsterdam: John Benjamins), 77–98.

HOFSTADTER, Douglas, and Emmanuel SANDER.
 2013.   *Surfaces and Essences: Analogy as the Fuel and Fire of Thinking* (New
          York: Basic Books).

HON, Giora, and Bernard R. GOLDSTEIN.
 2008.   *From Summetria to Symmetry: The Making of a Revolutionary Scientific
          Concept*. Archimedes: New Studies in the History of Science and Tech-
          nology vol. 20 (Berlin: Springer).

JOHNSON, Mark.
 2007.   *The Meaning of the Body: Aesthetics of Human Understanding* (Chicago:
          University of Chicago Press).

LAKOFF, George.
 1987.   *Women, Fire, and Dangerous Things: What Categories Reveal about the
          Mind* (Chicago: University of Chicago Press).

LAKOFF, George, and Mark JOHNSON.
 1980.   *Metaphors We Live by* (Chicago: University of Chicago Press).

LÉVI-STRAUSS Claude (1908–2009).
 1962.   *Totemism*, trans. Rodney Needham (London: Merlin Press).

LEVINSON, Stephen C., and Penelope BROWN.
 1994.   "Immanuel Kant among the Tenejapans: Anthropology as Empirical
          Philosophy", *Ethos* 22.1, 3–41.
          doi: https://doi.org/10.1525/eth.1994.22.1.02a00010

LIDDELL, Scott K.
 1998.   "Grounded Blends, Gestures, and Conceptual Shifts", *Cognitive Linguis-
          tics* 9.3, 283–314. doi: https://doi.org/10.1515/cogl.1998.9.3.283

MAALEJ, Zouheir A., and Ning YU, Editors.
 2011.   *Embodiment Via Body Parts: Studies from Various Languages and Cultures*.
          Cognitive Processing vol. 31 (Amsterdam: John Benjamins).

MATISOFF, James A.
 1978.   *Variational Semantics in Tibeto-Burman: The Organic Approach to Lin-
          guistic Comparison*. Occasional Papers of the Wolfenden Society on
          Tibeto-Burman Linguistics. (Philadelphia: Institute for the Study of
          Human Issues).
 1992.   "The Mother of All Morphemes: Augmentatives and Diminutives in
          Areal and Universal Perspective", in *Papers from the First Annual Meeting
          of the Southeast Asian Linguistics Society 1991*, ed. Martha Ratliff and

Eric Schiller (Phoenix: Arizona State University Program for Southeast Asian Studies).

MERLEAU-PONTY, Maurice (1908–1961).

1945. *Phénomènologie de La Perception* (Paris: Editions Gallimard). Trans. Colin Smith as *Phenomenology of Perception* (New York: Routledge, 1962).

c.1960. *Le Visible et L'invisible* (Paris: Editions Gallimard, 1964). Trans. Alphonso Lingis as *The Visible and the Invisible*, ed. Claude Lefort (Evanston: Northwestern University Press, 1968).

MIDDLETON, John.

1960. *Lugbara Religion: Ritual and Authority Among an East African People* (Oxford: Oxford University Press).

MONGRÉ, Paul (= Felix Hausdorff, 1868–1942).

1897. *Sant' Ilario. Gedanken aus der Lanschaft Zarathustras* (Leipzig: C. G. Naumann).

MYERHOFF, Barbara G.

1978. "Return to Wirikuta: Ritual Reversal and Symbolic Continuity on the Peyote Hunt of the Huichol Indians", in *The Reversible World: Symbolic Inversion in Art and Society*, ed. Barbara A. Babcock (London: Cornell University Press), 225–239.

NORRMAN, Ralf (1946–2000).

1999. "Creating the World in Our Image: A New Theory of Love of Symmetry and Iconicist Desire", in *Form Miming Meaning: Iconicity in Language and Literature*, ed. Max Nänny and Olga Fischer (Amsterdam: John Benjamins), 59–82.

OVID (43BCE–CE17).

8CE. *Metamorphoses*, trans. Charles Martin (New York: Norton, 2005).

PAUL, Robert A.

1973. "The Eyes Outnumber the Nose Two to One", paper presented for the symposium *Images of Body States*, Annual Meeting of the American Anthropological Association, New Orleans, 12pp.

PELKEY, Jamin.

2011. *Dialectology as Dialectic: Interpreting Phula Variation*. Trends in Linguistics: Studies and Monographs 229 (Berlin: De Gruyter Mouton).

2011a. *A Phula Comparative Lexicon: Phola, Phuza, Muji, Phowa, Azha*. SIL Language and Culture Documentation and Description 18. (Dallas: SIL International).

2013. "Analogy, Automation and Diagrammatic Causation: The Evolution of Tibeto-Burman *lak", *Studies in Language* 37.1, 144–195. doi: https://doi.org/10.1075/sl.37.1.04pel

2013a.   "Chiastic Antisymmetry in Language Evolution", *The American Journal of Semiotics* 29.1, 39–68. doi: https://doi.org/10.5840/ajs2013291-43

2015.   "Shoes that Fit Like a Glove: The Visceral Roots of Human Cognition", in *SemiotiX* 13.1, online: bit.ly/29xmF5j.

2016.   "Semiotic Animal: Waking up to Reciprocity", a review of John Deely, 2010, op. cit., *Chinese Semiotic Studies* 12.3, 445–453.

2016a.   "Symbiotic Modeling: Linguistic Anthropology and the Promise of Chiasmus", *Reviews in Anthropology* 45.1, 22–50.
doi: https://doi.org/10.1080/00938157.2016.1142294

forthcoming.   "Greimas Embodied: How Kinesthetic Opposition Grounds the Semiotic Square", *Semiotica* 208.1.

PENNER-WILGER, Marcie, Lisa FAST, J. LEFEVRE, B. L. Smith-Chant, S. SKWARCHUK, D. KAMAWAR, and J. BISANZ

2007.   "The Foundations of Numeracy: Subitizing, Finger Gnosia, and Fine-motor Ability", in *Proceedings of the 29th Annual Cognitive Science Society*, ed. D. S. McNamara and J. G. Trafton (Austin: Cognitive Science Society), 1385–1390.

RICE, Sally.

2002.   "Figure/motion/manner/path Conflation Patterns in the Dene Sųłiné Verb", paper presented to the 2002 Athapaskan Languages Conference, Fairbanks, Alaska, 16–18 June 2002.

2014.   "Corporeal Incorporation and Extension in Dene Sųłiné (Athapaskan) Lexicalization", in *The Body in Language: Comparative Studies of Linguistic Embodiment*, ed. Matthias Brenzinger and Iwona Kraska-Szlenk (Leiden: Brill), 71–97.

ROHRER, Tim.

2007.   "The Body in Space: Dimensions of Embodiment", in *Body, Language, and Mind, Vol. 1: Embodiment*, ed. Tom Ziemke, Jordan Zlatev, and Roslyn M. Frank. Cognitive Linguistics Research 35.1 (Berlin: Mouton De Gruyter), 339–377.

ROSSI-LANDI, Ferruccio (1921–1985).

1978.   *Ideologia* (Milan: ISEDI; reprinted Milan: Mondadori, 1982; and with a new Introduction by Augusto Ponzio, Rome: Meltemi, 2005). Trans. into English by R. Griffin as *Marxism and Ideology* (Oxford: Clarendon Press, 2005).

SAVAN, David (1916–1992).

1976.   *An Introduction to C. S. Peirce's Semiotics* (Toronto: Victoria University).

SEBEOK, Thomas A. (1920–2001).

1984.   "Vital Signs", presidential address delivered 12 October 1984 to the ninth Annual Meeting of the Semiotic Society of America, Bloomington,

IN, October 11–14; subsequently printed in *The American Journal of Semiotics* 3.3, 1–27.

SHAPIRO, Michael.
1983. *The Sense of Grammar* (Bloomington: Indiana University Press).

SHEETS-JOHNSTONE, Maxine.
2011. *The Primacy of Movement*, 2nd ed. Advances in Consciousness Research 82 (Amsterdam: John Benjamins).

SILVERMAN, Kaja.
2015. *The Miracle of Analogy* (Stanford: Stanford University Press).

SLINGERLAND, Edward G.
2005. "Conceptual Blending, Somatic Marking, and Normativity: A Case Example from Ancient Chinese", *Cognitive Linguistics* 16.3, 557–584.

STAMPE, David.
1976. "Cardinal Numeral Systems", *Chicago Linguistic Society* 12, 594–609.

TURNER, Victor (1920–1983).
1966. "The Syntax of Symbolism in an African Religion", *Philosophical Transactions of the Royal Society B* 772.251, 295–303.

VAN LIER, Henri (1921–2009).
2003. *Around Homo in 80 Theses: A Fundamental Anthropogeny*, ed. Micheline Lo, trans. Pierre Lottefier, abridged version of Henri Van Lier c.2009, op. cit., *Anthropogénie* (Brussels: Anthropogenie.com), online: bit.ly/2drXX3W.
c.2009. *Anthropogénie* (Brussels: Les Impressions nouvelles, 2010).

VIOLI, Patrizia.
2008. "Beyond the Body: Towards a Full Embodied Semiosis", in *Body, Language, and Mind, Vol. 2: Sociocultural Situatedness*, ed. Roslyn M. Frank, René Dirven, Tom Ziemke, and Enrique Bernárdez. Cognitive Linguistics Research 35.2 (Berlin: Mouton De Gruyter), 53–76.

VORBICHLER, Anton.
1965. *Die Phonologie und Morphologie des Balese (Ituri-Urwald, Kongo)*, Afrikanistische Forschungen 2 (Glückstadt: J. J. Augustin).

WEGENER, Claudia.
2006. "Savosavo Body Part Terminology", *Language Sciences* 28.2–3, 344–359. doi: https://doi.org/10.1016/j.langsci.2005.11.005

WIERZBICKA, Anna.
2007. "Bodies and Their Parts: An NSM Approach to Semantic Typology", *Language Sciences* 29.1, 14–65. doi: https://doi.org/10.1016/j.langsci.2006.07.002

WILKINS, David P.

    1996.   "Natural Tendencies of Semantic Change and the Search for Cognates", in *The Comparative Method Reviewed*, ed. Mark Durie and Malcolm Ross (Oxford: Oxford University Press), 264–304.

WITKOWSKI, Stanley R., and Cecil H. BROWN.

    1985.   "Climate, Clothing, and Body-Part Nomenclature", *Ethnology* 24.3, 197–214. doi: https://doi.org/10.2307/3773610

Semiotic Animal on the Path of Evolutionary Love

Farouk Y. Seif
Antioch University Seattle

Abstract: John Deely uses the way of signs not only to establish the contact and dependencies between human thought and action and the surrounding physical universe, but also to account for a social construction of reality as part of human experience beyond mere "thinking thing". Experiencing evolutionary love is a reciprocal exchange of desire, which is the primary strength of Eros, where eroticism and semiotics intertwine. When Deely states that all animals signify, but only human animals are capable of developing semiotics, he opens a whole way of understanding for us to move beyond the definition of human being as a rational animal into a "semiotic animal" that is also capable of love.

Keywords: agapasm, John Deely, eros, evolutionary love, Charles S. Peirce, postmodernity, semiotic animals, transmodernity, wholophilia

1. Introductory Anecdote

The connection between the "semiotic animal" and the notion of "evolutionary love" is captivating. Although a few semioticians hinted at semiotic animals and love, nothing that I am aware of that have been explicitly communicated. My interest in semiotic animals and their love relations with other-than-human animals goes back to the time when I experienced the loss of my golden retriever *Kishtta* in 2008. When John Deely visited me on Orcas Island, Washington, May 6–10, 2013, he noticed a draft of an article "Dialogue with Kishtta: A Semiotic Revelation of the Paradox of Life and Death" (Seif 2013) that was lying on my desk, which I had presented at the International Conference: *Zoosemiotics and Animal Representations* in Tartu, Estonia, on April 6, 2011. After reading the last line of the article, John

ISSN 0277-7126

doi: 10.5840/ajs201610512

Online First: October 6, 2016

The American Journal of Semiotics 32.1–4 (2016), 127–142.

said in a tender voice with teary eyes: "Farouk, this is wonderful, you must publish this article in *The American Journal of Semiotics.*"

Deely's work on semiotic animals is undoubtedly one of his most significant contributions to the development of semiotics and the doctrine of signs. Even though his book, the *Four Ages of Understanding*, is considered to be his major contribution to semiotics and philosophy, his many published articles, of varying sorts, with slighter versions concerning semiotic animals are of special interest to me. As a matter of fact, the thesis of his book focuses on finding the "way of signs" and is the best hope for us to realize the ancient advice of Socrates: "Know thyself" (Deely 2001: 736). In Deely's oeuvre, the phrase "semiotic animal" first appeared in 1999, in *Basics of Semiotics*, and in several other versions until it was put together in a whole, extensive monographic form entitled, *Semiotic Animal: A Postmodern Definition of "Human Being" Transcending Patriarchy and Feminism.*

The idea of human beings as semiotic animals was conceptually established in several lectures delivered at conferences and seminars, and communicated in published articles with slight variations. Deely's first usage of the expression was a coinage made in passing. However, two other scholars had independently used this expression, Paul Mongré, who was known as Felix Hausdorff, in 1897: "The human being is a semiotic animal"; and Ferruccio Rossi-Landi in 1978: "The human being, as a semiotic animal, is semiotic through and through" (Deely 2010: xi, 29–30). The term independently appeared again in an Italian book by Susan Petrilli in 1998, which opened the way for semiotic dimension of ethics in the human animal (Deely 2010). In addition, Deely, Petrilli, and Ponzio worked together in a conference in Milan to establish "semiotic animal" as semiotic development (Deely, Petrilli, and Ponzio 2005). It is necessary therefore to cite Deely's several versions in order to give a full understanding of the idea of semiotic animals and the connection to the notion of evolutionary love.

2. The Shift from a Rational Animal to a Thinking Creature

John Deely describes how modernity "opened under the sign of the *Res Cogitans*, the thinking thing"—"I think, therefore I am", proposed by Descartes as a replacement of the definition of human being as a "rational animal". This modern definition of the human being left much to be desired, but, ironically, the modern mainstream adopted this definition for more than three centuries (Deely 2005). Confronting Descartes' proposition, "I doubt, therefore I think, therefore I am", Deely uses the very act of thinking to doubt the proposition and to turn the "thinking thing" on its head! And by divorcing objects from things, the mainstream of modern philosophy has become enshrined in the dogmatic formula of thinking thing (*res cogitans*). "Modern philosophy came to an understanding of the difference between objects existing in knowledge and things existing independently of knowledge, but at the price of failing to show how things can themselves become objects", says Deely (2010: 41). "The connection between objects as what is known and things as existing became the nub of the issue." This way of thinking sets the human being apart from nature—patriarchy apart from feminism—and launches man above woman as supposedly more rational, but paradoxically, *"what sets us apart is an awareness of the very process that ties us into nature as a whole. ... What distinguishes the semiotic animal is the awareness of what ties its being in with the whole of nature,* what makes it a part of the unfolding cosmic whole" (Deely 2010: 103).

By tracing the development of the "way of signs" through the Latin and Medieval Ages, from St. Augustine (354–430) through St. Thomas Aquinas (1225–1274) and into the work of John Poinsot (1589–1644), Deely persuades us to re-evaluate modernity and to contrast it with postmodernity, where the later distinguishes human understanding and the realization that suggests the need for a new definition of human being, one that surpasses *res cogitans* just as *res cogitans* surpassed rational animal. As Deely argues:

> Since the knowledge that arises from this realization of the role of signs is called "semiotics," the definition of the human being as "semiotic animal" best captures and expresses the understanding of human beings that corresponds to the exploration of the "way of signs", the postmodern path of understanding the web of human experience not as subjectively isolated from, but rather as inextricably entangled with, the physical universe. (Deely 2005: 464)

The above statement highlights the significance of what makes human thought and action distinctive in the postmodern world: the realization of the role of signs and that "there are signs upon which the whole of life depends for successful continuance" (Deely 2005: 463). Certainly, the notion of semiotic animal (*animal semeioticum*) captures the very essence of being human. Although all animals signify, only human animals are capable of developing semiotics, which is postmodern; however, we may squabble over whether this development is postmodern or transmodern.

3. Semiotic Animal at the Core of Transmodernity

John Deely (2005) maintains that philosophy became postmodern when the work of Charles S. Peirce recovered and thematically developed the semiotic consciousness of the Latin Age. Even though John Poinsot traced the genesis and development of the action of sign, which was proposed by Augustine of Hippo, and was the first to establish the foundations of semiotics as a distinct subject matter, the action of signs gradually made its way to becoming a singular exemplification of *relation*. Relation could not be seen, nor heard, nor touched, nor perceived directly by any of the senses. Relation is "the most elusive of all the ways of being" and is often not recognized as an element of reality (Deely 2005: 469). Yet, relation can be real, true, or imaginary (Seif 2016). What is remarkable about relations is "their permeability to the otherwise distinct orders of what does and what does not exist independently of finite mind" (Deely 2005: 470).

Deely (2010: 57) goes on to say: "The animal, *rational or not*, perforce constructs *a plethora* of *entia rationis* unwittingly, not known as such, but as facilitating its function and orientation within the environment". Ultimately, the presence of *entia rationis* in the experience of cognitive organisms is inevitably a necessary one in order for their surrounding environment to become a meaningful world within which cognitive organisms can orient themselves within their *Umwelt* in order to survive and thrive. Indeed, relation forms the fabric of the experience of animals through sign-processes. The semiotic animal is a unique self within the species, and is aware of its world, but not just via mere *res cogitans* and concerns with the reason for being. Deely explains:

> Of all living things we can say that they are semiosic creatures, creatures which grow and develop through the manipulation of sign-vehicles and the involvement in sign-processes, semiosis. If this is true of all the living, a-fortiori is it true of all animals: every animal is a semiosic animal, able to survive and thrive only thanks to whatever semiosic competence it is able to manage. (Deely 2005: 479)

Yet, what distinguishes the human being among the other animals is not any means of semiosis; it is that "*only human animals* come to realize that *there are signs* distinct from and superordinate to every particular thing that serves to constitute an individual … in its distinctness from its surrounding" (Deely 2005: 479). Although the idea of the semiotic animal was conceived to overcome the human-animal dualism, many zoosemiotics supporters still remain anthropocentrically biased. Deely's idea of semiotic animals overlaps anthroposemiosis and zoosemiosis, and hints indirectly at the integration of both (Seif 2013). In fact, expanding on the work of Susan Petrilli and Augusto Ponzio, Deely (2010: 117) comes closer to the understanding that humans as semiotic animals are moving from merely being aware of their own being and action into seeing themselves accepting the burden of responsibility of becoming aware that "*the welfare of the human race is inseparable from the whole biosphere* from which the race of semiotic animals is inseparable" (117), which also includes human and more-than-human animals. If the semiotic animal transcends the gender divide of "patriarchy and feminism" (Deely 2010), one wonders, why not go beyond the human animal-other animal schism! In their own way, more-than-human animals think just as well as humans (or even better than they do), only semiotic animals love—although one cannot affirm that more-than-human animals love or not (Marion 2003).

Moreover, building on Petrilli's work, Deely upholds that human beings, as semiotic animals, are able to deal with otherness reasonably, a process which cannot be developed in isolation but necessitates the experience of a web of relations through love. Following Deely's earlier statement about relations, we can say that the sign of love is a relation that is not perceived directly by any of the senses. For example, would we consider the kiss of Judas on Jesus's cheek a sign of love or a sign of deception? This kiss was not a sign of a love relation.

Love is certainly the domain within which ethical concerns, responsibility, and freedom exist; "to have ethical concerns, to be responsible, to be free, one must see the other and oneself in his or her legitimacy" (Maturana and Verden-Zöller 2008: 80–81). Bear in mind that "ethics belongs to the domain of emotions, not of reason, and as such it belongs to the domain of love" (80–81). This domain of love that embodies ethical responsibility undoubtedly falls in the very core of semiotics and is of great interest to semiotic animals.

> Human beings are invested biosemiosically and phylogenetically with a unique capacity for responsibility toward life, for care of life in its joyous and dialogical multiplicity, for listening and accountability. This ensues from the global condition of intercorporeity, dialogical interrelatedness, creative awareness of the other. The capacity for making decisions, taking a stand, intervening upon the course of semiosis over the entire planet implies nothing less. In this sense the "semiotic animal" is also a "semioethic animal" (Petrilli 2013: 200).

Semioethics tenders us to genuinely engage with others, to love and care for each other. To recognize not just the presence of the other beyond self, but also the self's very own other (Petrilli 2013). Semioethics is "the extension of semiotic awareness to that *unfixed* boundary between nature and culture" (Deely 2010: 123), and the paradoxical love relation between self and others. The semiotic animal as the birth of "a new form of humanism" is "reconceptualizing the whole matter of interdependency" of a semiotic reality that is "never fixed and always shifting" (123).

In a semioethical sense, the relation between semiotic animals and the whole cosmos is inseparable. Relations, through love, not only convey the connections of humans to their innerworld (*Innenwelt*) and their environment (*Umwelt*), but also imply the meaning of being in the lifeworld (*Lebenswelt*). For without an *Innenwelt* there is no *Umwelt* (Deely 2007), and without both there is no *Lebenswelt*. In this context, postmodernity is recognized as the sphere within which the semioethical responsibility of semiotic animals is to be realized (Deely 2010).

Different causes put aside, both modernity and postmodernity seem to be indistinguishable; there seem many more similarities than differences between modernity and postmodernity (Seif 2008). Observation has shown that postmodernity has been superseded by transmodernity,[1] which embodies many diaphanous and integrative qualities that do not imply mixing and dissolving differences; rather it reveals the transparency between entities and boundaries. In this sense, transmodernity does not reject either modernity or postmodernity. Because transparency or seeing through—what Jean Gebser (1949) calls "diaphanous perception"—is the hallmark of transmodernity and is more inclusive of modernity and postmodernity and resonates with both Gebser's "aperspectival world" and Peirce's notion of "synechism".

Peirce says, "I have proposed to make synechism mean the tendency to regard everything as continuous" (CP 7.566), and "I carry the doctrine so far as to maintain that continuity governs the whole domain of experience in every element of it" (CP 7.567). However, while this idea of synechism means continuity, it is not something thought of as infinitely divisible and does not propose sameness; rather, in this context, continuity implies an ongoing shifting whole. It follows, then, that Peirce's principle of continuity behooves us to engage in the process of evolution, whereby the *love for wholeness* manifests in our thoughts and actions in a shifting semiotic reality.

With this understanding, one can say that Peirce's semiotics and Deely's semiotic animal are thoroughly transmodern developments. In the transmodern world, semiotic animals can cross the threshold between what is real and what is true, between the real and unreal (Seif 2016), transcend the fixed boundary between nature and culture, between patriarchy and matriarchy, and between human animals and other-than-human animals, yearning for wholeness as a manifestation of love.

---

[1] Transmodernity is a major shift in our philosophical understanding of modernism and postmodernism. What catches our attention in the term "Transmodernity" is the prefix "trans," which comes from the Latin *across*, indicating beyond and through. This seems to be the rationale behind favoring of the term "beyond" over "post."

4. Semiotic Animal's Yearning for the Love of Wholeness

The semiotic animal as a whole is ephemerally autonomous, yet, as a part, it is alienated and disconnected from those contexts that are beyond its own awareness; until this whole takes the larger and infinite semiosis into account, its incompleteness tear at its boundaries, hinting at a deeper realm and more meaningful spectrum. Yet this infinite semiosis is "an unfinalizable process that is never definitively concluded, that propelled by the search for the other, seduced and called forth by the other, never reaches 'the end'" (Petrilli 2013: 21). As semiotic animals, human beings are always vulnerable to being seduced by Eros, simply because they lack a sense of completeness. While the conventional view arrests Eros in the domain of eroticism, it does not necessarily reject the sensuous and seductive features of Eros toward never-ending wholeness.

Peirce's doctrine of *synechism* comes handy here. Again, he says, "I have proposed to make synechism mean the tendency to regard everything as continuous" (CP 7.566), and "I carry the doctrine so far as to maintain that continuity governs the whole domain of experience in every element of it" (CP 7.567). The self, as a semiotic animal, "is not a separate entity, a compact unit, but rather a semiosic continuum characterized by incompleteness and unfinalizability" (Petrilli 2013: 19). In Peirce's sense, the semiotic animal must acquire the propensity for humility and surrendering to others, to put aside its own identity, to move from self-monolog to dialogical intimacy with the other (Seif 2013).

A whole must achieve a degree of coherence and consistency in order to endure at all as the same entity across space and time. But as a part of some other whole, it must embrace its incompleteness, or otherwise it will not fit in, and drift off into its own isolated whole.[2] Jean Gebser (1949) reminds us that nothing exists in life autonomously for its own sake, it exists for the sake of the whole; it also exists to relentlessly seek to be in a larger whole. As Hegel (1807: 11) declares, "the whole is nothing other than the essence consummating itself through its development". Echoing Aristophanes's speech in the *Symposium*, Marcel Proust says: "Love, in the pain of anxiety as in the bliss of desire, is a demand for a whole" (in Martin 2015: 165). It seems that the ultimate purpose of life is to seek wholeness and to be nested in a larger whole. This nesting phenomenon of life, which I call *wholophilia* (love of wholeness), is the relentless desire to engage in a co-evolutionary

---

[2] Contrary to the English dictionary's definition, the "whole" is never complete because it always seeks perfection and integration. *A complete whole is a dead whole!*

process seeking a larger whole through creative love. Eros represents a triadic phenomenon of creative love that includes our present ontological incompleteness, our recognition of our incompleteness, and our desire to overcome our experience of incompleteness to achieve our longed-for wholeness (Hyland 2008).

As a creative love, agapasm is dominated by the forces of affinity, attraction, and desire in the relation among semiotic animals that come into being in the continuous flux of infinite semiosis. Genuine creative love "is regulated by the logic of otherness; love for the other, love that does not calculate returns, love directed to the other as other" (Petrilli 2013: 94). Experiencing love is really a reciprocal exchange of seductive desire, which is the primary strength of Eros *par excellence*. The relationship between humans and Eros as the *generator-of-desire* constitutes the desire for seeking mutual fulfillment in the creation and experience of love. As St. Thomas Aquinas, Pierre Teilhard de Chardin, Archimandrite Sophrony, and Alfred North Whitehead, to name a few, insist to love others and the world, we must see them as the manifestation of God's loving creation.

Eros which drives us, as semiotic animals, toward completeness "leads us to seek both to include all knowledge there is to include and to include it in a meaningful whole" (Hall 1982: 213). In a Socratic sense, it is through Eros that lovers are taken out of themselves and into a larger and wider union with the beloved, moving from the body to the mind to the soul, and ultimately, to self-transcendence toward evolutionary love. Eros is humans' way to connect with each other and reach the Divine (Nygren 1953). In the words of Pierre Teilhard de Chardin (1955: 265):

> Love in all its subtleties is nothing more, and nothing less, than the more or less direct trace marked on the heart of the element by the psychical convergence of the universe upon itself. … Love alone is capable of uniting living beings in such a way as to complete and fulfill them, for it alone takes them and joins them by what is deepest in themselves.

Indeed, love is part of who we are as *homo sapiens*; it is innate in human nature. Again, love is the emotion that constitutes communal life within which our intelligence can expand. We are love-dependent animals, *Homo sapiens amāns* (Maturana and Verden-Zöller 2008). The love for wholeness is recognizable by its fruits. To be able to be known by the fruit we bear is indeed the manifestation of love through our creative action in our *Lebenswelt*. We are indeed loving animals; and our intelligence and imagination depend on our being loving animals. The open-ended semiotic process of wholeness is the pathway for semiotic animals to experience evolutionary love.

5. Semiotic Animals on the Path of Evolutionary Love

Deely does not explicitly link semiotic animals to love, however, his entire work hints at the love and desire for wholeness. This is an interesting point. One would wonder whether Deely intentionally inclines to hint or prefer a suggestive notion to a direct utterance of love. We experience love but, ironically, as soon as we attempt to define it, it moves away from us (Marion 2003). In addition, it is really difficult to speak about love without facing the unjustifiable attitude toward eroticism as a mere satisfaction of carnal appetite, and the narrow understanding of Eros as a primarily sexual desire.

The relationship between love and sexual desire of the semiotic animal is a complex one. Love may exist without sexual desire and sexual desire may be triggered without love. However, "the feelings of being in love with, and sexually attracted to, another person are frequently intertwined", as in the case with romantic and sensual kisses (Danesi 2013: 74). Although the role of sexuality in love is not clear, the relationship between sexual desire and love is more paradoxical than dualistic.

Aside from modernity's emphasis on biological needs for sex that views love as an erotic drive similar to hunger, or thirst, or as a cognitive social phenomenon, the concept of love is a difficult phenomenon to explain. What is most relevant in the present context is the paradoxical interconnection between Eros and love, between love and eroticism. While eroticism may seem mysterious, it is the least straightforward human nature. Humans cannot escape their own nature (Bataille 1957). But whenever we talk about love we unavoidably bring up the notions of Eros, erotica, and semiotics. The connection between erotica and love is not radically new. The roots of our understanding of the nature of Eros extend back to Plato's (c.385–370 BC) dialogue *Symposium* and *Phaedrus's* speech. The *Symposium*—the most artfully and paradoxical form of philosophy ever written—is particularly essential in establishing the connection between the semiotic animal and evolutionary love.

While *Philia* is the Greek word for "love", *Érōs* generally refers to the notion of "erotic desire" and attachment. But since Plato's erotic activity is not divorced from philosophy—*philo-sophy*—the love of wisdom and erotica are inseparable. Semiotics, the doctrine of signs, is at the heart of philosophy. In fact, the founding father of semiotics, Charles S. Peirce, is a philosopher, that is to say, a lover of wisdom. As semiotic animals, we live semiotically; that is, to live in relation to others, to become aware of the "otherness of every other" (Petrilli 2013: xxiv); and to be in relation with others is to have the capacity of engaging in the process of creative love, to surrender to the seductive force of Eros. Again, it is through Eros that lovers are taken out of their ephemeral autonomous self by desire into a larger and wider union with the beloved, moving from the body to the mind to the soul, and ultimately, to self-transcendence toward the path of evolutionary love.

Because the term "erotica" etymologically derives from the Greek word *Érōs*, which associated love with desire, the worldview of Eros has been focused mainly on sexual love and mere erotic sensation. But by liberating Eros from the narrow understanding of eroticism, we can not only reinterpret the relation between *erotica* and *semiotica*, but also reveal the primordial meaning of love as divine insemination for creation and the trigger of evolution. Evolutionary love urges us to perceive Eros beyond the misinterpreted eroticism as a mere sexual act. *Experiencing evolutionary love is really a reciprocal exchange of seductive desire, which is the primary strength of Eros, where eroticism and semiotics intertwine.*

When John Deely (2005) argues that only human animals are capable of developing semiotics, he opens a whole way of understanding for us to move beyond the definition of human being as a rational animal into a semiotic animal who is also capable of love. As semiotic animals, human beings are love-dependent animals. According to Maturana and Varela (1987), to love is to make space and time for one another so that each becomes a part of the domain of knowing and the existence of the other. The lure of certainty about intellectual dogma can blind us, for the more we are certain the less we see. Genuine knowing requires dialogue, and dialogue cannot occur without love. The only emotion that expands intelligence is love, because intelligence has to do with mutual acceptance, the legitimacy of the other, and the expansion of the possibility for consensual relations (Maturana and Verden-Zöller 2008). Only love creates and expands intelligence among members of a community of inquirers.

> Such a community, in turn, needed to support intelligence in those scientific and literary aspects found as expressions only of semiotic animals. … In such knowledge the human being realizes the source of its difference from the other life forms, the *humanitas* of the human animal, as well as the universality of the process on which all the life forms depend. (Deely 2001: 737)

Our relations and identities as semiotic animals depend on our manner of living and, for the most part, on our love for each other that expands over generations in an evolutionary process. To live in love, in the acceptance of the other, and in the acceptance of the conditions of existence, as a source and not as a mere opposition, restriction or limitation, has been the evolutionary manner of conservation of the origin of our humanness and continuous expansion of our intelligence (Maturana and Verden-Zöller 2008), which indeed transcends rationality. Love is an expression among people with no rational reason. As semiotic animals, we fall in love for no rational reason. Rationality is not quite reasonableness; both Deely (2005, 2010) and Petrilli (2013) maintain that reasonableness is the capacity to respond to the attraction is that exerted upon the self by the other. Rationality has nothing to do with love. "We may resist the notion of love in a scientific reflection because we fear for the objectivity of our rational approach" (Maturana and Varela 1987: 247).

Despite the debates over the ideas of philic love and agapic love, all kinds of love share one thing in common—that is, simply, love. For instance, we "find in Aristotle the Eros of Plato raised to the level of a cosmic force" (Nygren 1953: 184). This is also why Aristotle's *philia* bears some resemblance to Plato's *eros*; there cannot be any contradiction between Agape and Eros, only paradox. Certainly, Peirce's *Agapasm* bridges the gap between Agape-Eros—an integration that maintains the teleological aspects of evolution. This may explains why Peirce uses *agapasm* to talk about the law of love as a cosmic evolution. *Agapasm* draws our attention to the paradoxical relation between Agape and Eros.

Agape is love that is expressed by an agent's concern for the beloved, exemplified by brotherly-sisterly love or parental love, and is the energy that overflows in interdependence toward others. Eros is love that seeks perfection and is dependent on the beloved for this fulfillment. But fulfillment of perfection is not present at the act of engagement; it needs the participation of Agape. Therefore, the integration of Agape and Eros is the dynamic principle in the evolutionary process that forms the intentional passage from incompleteness toward completeness. Eros requires the telos to give it direction as much as the telos needs Eros to be actualized in the emergent outcome of the evolutionary process (Hausman 1974).

Peirce tells us that there are three modes of evolution: "evolution by fortuitous variation, evolution by mechanical necessity, and evolution by creative love" (CP 6.302). The third mode, agapasm, incorporates the other two. In other words, genuine agapasm (agapastic evolution) is the synthesis of chance (anancastic evolution) and necessity (tychastic evolution). "In the very nature of things, the line of demarcation between the three modes of evolution is not perfectly sharp" (CP 6.306), just as the color gradient is a variant form of the *sorites paradox*. Yet, Peirce describes anancasm and tychasm as "degenerate forms of agapasm" (CP 6.303). Agapasm seems to englobe both anancasm and tychasm. It also seems that agapastic integration is the ultimate teleological aspect of evolution, in which Eros moves the world by gentle desire toward love; this generative spirit of Eros is, to use the Aristotelian notion, the creative *entelechy* in us surging from our deepest desire for evolutionary love.

Love transcends chance and necessity; it is by desire and intention. In-tentionality means "to signify"; therefore, one can infer that the very meaning and significance of love are reachable by intentionality. The linkages between intentionality and semiotics have already been explored by Deely (2007). While intentionality makes meaning-making possible, it does not follow a predetermined path of action or end, preconceived thought, or specific des-tination; rather, the ultimate intention of love is to engage in an unfolding emergent and evolutionary process of creation. I think this is what Peirce (CP 6.156) intends by his notion of "developmental teleology" as an ongoing transformation of intention.

Moreover, Peirce's idea of evolutionary love incorporates, yet transcends, the Christian belief of God as love. Christian fellowship with God "*depends exclusively on God's Agape*", simply because it is "His nature to love" (Nygren 1953: 75); and since human beings were created in the image of God, then the teleological nature of semiotic animals is to love. God's highest tran-scendence, the only one that does not dishonor Him, "belongs not to power, nor to wisdom, nor even to infinity, but to love. For love alone is enough to put all infinity, all wisdom, and all power to work" (Marion 2003: 222). By expanding on God-like attributes of human beings, Russian Orthodox Archimandrite Sophrony (1896–1993) challenges the idea of "incommen-surability" between God and human beings. Paradoxically, "there is and must be commensurability in spite of all that is incommensurable. To dismiss this idea of commensurability would make it totally impossible to interpret any form of cognition as truth—that is, as corresponding to the reality of primordial being" (in Sakharov 2002: 79); "to be a person is to love" (81). Actually, this idea of love "was anticipated by the early Egyptians" as well as "by the Stoics, by the Buddhists, and by Confucius" (CP 6.442). For ancient Egyptians, love meant the long desire of the heart for an ongoing mutual rela-tion that is sustainable, unselfish, and endless; they believed that the heart is the seat of love and intelligence; this is expressed through what they called the *intelligence-of-the-heart*.

In the transmodern world, where the absolute becomes obsolete,[3] the relation between God and humans is transparent and continuous. For if we are created in the image and likeness of God, according to Judeo-Christian

---

[3] The concept of the "Absolute God" as an entirely static, permanent entity is a fallacy that separates God from humans and, consequently, fabricates a deficient reality. For to *absolutize* God is to deny human beings the capacity to create and paralyzes them from performing the very nature of God's image—not only the act of creation, but also the desire for loving each other.

traditions, then we are created to delight in what is infinite and to carry in our minds and hearts evolutionary love. The link between God and Eros goes back to the Greek historian Zeller, who said: "The Creator, to form the universe, had first to transform himself into *Eros*, the love-god" (in Peirce 1892: 240). And because Eros triggers all sorts of love, it can best be perceived, as I said above, the *generator-of-desire* or G.O.D. The intimate relation between Eros (G.O.D.) and semiotic animals emerge as a necessary condition for Peirce's synechism.

Like any semiotic phenomenon, love is a sign that includes triadic relations, where the lover, the beloved, and love are only fixed at one semiotic moment; each element in the triad shifts its role and never remains the same. This means that love is in a constant expansion of an infinite and fluid process of semiosis, where we, as semiotic animals, become both lovers and beloved beings. Love of one's friends and colleagues, one's community and humanity at large, is at the core of evolutionary love. It is not surprising that Renaissance authors used the words "friend" and "lover" interchangeably. Intimacy of friendship means affection of kinship, where kinship does not simply imply blood or lineage but shared feelings. Intimacy thus marks the harmonious relation among the community of semiotic animals.

It has never been more essential in human history to cultivate the love for wholeness to overcome the widespread violence and fix the rampant fragmentation in our lives. For semiotic animals, only love in its various forms transcends survivability and sustainability into thriveability and liveliness, attracting them to seek new connections and make fresh meaning in the world. The semiotic animal can be seen as the birth of "a new form of humanism" (Deely 2010; Petrilli and Ponzio 2003). Semiotic animals, as loving animals, are able to become aware of their own synchronicity, taking "serious account of a past without which their present would not be at all, or of a future which offers unpredictable possibilities as well as mere extensions of the past" (Deely 2010a: 13). And yet, becoming aware of the path of evolutionary love is "much into the future it will perdure" (Deely 2010a: 15). Undoubtedly, Deely has paved the way for us to consider semiotic animals as *wholophilic* animals. We may join Archimandrite Sophrony in declaring that *I love therefore I am*. Deely's contributions deepen our understanding of ourselves as semiotic animals who are capable of love.

References

BATAILLE, Georges (1897–1962).
    1957.   *Erotism: Death and Sensuality*, trans. Mary Dalwood (San Francisco: City Lights Books, 1986).

DANESI, Marcel.

  2013.   *The History of the Kiss: The Birth of Popular Culture (Semiotics and Popular Culture)*. (New York: Palgrave Macmillan).

DEELY, John.

  2001.   *Four Ages of Understanding: The First Postmodern Survey of Philosophy from Ancient Times to the Turn of the Twenty-first Century* (Toronto: University of Toronto Press).

  2005.   "Defining the Semiotic Animal: A Postmodern Definition of Human Being Superseding the Modern Definition 'Res Cogitans'", *American Catholic Philosophical Quarterly* 79.3 (Summer), 461–481.

  2007.   *Intentionality and Semiotics: A Story of Mutual Fecundation, as told by John Deely* (Chicago, IL: University of Scranton Press).

  2010.   *Semiotic Animal: A Postmodern Definition of "Human Being" Transcending Patriarchy and Feminism* (South Bend, IN: St. Augustine's Press).

  2010a.   *Semiotics Seen Synchronically: A View from 2010* (Ottawa, Canada: Legas Publishing).

DEELY, John, Susan PETRILLI, and Augusto PONZIO.

  2005.   *The Semiotic Animal* (Ottawa, Canada: Legas Publishing).

GEBSER, Jean (1905–1973).

  1949.   *The Ever-Present Origin*, trans. Noel Barstad and Algis Mickunas (Athens, OH: Ohio University Press, 1985).

HALL, David L.

  1982.   *Eros and Irony: A Prelude to Philosophical Anarchism* (Albany: State University of New York Press).

HAUSMAN, Carl R.

  1974.   "Eros and Agape in Creative Evolution: A Peircean Insight", *Process Studies* 4.1 (Spring), 11–25.

HEGEL, G. W. Friedrich (1770–1831).

  1807.   *Hegel's Phenomenology of Spirit*, trans. A. V. Miller. (Oxford, UK: Oxford University Press, 1977).

HYLAND, Drew A.

  2008.   *Plato and the Question of Beauty* (Bloomington, IN: Indiana University Press).

MARION, Jean-Luc.

  2003.   *The Erotic Phenomena*, trans. Stephen E. Lewis (Chicago, IL: The University of Chicago Press, 2007).

MARTIN, Clancy.

  2015.   *Love and Lies: An Essay on Truthfulness, Deceit, and the Growth and Care of Erotic Love* (New York: Farrar, Straus and Giroux).

MATURANA, Humberto, and Francisco J. VARELA (1946–2001).

1987.   *The Tree of Knowledge: The Biological Roots of Human Understanding.* Revised Edition (Boston, MA: Shambhala Publications).

MATURANA, Humberto Romesin, and Gerda VERDEN-ZÖLLER.

2008.   *The Origin of Humanness in the Biology of Love*, ed. Pille Bunnell (Charlottesville, VA: Imprint Academic, Philosophy Documentation Center).

NYGREN, Anders (1890–1978).

1953.   *Agape and Eros*, trans. Philip S. Watson (Philadelphia: The Westminster Press).

PEIRCE, Charles Sanders (1839–1914).

1866–1913.   *The Collected Papers of Charles S. Peirce.* Vols. I–VI ed. Charles Hartshorne and Paul Weiss. Vols. VII–VIII ed. Arthur W. Burks. (Cambridge, MA: Harvard University Press, 1958). (References from this source are abbreviated as CP followed by numbers that refer to the volume and paragraph with a period in between.)

1892.   Lowell Lectures on the History of Science", in *Charles S. Peirce: Selected Writings (Values in a Universe of Chance)*, ed. Philip P. Wiener (New York: Dover Publications, Inc., 1958).

PETRILLI, Susan.

2004.   "Crossing Out Boundaries with Global Communication: The Problem of the Subject", *The American Journal of Semiotics* 20.1–4, 193–209. doi: https://doi.org/10.5840/ajs2004201/45

2013.   *The Self as a Sign, the World, and the Other: Living Semiotics* (New Brunswick, NJ: Transaction Publishers).

PETRILLI, Susan, and Augusto PONZIO.

2003.   *Semiotica* (Rome: Meltemi).

PLATO (c.385–370 BC).

Plato Symposium, trans. Alexander Nehamas and Paul Woodruff (Indianapolis: Hackett Publishing Company, 1989).

SAKHAROV, Nicholas V.

2002.   *I love Therefore I am: The Theological Legacy of Archimandrite Sophrony* (New York: St. Vladimir's Seminary Press).

SEIF, Farouk Y.

2008.   "At Home with Transmodernity: Reconstructing Cultural Identity in a Globalizing World", in Transmodernity: Managing Global Communication, ed. Doina Cmeçiu. Proceedings of the 2nd ROASS Conference, Slavic-Moldova, Romania, 23–26 October 2008 (Bacău, Romania: Alma Mater Publishing House, 2009), 248–256.

2013.   "Dialogue with Kishtta: A Semiotic Revelation of the Paradox of Life and Death", *The American Journal of Semiotics* 29.1–4, 101–115. doi: https://doi.org/10.5840/ajs2013291-44

2016. "What Is Real Is Not Always True! Reconstruction Reality in a Transmodern World", in *Is It Real? Structuring Reality by Means of Signs*, ed. Zeynep Onur et al. (Cambridge Scholarship Publications).

TEILHARD DE CHARDIN, Pierre (1881–1955).

1955. *The Phenomenon of Man*, trans. Bernard Wall (New York: Harper & Row Publishers, 1965).

Replacing Descartes's "Thinking Thing" With Deely's "Semiotic Animal"

Resolving Our Species Sustainability Dilemma and Establishing the Semiotic Age

Richard Currie Smith

Case Western Reserve University and Kent State University

Abstract: French mathematician and natural philosopher René Descartes in the early seventeenth century developed his "thinking thing" definition of human being. This ontological construct that places the rational intellect of mankind as separate and superior to the natural world became the centerpiece of the Enlightenment and established the Modern Age. Descartes's definition underlay the scientific and industrial revolution, colonialism, and the cultural imperialism of the West to become globalized along with modernity. With the marvelous technological advances of the worldwide spread of modernity also came devastating climate change and massive biodiversity loss that threatens our species' sustainability. The American philosopher John Deely in the early twenty-first century developed his "semiotic animal" definition of human being that places our species within the natural world while being endowed with a unique responsibility toward its preservation and restoration. Deely's definition is viewed as in consonance with our sustainable Paleolithic animistic ontological orientation centered on accurately interpreting relational being while going beyond it through clarifying the semiotic processes involved in accurate discernment of sustainable activities. It is asserted that replacing Descartes's thinking thing definition with Deely's semiotic animal and globalizing it through contemporary communication technology such as the Internet will launch a Semiotic Age and resolve our sustainability crisis.

Keywords: semiotics, semiotic animal, sustainability, John Deely, Semiotic Age, relational being, relational ontology, animism, Gregory Bateson, cybernetics, ecological anthropology

ISSN 0277-7126

doi: 10.5840/ajs201711819

Online First: January 19, 2017

The American Journal of Semiotics 32.1–4 (2016), 143–204.

> *As semiotics comes of age, it must increasingly free itself from the drag*
> *of pre-existing philosophical paradigms … it is the task of semiotics to*
> *create a new paradigm—its own—and to review, criticize, and improve*
> *wherever possible all previous accounts of experience, knowledge, and*
> *belief in terms of that paradigm.*
>
> John Deely (1990: 124)

1. Introduction

Because you are reading this article it is highly likely that you are the Earth walking through the sky with awareness. You are a creature who resides on a small planet orbiting a minor sun in a dense galaxy you can observe hovering above you on a cloudless night, insignificant but for the earth being the single place in the vast known universe that for certain harbors life. You have emerged from a delicate rim of life whose oceans' depth is shallower in proportion than to the ink on a typical desk globe. Possessing a complex learned and shared oral and written symbol system, you are a member of the only species ever to have existed both to engage in the grand semiotic or communicative enterprise of life in which meaning is created, and also to reflect upon that process. The self-organizing and self-replicating processes of your body made up of the minerals and moisture of the earth allow you to engage in the miraculous semiotic feat of making sense by having something you perceive or think about represent something else. The heart in your chest is beating blood, your bilateral lungs are breathing air, billions of neurons in your brain and gut fire signals at speeds beyond your comprehension to enable you to *interpret* ink on paper or digital image on screen while associating them with emotional nuance; all this and so very much more is done without any need for assistance on your part. William Shakespeare's Hamlet said it well,

> What a piece of work is a man, how noble in reason, how infinite in faculties,
> in form and moving how express and admirable, in action how like an angel,
> in apprehension how like a god! The beauty of the world, the paragon of
> animals. (Shakespeare 1623: Act II, Scene II)

After 200,000 years of our species performing marvelous accomplishments no creature had come close to in 3.8 billion years of evolution, the renowned philosopher René Descartes formed a definition of human being as the *thinking thing* or *res cogitans*. This definition, which saw humans as superior and separate from the natural world, would go on to launch the Enlightenment period of Europe. The Modern Age that also "was enshrined in the formula 'thinking thing'" (Deely 2003a: 111) would soon globalize this

Cartesian definition and put us on a rapid trajectory to extinction, challenging not only our survival but also that of life on earth as we know it (Jorgenson 2006; Spaargaren 2000).

Descartes's notion about what it means to be human, formed around assumptions on both the nature of reality and how we know the world, was complemented by other Enlightenment philosophers such as Francis Bacon and Isaac Newton. Later Enlightenment philosophers, most notably Immanuel Kant whose work is frequently seen as the cornerstone of modernity, continued refining Descartes's thinking thing definition (Rohlf 2016).

Because of the successful globalization of modernity based on what became the revered thinking thing definition of humankind by Descartes, a grand sustainability dilemma or a choice between two undesirable alternatives has now come to the center on the world stage (Sachs 1993; Sachs and Santarius 2007). It has placed in front of humanity the pressing need to resolve immediately the most crucial conundrum our species has ever faced. If humankind chooses to continue to follow the modern Cartesian view of humankind, material abundance will flourish and the inventions of technology will become ubiquitous in the short-term foreseeable future; however, our planetary life support systems will also decay in the long-term leading to our demise (Barnosky 2011; IPCC 2015; Rockstrom 2009). If humankind chooses to refute the globalization of modernity and its concomitant Cartesian definition of humanity, millions will not experience modern economic development and the benefits of the other wondrous achievements that have occurred because of the globalization of modernity (Rodrik 2011).

This article asserts that a way out of our ominous sustainability dilemma has been created. This bold assertion derives from the success of the recent endeavor by John Deely, who was termed "arguably the most important living American philosopher" (Cobley 2009: 3), to "thematize the notion and to establish conceptually" (Deely 2010: xii) a "semiotic animal" or *animal semeioticum* (Deely 2010: 43) definition for human being[1] as the only animal "able to recognize that there are signs and to investigate their action" (Deely 2010a: 52). This is because the semiotic animal definition of Deely is viewed by your author as a *replacement* for the "thinking thing" definition of Descartes (Deely 2016a).[2]

---

[1] Human being in anthropology can be described as occurring with the genus Homo, for this article it will mean our species Homo sapiens. There is debate on whether Human being should be termed as our sub species Homo sapiens sapiens because of the discovery of what some anthropologists are calling Homo sapiens idaltu.

[2] Deely was asked, "Do you think the title of my article should be replacing or recasting Descartes's definition by Deely's definition? I think replacing". Consistent with Deely's intent

The semiotic animal definition of Deely is given such consequential weight in resolving our species' sustainability dilemma because this definition of humanity provides a fundamental ontology centered upon humility and connection with the natural world that allows for the benefits of modernity to be experienced by the world's people without the decay of the life-support systems upon which we depend. Support will be presented for this definition of humanity as an effective replacement of the presently globalizing modern thinking thing definition, which separates humans from the natural world and provides a fundamental ontology centered upon hubris that lies at the root of the non-sustainable trajectory of our species (Bateson 1972: 496–501; Roszak 1975; Sutton and Anderson 2009). Finally, the article will further contend that the globalization of the semiotic animal definition, which is in consonance with how we have sustainably defined ourselves for 95 percent of our time on earth (Bateson 1972: 496–501; Roszak 1975; Sutton and Anderson 2009), will led to a new age for humankind. That is, just as the thinking thing definition led to the Modern Age, in the view of your author the semiotic animal definition will usher in a *Semiotic Age*[3] (Smith 2016) that will facilitate our survival into the far distant future (Deely 2016).[4]

This modern enculturation process of globalization occurred through diverse avenues that included colonialism, the industrial revolution, two World Wars, multinational corporate capitalism, oligarchical communist materialism, mass media, and finally the Internet and new media. Seemingly immune to resistance by the diverse cultures of the world, the entrenchment of globalization, especially since the end of World War II, has enabled the definition of what it means to be a human being of modern Western culture to become the dominant contemporary way humankind defines itself (Sachs: 1993; Spaargaren 2000).

The essential cultural creation of defining what it means to be human, which was centered upon being embedded within the natural world as expressed by a multitude of diverse cultures around the world for thousands of years, has now become one of separation from nature derived from the mono-cultural production of the modern West. It is crucial to note that this

---

in writing his *Semiotic Animal* book, "to supersede the ancient and medieval 'animal rationale' along with the modern 'res cogitans'" (Deely, 2010: iii), Deely replied: "replacing!"

    [3] The establishment of the Semiotic Age to replace modernity is conceived by your author just as Deely states "in principle, not in sociological fact, of course" when he describes Peirce's 'New List of Categories' in regard to their creation effectively closing the era of modern philosophy and bringing in "authentic" postmodernism (Deely 2010: 101).

    [4] Deely stated informally to your author, "This is a great project that you have defining the Semiotic Age." He suggested later that this age "beyond modernity" could be termed "the age of relation", and that he saw benefit in both designations.

globalized definition of human being is not that of "Western" culture—what most writers stress when critiquing globalization. It is instead a definition that is unique to one particular social and historical period of time within this culture, the "modern" West, which has existed for only about 350 years.

During the globalization of this modern definition—built upon a Cartesian model not only of human nature but all of nature (Hornborg 2006)—science and technology have flourished. Marvelous discoveries and their applications have produced wondrous achievements in a myriad of diverse domains, including medicine, communication, transportation, construction and energy. However, with the globalization of the modern view of humankind the planet has undergone prodigious environmental decay. This is because at its core, modernity affirms our inherent separation from the "inferior mechanistic natural world" whose non-thinking creatures are intrinsically unknowable and alien to us. Many social theorists contend that the technological accomplishments and social expressions of modernity have been founded on this categorical distinction between humanity and nature, and that this separation lies at the heart of the "modern project" (Hornborg 2006: 21). This degradation is most notably expressed in the form of devastating climate change and massive biodiversity loss that has come in response to modern hubris like the sword of Damocles to threaten our very survival (Barnosky 2011; Bateson 1972: 494–498; IPCC 2015).

To support this assertion that the semiotic animal definition provides a foundation for a way out of our pressing sustainability dilemma, the general academic context and specific approach that guides the argument will be discussed. This context is covered in relative detail to demonstrate the importance of culture as the medium guiding human interaction with the natural world. An in-depth exploration of the long held sustainable definition embraced by our species as animistic foragers follows, which highlights how we were embedded in a semiotic or communicative web of interaction within the natural world—a definition that was adopted for the vast majority of our species' time on earth. Next, the Enlightenment definition of human being by René Descartes and its elaboration by the premier later enlightenment philosopher, Immanuel Kant, which further fueled the modern era and its globalization will be explored. Special emphasis will be placed on the ontological and epistemological assumptions of modernity leading to our current sustainability crisis. Following this, a chronological account of the historical semiotic context that informed the creation of the semiotic animal definition of human being by Deely, and the Semiotic Age by your author that this definition led to, will be discussed with particular attention on how

Deely's definition contrasts with that of Descartes and how modernity and postmodernity "falsely so called" (Cobley 2009: 5; Deely 2010: 118) contrast with the Semiotic Age.

It is important to add the caveat that because of the large scope and potential consequence of the fundamental sustainability assertion of this article, the supporting argument will only be able to be touched upon. Greater depth and breath will necessarily follow in subsequent work by your author and perhaps by others better versed in certain aspects of the assertion.

2. Context and Approach

The general academic context that guides this article is anthropology, whose principal task is defining what it means to be human. Derived from the Greek *anthropos* ("human") and *logia* ("study"), anthropology performs this task through its position as the only academic discipline to be both a humanity and a science, holistically studying humankind from a large-scale spatial and long-term temporal or evolutionary perspective. Semiotic anthropology and cultural ecology, two intertwined sub-disciplines of anthropology further guide this exploration. Semiotic anthropology focuses on sign-based communication as it relates to humans (Mertz 2007), whereas cultural ecology focuses on the mediation of human interaction with the natural world through culture (Sutton and Anderson 2009). The specific approach that is utilized is a cybernetic or living system orientation to cultural change centered on the work of the semiotic and ecological anthropologist Gregory Bateson. The approach of Bateson was chosen because of his focus on clarifying the semiotic dynamics of major cultural change, especially in regard to human interaction with the natural world; this approach fits especially well with the emphasis of this article, the transition from the Middle Ages to the Modern Age and the proposed transition from the Modern Age to the Semiotic Age (Capra 1996; Deely 2016; Harries-Jones 1995; Hoffmeyer 2008; Smith 2016).

Exploring our sustainability crisis through the lens of the holistic academic discipline of anthropology, the sub-disciplines of semiotic and ecological anthropology and the cybernetic approach to living systems, the article begins at the inception of life on earth 3.8 billion years ago with the grand stochastic process of the evolution of life that eventually led to our species being present on the earth (Bateson 1972). It is important to point out that the cybernetic or living systems approach utilized by Bateson to address our contemporary sustainability dilemma and to frame evolution as a stochastic process contrasts significantly with the routinely accepted notions of Darwinian evolution (Bateson 1979). For a cybernetic evolutionist (Levin 2005; Montagnini 2007) like Bateson the emphasis of evolution is not on the competition between and among species as in Darwinian thought, but in consonance with the original meaning of the term "competition" from the Latin *competere*: to strive together for a common purpose. For Bateson, the definition of life used by Darwin that inaccurately framed organisms as separate from the environment was a crucial mistake, one that remains central to the contemporary degradation of the natural world.

> It is now empirically clear that Darwinian evolutionary theory contained a very great error in its identification of the unit of survival under natural selection. The unit which was believed to be crucial and around which the theory was set up was either the breeding individual or the family line or the sub-species or some similar homogeneous set of conspecifics. Now I suggest that the last hundred years have demonstrated empirically [through cybernetics] that if an organism or aggregate of organisms sets to work with a focus on its own survival and thinks that that is the way to select its adaptive moves, its "progress" ends up with a destroyed environment. If the organism ends up destroying its environment, it has in fact destroyed itself. (Bateson 1972: 456–457)

The cybernetic approach toward evolution and the workings of living systems affirms the absolute necessity of defining the unit of survival as the organism in semiotic communication with environment, and plays a crucial role in addressing the main sustainability thesis of this article. As such, the highly germane field of cybernetics will be covered in relative detail.

Cybernetics traces it origins to the early 1940s when the U.S. military presented a team of diverse scientists and engineers with a vexing problem that had occurred during World War II. They were asked to create a better way to shoot down enemy planes whose pilots were performing unpredictable and effective evasive gyrations and causing extensive damage to navy ships (Capra 1996: 52; Gerovitch 2009).

From the novel work of several twentieth-century disciplines, including Gestalt psychology, organismic biology and quantum physics, the team approached the anti-aircraft task from a living or *open systems* perspective (Capra 1996: 30, 52; Gerovitch 2009; Montagnini 2007; Smith 2005; 2016). The organismic biologist Ludwig von Bertalanffy first called living systems, such as organisms, *open* because in order to survive they needed a continual flow of matter and energy from their external environment (Capra 1996: 48; Von Bertalanffy1950). Since Bertalanffy's work focused on problems organisms face in attempting to survive and the solutions that they devise to solve these problems, he needed to understand the whole organism in the context of its environment (Bartholomew 2005). Bertalanffy understood that problems of survival have been creatively solved by millions of organisms in a multitude of diverse ever-changing environments through evolution or the stochastic process of natural selection (Bartholomew 2005; Bateson 1972; 1979). Through biological adaptation in association with the environment, this purposeful process of evolution is seen by organismic biologists as "so central as to be inseparable from life itself" (Bartholomew 2005: 330).

The work of the team regarding this interplay of organism and environment was greatly advanced by physiologist Arturo Rosenblueth, who brought to the forefront how for living organisms the semiotic process of information "feedback" through multiple circular loops was essential in the accomplishment of purposeful behaviors. Seemingly simple activities that engaged the environment such as picking up a pencil, were shown to rely on the complex communication of information that "feeds back" into the system through circular causality where the effects of an event return indirectly to influence the original purposeful event. It is this nonlinear network of numerous connected parts centered on a semiotic process of communicative feedback of information found within living systems and their interaction with their environments that allows them to have the capacity to self-correct and solve complex problems creatively, such as a cat catching a mouse or a dog following a trail (Capra 1996; Montagnini 2007; Rosenblueth 1943).

The team of scientists and engineers quickly integrated the living system model into the U.S. military's problem of shooting down enemy aircraft. The evasive actions of enemy pilots were effectively anticipated and countered with great success through the integration of the living systems nonlinear-feedback model formulated by the team into the use of computers and radar.

The leader of the team, Norbert Wiener, realized the importance of their findings and called this new revolutionary field of study *cybernetics*, from the Greek *kybernetes* ("steersman"). He decided on this term because he viewed the process of solving vexing complex problems through *information-centered* communication based on feedback from multiple environmental sources to be like the process involved in steering a boat (Wiener 1948). When sailing a boat from one location to another a sailor must take in feedback or information from multiple environmental sources and creatively make adjustments and readjustments in a stochastic or calibrated fashion to reach the desired destination. The force of the current, direction and velocity of the wind, and the size and frequency of the waves are just some of the environmental factors that must be continually monitored. As in living systems, it is the semiotic circular system of information feeding back through a nonlinear cycle of communication between sailor and the environment that keeps the boat on course.

Wiener's cybernetic analogy clarified how the complex goal-directed problem of the sailor is solved through the feedback of information from diverse sources. His steersman analogy demonstrates how the *emergence* of innovative "self-corrective" solutions occurs in living systems (Wiener 1948; 1950) through calibration and recalibration derived from diverse environmental information.

For Bateson and the cybernetic evolutionists, this means the organism that fits its biotic and abiotic environment best through accurate interpretation of diverse feedback from multiple sources is the one that flourishes and remains. This is because for life to occur and be sustained, the formula for all organisms is simple and inexorable: organism = biology + environment (Bateson 1972: 491). From the cybernetic perspective, every organism on earth must resolve the same sustainability challenge, how to acquire enough from the environment to survive and thrive, but how to do so without degrading the environment upon which the organism is dependent. Therefore, in the ongoing quest for sustainability by organisms in the interrelated semiotic matrix of living systems that makes up life on earth, evolution requires *survival of the organism that best fits its environment.*

3. Paleolithic, Neolithic, and Ancient Eras

> *Is not the sky a father and the earth a mother, and are not all living things with feet or wings or roots their children?*
>
> Black Elk, Lakota (1932)

> *Praised be You, my Lord, through Sister Moon and the stars, In the heavens you have made them bright, precious and fair. … Praised be You, my Lord, through our Sister, Mother Earth who sustains and governs us, producing varied fruits with coloured flowers and herbs.*
>
> Saint Francis of Assisi (1225)

With the emergence of culture approximately 2.5 million years ago, and along with it the genus Homo or human and the Paleolithic Era as designated by anthropology, the essential aspect of sign interpretation and production or semiosis (Deely 2010: 57–60; Sebeok 1979) that we share with all species was radically altered. Our use of culture—defined as the learned and shared complex semiotic communication system of a group that guides perception and action (Geertz 1973)—made us distinct from the many millions of species that have existed on the earth. While culture had appeared in very rudimentary form for around 16 million years in some primates including chimpanzees and orangutans, its elaboration through the use of symbols or signs that arbitrarily stand for something else and their integration into our existing primate semiotic apparatus made culture the central distinguishing feature in humankind's pursuit of sustainability (Buss 2003; Palagi 2006; Sebeok 1979).

Like all other organisms engaged in the quest to survive through living in consonance with their environment, humankind was semiotically interdependent, needing to produce and to interpret or make "sense" of signs, which the renowned semiotician Charles Sanders Peirce saw as "something that stands for something, to someone in some capacity" (Danesi 1999), in order to act effectively within our environment (Stutz 2014). Utilizing our senses, applying our cognitive and cathectic abilities and integrating what we had learned from our previous experiences, we continually scanned our environment in an attempt to interpret accurately the signs in our surroundings in order to survive and thrive (Deely 2010: 82; Stutz 2014).

Like all other organisms we engaged in semiosis by transforming things in our environment into objects of perception (Deely 2010: 57–60; Sebeok 1979). We then acted upon these objects through nuanced gradations of: "plus" go toward, "minus" go away from, and "zero" neutral or ignore (Deely 2010: 78). Every moment of life involved active participation in semiosis to ascertain what expression in our biotic and abiotic environment represented sustenance, danger, or inconsequence and then discerning the feedback in regard to the efficacy of those appraisals. Accurate interpretation of signs determined whether our species went on to procreate and continue our existence on earth; these signs requiring interpretation included the calls of birds, the scents and the movements of animals, the tastes and effects of plants, the color of the sky, the direction of the wind, the amount of moisture in the air, and even the length of day.

Moreover, in the evolutionary short-time period of approximately 2 million years, the integration of culture into our existing primate semiotic apparatus became for Paleolithic humans the "big bang" or the catalyst for a tripling of brain size to 1300 cubic centimeters in vast disproportion to body mass. The rapid refinement and application of culture also triggered and encouraged the development of intricate prefrontal cortex complexity that no organism on earth had ever remotely expressed (Hofman 2014). In addition, culture fostered an unprecedented growth in the creation and dissemination of stone tools within and between human groups, making culture instead of physiological change the major component of adaptation to the surrounding environment (Van Schaik 2003).

When our species Homo sapiens emerged approximately 200,000 years ago as anatomically modern humans, it was the highly elaborated expression and utilization of culture, seen especially in symbolic or arbitrary sign production and application that primarily defined us. The further refinement of culture, as expressed most notably in the high-level semiotic expressions of language and art helped enabled us to move from our original savanna environment in East Africa approximately 70,000 years ago to begin our eventual global migration (Derricourt 2005).

We took culture with us as we moved across the planet engaging in semiosis within the diverse environments that were encountered. As nomadic subsistence hunters and gatherers, or foragers as termed today, we continued to sustain ourselves by interpreting natural signs while increasingly relying more on anthroposemiotic or human signs. Survival was dependent upon an intricate knowledge of the various flora and fauna that was present in the environment (Sutton and Anderson 2009). We remained environmentally opportunistic, gathering plants and hunting available animals in rigorously created seasonal rounds engaged in an adaptive strategy that kept us semiotically embedded in the new environments we inhabited. With enhanced application of language, this knowledge was attained through circular feedback loops centered on creative and rigorous research or ethnoscience derived from trial and error experimentation and application over immense timeframes.

Through an encounter with a rich diversity of environments and microenvironments, such as lush tropical forests, grassy savannas, wind-blown deserts and frozen tundra, the cultural creation and application of abstract signs facilitated our successful adaptation. Thousands of diverse foraging cultures populated the planet in a dynamic interactive self-organizational dance of stochastically calibrated creative adaptation to varying environments. Culture allowed for the creation of a repository of information, which means to "bring into form" through representation (Hoffmeyer and Emmeche 1991), concerning interaction with the environment that could be passed down from generation to generation over thousands of years.

In small nomadic bands typically of twenty-five to fifty members we shared our foodstuffs among the group and cared for each other in a manner so intimate that the expression *thank-you* was often non-existent. Although becoming a leader in these nomadic bands typically meant displaying exceptional ability in physical, emotional, and intellectual endeavors, the primary and essential attribute for leadership frequently was social and semiotic in the form of empathy and generosity (Fehr and Fischbacher 2003; Kottak 2011; Sutton and Anderson 2009). Furthermore, because of the uncertainty of foraging and the value of working in coordinated gathering and hunting groups, by necessity we were interdependent and defined ourselves as close-knit kin and fictive kin relatives. In consonance with cybernetics, the stochastic focus of survival was the group in relationship with the surrounding environment.

The most defining characteristic of Paleolithic humans in regard to the sustainability assertion of this article was the development of intimate, personal, and spiritual relationships between them and the biotic and abiotic environment. Anthropologist Edward Tylor coined the term "animism" from the Latin term "*anima* or soul" for the perspective of viewing the natural world as being made up of "spiritual beings" (Tylor 1871). He speculated that "primitive" people were intrigued and perplexed by the experience of death and of images in dreams and trances that they sometimes remembered upon waking up or coming out of a trance. To explain these occurrences, the notion of a double or second ethereal body inhabiting the physical one arose and became generalized from humans to plants, animals, and physical manifestations in the environment. Tylor saw animism as the first form of religion, a "childlike" expression in a maturing progression to polytheism, monotheism and eventually to the end of religion with the establishment of science.

While Tylor's pejorative and ethnocentric progression of religion has been rejected by anthropology, his insights became widely accepted as well-founded concerning the prevalence of diverse foraging peoples who affirmed personal and often sacred relationships with nature, and assigned supernatural designation to biotic and abiotic expressions of the natural world. While being mindful of overgeneralization (Sutton and Anderson 2009: 2), many anthropologists have gone on to utilize animism (the projection of meaning from culture to nature) to bring understanding to the benevolent tendency of native people toward the natural world they encountered (Bird-David 1999; Descola 1992; Hornborg 2001). Bird-David describes this reevaluation process undertaken by anthropologists as "Animism Revisited."

> "Animism" is projected in the literature as simple religion and a failed epistemology, to a large extent because it has hitherto been viewed from *modernist* perspectives ... [alternatively] hunter-gatherer animism constitutes a *relational* (not a failed) epistemology. This epistemology is about knowing the world by focusing primarily on relatednesses, from a related point of view, within the shifting horizons of the related viewer. The knowing grows from and *is* the knower's skills of maintaining relatedness with the known. This epistemology is regarded by Nayaka [of India] (and probably other indigenous peoples we call hunter-gatherers) as authoritative against other ways of knowing the world. (Italics added)

For instance, while indigenous Amazonian people have developed their own cultural lens for interpreting their environment, some animistic themes pervade the region. One of high significance in regard to a cybernetic or relationship centered environmental orientation is "the notion of perspective" (Hornborg 2001: 133). Several Amazonian ethnographies have shown that perception and meaning are recognized as active processes dependent upon the vantage point of the perceiver. The Makuna of southeastern Columbia, for example, see any class of beings as classifying all other beings as either predator (*yai* for jaguar) or prey (*wai* for fish). In regard to the cosmology of the Campa people Weiss states:

> It is a world of relative semblances, where different kinds of beings see the same things differently. Thus humans can normally see good spirits only in the form of lightning flashes or birds whereas they see themselves in true human form, and similarly in the eyes of jaguars human beings look like peccaries to be hunted. (Weiss 1974: 264)

A crucial element of Amazonian animistic cosmologies that follows from the notion of perspective is the belief that all beings are essentially "humans" or "persons." Personifying animals and spirits endows them with conscious intention and social agency as knowing subjects. For Amazonians *"the surface appearance of animals disguises their human aspect"* (italics added), this is why for them it is through personification that an animal is best known (Viveiros de Castro 1999: 3–4; Hornborg 2001: 134). "In the animic ontology, beings do not simply occupy the world, they inhabit it" (Ingold 2006: 14).

A concept closely associated with animism is "totemism," derived from the Native American Ojibwa word *dodaem*, for spiritual being or sacred object or symbol. Pacific Northwest Native American totem poles of tribes such as the Kwakiutl and the Nuu-chah-nulth are perhaps the most well-known expressions. Made from large trees placed upright into the ground in which sculptures are carved of creatures such as fish, birds, bears and supernatural beings, the poles are typically placed outside of lodges to depict clan association (Sutton and Anderson 2009). Ethnologist J. F. McLennon (1885) used totemism in a similar fashion to Tylor's use of animism, seeing it as a stage in the religious progression of humans. Like animism, the concept of totemism was rejected since it was viewed as evidence of an immature state in the progression of religion and then later found to be useful in regard to understanding human interaction with the natural world. Totemism as a concept clarifies the emphasis of Paleolithic foragers on forming benevolent relationships with nature that derive from the projection of nature to human society.

The dynamic interplay between animism and totemism in the personalization of nature by foraging cultures often makes it difficult to distinguish between the two notions (Ingold 1996). This difficulty is exemplified well in a description of *the offering of the pipe* ceremony by Black Elk, the Ogallala Lakota (Sioux) *wičháša wakháŋ* or sacred healer, whose narration of his life in 1932 to the writer John Niehardt made him one of the most well-known persons to have lived a Paleolithic life that intersected with the modern world.

> [B]ecause no good thing can be done by any man alone, I will first make an offering and send a voice to the Spirit of the World, that it may help me to be true. See, I fill this sacred pipe with the bark of the red willow but before we smoke it, you must see how it is made and what it means. These four ribbons hanging here on the stem are the four quarters of the universe. The black one is for the west where the thunder beings live to send us rain; the white one for the north, whence comes the great white cleansing wind; the red one for the east, whence springs the light and where the morning star lives to give men wisdom; the yellow for the south, whence come the summer and the power to grow. But these four spirits are only one Spirit after all, and this eagle feather here is for that One, which is like a father, and also it is for the thoughts of men that should rise high as eagles do.

Paleolithic members of our species, as exemplified by the Nayaka, Amazonians, and the Lakota, sustained themselves as foragers for nearly 200,000 years by embedding themselves within the natural world through an animistic and totemistic *relational way of being* (Ingold 2006: 12). This underlying *relational* ontological orientation and consequent relational epistemology guided their interaction with both abiotic and biotic environmental expressions. These foragers took advantage of elaborate learned and shared semiotic systems of our species that included language and art to disperse from East Africa to the far reaches of Eurasia, Australia, and the Americas. It is crucial to point out that while Paleolithic humans had recognizable ecological impacts on flora and fauna primarily through the use of fire and the hunting of megafauna, the environments they inhabited did not undergo large-scale degradation in anyway comparable to the ways that our species defined itself in regard to the natural world that followed (Boivin 2016).

Approximately 12,000 years ago, or at 5 percent of the existence of our species, our foraging style of interaction with the natural environment changed radically when plants and animals became domesticated. With the beginning of the "Neolithic" era, the foraging way of sustaining ourselves that emerged with the elaboration of culture and had acted to shape human physical, psychic, and social development (Barker 2009) began to be replaced through our second evolutionary "big bang". This change in human adaptation to the environment away from foraging to horticulture, pastoralism, and agriculture not only altered the definition of our species, but also changed and sealed the fate of innumerable other species and the habitats around the globe in which these affected species had coevolved (Barker 2009; Boivin 2016).

Human semiotic attention shifted away from the diverse natural world of wild plant and animals toward interpreting the signs of a few species chosen from the vast pantheon of the earth's flora and fauna. Heretofore inconsequential characteristics such as the species' storage capacity and reproductive success, as exemplified by corn and wheat or cattle and goats, now became of crucial importance to humankind. For newly sedentary Neolithic and ancient peoples, anthroposemiotic signs quickly became the focus of attention; the accurate interpretation of signs within human-created croplands, pastures, villages, towns and ancient cities became of highest importance for survival. This shift in semiotic engagement with the environment was in direct contrast to the focus on the natural environment of their Paleolithic nomadic ancestors. While natural or human unaltered landscapes continued to be viewed by many Neolithic and ancient people partially through the animistic personalized view of nature, with polytheism and monotheism such landscapes began to become fear-inducing places best to be avoided.

The environmentally sustainable Feng Shui system of southeastern China is a Neolithic and ancient adaptive strategy that exemplifies the integration of the animistic ontological perspective into the domestication of plants and animals. This philosophical system began approximately 6000 years ago, continued through ancient times and is still present even today, albeit in a highly degraded fashion because of communist influence. The peasants living in this area developed a "wind and water" approach that emphasized balance between multiple human and environmental components. Over millenniums they employed experimentation and innovation to create an effective intensive agricultural strategy to a landscape of mountainous land with well-watered rivers, streams and fertile valleys. The area went on to produce a large portion of the world's rice and pigs along with vast quantities of fruits and vegetables while raising and catching immense amounts of fish and other seafood. Throughout the years the fine-tuned system in true cybernetic fashion took in and utilized feedback at every juncture to regulate what and when to plant, along with how to maximize and recycle waste to increase soil fertility and lessen the possibility of infection for people. The positioning of roads, towns, and fields were all regulated for maximum advantage of each individual component as well as the overarching system (Sutton and Anderson 2009).

For the inhabitants, the Feng Shui belief system was centered on an animistic ontology that created personalized intimate spiritual relationships with the environment. This is vividly illustrated by the belief in the sacredness of particular groves of trees located in mountain valleys. To preserve the groves meant good fortune, whereas to destroy them would harm the "dragon" whose task it was to protect the mountain. This morally wrong action would "cut the dragon's pulse" and bring bad fortune to the actor and ruin to the people. In cybernetic fashion, this animistic expression of Feng Shui persuaded millions of peasants for thousands of years to forgo the short-term gain of felling the trees and similar prohibited actions because of the potential long-term pain that would come to them and to their community (Bateson 1972: 309–337, Sutton and Anderson 2009).

While the animistic ontology was vividly expressed in Neolithic and ancient cultures of Western Europe, the response of Christianity beginning in the fifth century was to contest harshly and label animistic beliefs by the pejorative terms *pagan* and *heathen*. With the widespread adoption of Christianity in the early Middle Ages, for the European people who would become the direct ancestors of the modern culture, the animistic natural world ontology was now dangerous and forbidden. Untamed nature was no longer a "plus" place of affinity to establish clans and gather medicine; instead the natural world became a "minus" place or fear-inducing 'wild-deer-ness' (Cronon 1995: 382).

4. Thinking Thing—The Enlightenment and The Modern Age

> *Thinking Thing, Res Cogitans,*
> *I think therefore I am, Cogito ergo sum,*
> René Descartes (1641)

The third evolutionary "big bang" directly related to the semiotic animal theme of this article is the definition of humankind as "modern" that emerged at the end of the European Middle Ages (fifth through fifteenth century). The predominant historical depiction of this era in Western culture is that of the European so-called "dark ages" (Deely 2001). Devastating diseases and plagues, tyrannical theological dogmatism, and the bewilderment of shadowy pagan superstition eventually gave rise in the sixteenth–seventeenth century to the Enlightenment era (Merchant 2013). To lift the proverbial cloud of "darkness" enveloping Western culture and the societies of Europe, the accumulated knowledge of the Neolithic peoples, that of the "ancients" including the polytheistic Greeks and the Christian Latins and scholastics that had replaced the previous animistic orientation in Europe, was now itself being replaced. An "enlightened" modern ontology or way of being along with an "enlightened" epistemology or way of knowing was affirmed that would rapidly be globalized in a few centuries. This precipitous change in the definition of our species would affect our species in a manner as grand as the Paleolithic, Neolithic and Ancient eras.

The philosophers Francis Bacon (1561–1626), René Descartes (1596–1650), and Isaac Newton (1643–1727) led the Enlightenment charge (Capra 1996, Hollinger 1994). Bacon and Descartes shared the desire to create a "new beginning" in philosophy and a belief in the need to discard the Latin philosophical tradition that had come before them (Deely 2001: 506). It was Descartes's development of the definition of human being as the thinking thing or *res cogitans* in Latin that became the ontological and epistemological centerpiece of the Enlightenment period between the seventeenth and eighteenth century of Western European culture. This definition led Descartes to be seen as the founder of modernity, most recognized by the phrase *I think, therefore I am* or *Cogito ergo sum* in Latin (Descartes 1641; Hollinger 1994: 21).

The Enlightenment can be said to have begun when Descartes, who was educated as both a mathematician and philosopher, had a series of dreams concerning what path he should take on the night of November 10, 1619, at the age of twenty-three, while staying near the German town of Ulm (Deely 2001: 512). His interpretation of the dreams, which ironically became known as the "great dream of reason" (Deely 2010a: 37), was that it would be his mission in life to create a new basis for science or "natural philosophy" built on the example of mathematics to find out what is real and true. It was the field of mathematics that since his youth he "delighted in above all ... [feeling that] nothing more exalted had been built upon such firm and solid foundations" (Descartes 1637: 114). His adulation with mathematics led to his belief that he could add nothing more to philosophy. Using the lens of mathematics, he held that anything which was merely probable was false, stating that philosophy "has been cultivated for many centuries by the most excellent minds and yet there is still no point in it which is not disputed and hence doubtful ... even though it is impossible for more than one to be true" (Descartes 1637: 114).

In order to find a way to uncover truth modeled after mathematics, Descartes developed *the method of universal doubt* in which a proposition clearly stated and understood is presented and from it deductions and other propositions are derived with certainty. The starting point for his method is to doubt anything that concedes the possibility of error, and if it does it must be viewed as false. He began his method of inquiry from the ontological assumption that mind and matter were separate substances having an independent existence with an infinite difference between the two (Descartes 1641; Fuenmayor 1991; Heidegger 1962), and in this process rejected anything related to the senses because of the verities of physical sensation, which includes experiences of the physical world and the body.

What Descartes determined to be beyond doubt was his existence as a thinking being, which he concluded is beyond doubt because *in order to think he must be or exist.* However, a key aspect of his proof is that it proves the existence of him as a *thinking being,* not a *thinking being that has a body.* For Descartes it is thinking and existence that are correlated with the method of doubt made pure through rejecting the senses and bodily experience. Therefore, by relying on thinking that is clearly and evidently formulated, his method could allow philosophy to be like mathematics—able to find certainty and truth (Deely 2001: 512–513).

Descartes's ontological justification for giving preeminence to thinking in his method is the placement of God at its center. He argues that his ability to think of himself as an imperfect being adrift in an uncertain ocean of doubt can only arise in contrast to the idea of a perfect being, or God. For Descartes, the starting point for the ability to think of God in his perfection comes from the *idea* of God instilled into the soul before coming into worldly existence. The perfect idea of God, all-powerful and good and removed from the ambiguity of sensations, both from the body and the external environment, becomes the foundation for relying on thinking to discern truth in his method (Deely 2001: 513–514).

Building upon his method of doubt and his notion of the idea of God, Descartes went on to contend that the rational intellect of humans was therefore the superior expression of God in the universe. However, he believed that the intellect of women did not fall into this category because they were encumbered even more than men by bodily distractions, such as fertility, which inhibited the clarity of their thinking. By placing the human intellect in a pinnacle and distinct position among beings, the linguistic animal of the ancients and the rational animal or *animal rationale* definition of the Latins that saw humans as unique among animals although still one of the animals was replaced by a severe separation from our bodies, animals and the environment. The natural world was no longer a place for us to learn from, to better know "'the way of things' as they really are, whatever mistakes might befall along that way" (Deely 2010: 41). This was because nature now occupied a lesser position than that of our masterful intellect, as did our body and its sense interactions with the environment. Humankind and the rest of nature were split from each other, as our minds were cleaved from our bodies.

The influence of Descartes's work in redefining what it means to be human and ushering in the Enlightenment period and the scientific revolution was immense both in terms of scope and scale. This influence was shown vividly by the state funeral given to him by France when he died, something unprecedented for philosophers (Deely 2001: 521). The foundation upon which he built his celebrated new system of thought was his belief in the certainty of knowledge or truth, which provided an exact science or natural philosophy to replace ancient knowledge and theological dogma, and became recognized as 'Cartesian belief'. His analytic method, involving breaking up the parts of a problem into smaller pieces and then arranging them in a logical order, became the 'Cartesian method' or reductionism. His Cartesian method was derived from the rational characteristic of the human soul, which became the 'Cartesian doctrine'. Finally his view of the universe as a machine designed by God through divine reason became what is known as the 'Cartesian dogma' (Capra 1983; Descartes 1637; 1641).

The work of Francis Bacon (1561–1626), which as mentioned earlier had actually begun shortly before Descartes, helped to further usher in the Enlightenment era and the scientific revolution. Both men advocated the complete overthrow of the methods of science or natural philosophy that came before them, demanding a greater standard of precision, a common commitment to the value of doubt, a concern about the "deceptions of the senses" (Dick 1955: 474), and a belief in the general principle of the reduction of problems to their smallest constituent parts. Nevertheless, some key differences existed between the two philosophers. While Descartes began with intuitive principles in the standard deductive method of reasoning, Bacon began with empirical observations used inductively to discern higher axioms. The reason was that Descartes was a mathematician familiar with premises and Bacon was a lawyer familiar with empirical observations as evidence to build a case in a court, which he had used frequently against scholasticism and its reliance on accepted authority.

Bacon's major contribution, it could be said, was to contend that the purpose of knowledge was to gain power over nature. Science was to "put nature on the rack" and "expose her secrets" (Merchant 2008). Like Descartes, Bacon was proposing a severe break with the animists and ancients to whom the purpose of knowledge was to learn from and to seek understanding of nature in order to survive and thrive. Humankind was no longer to adapt to the larger nature on which we were dependent; instead knowledge was for the purpose of prediction in order to control nature and bend it to human will. Therefore, for Bacon, knowledge increases only when humankind's power over lesser nature increases; as such, technology in the service of science would regain the "dominion over nature" lost in mankind's fall from grace in the Garden of Eden (Merchant 2013).

Fortified by Bacon's notions of humankind's relationship to the natural world, wise earthy elderly women or goddesses trained in centuries-old knowledge of herbal remedies known today as ethno-pharmacology, became demeaned and dangerous "wyrd hags". They were considered to be witches whose healing remedies became the expression of pagan superstition and cause for judicial inquires and the wrath of the Inquisition (Merchant 2008; 2013).

A few decades later, natural philosopher Issac Newton's notions about how to conduct research on nature, such as developing rules for constructing and using hypotheses, arose to become the dominant model or prevailing paradigm for understanding not only the non-living world of matter, but also for understanding life. For him nature was like a mechanistic clock, reducible to rationally understandable universal laws. His impact was not only great for those who practiced as natural philosophers, later to be called scientists in the nineteenth century, but also influenced many Enlightenment social philosophers that followed.

While Descartes, Bacon and Newton are seen as the founders of the Enlightenment, the most influential figure and with whom modern philosophy culminated is arguably Immanuel Kant (1724–1804). Born just a few years before the death of Newton, to whom he was most attuned, Kant attempted to synthesize early rationalism and empiricism (Deely 2010: 15). The rationalists following from Descartes contended that knowledge must start from certain innate ideas in the mind. The empiricists following Bacon and Locke contended that knowledge must start with sensory experience. In his famous *Critique of Pure Reason*, Kant argues that humans experience only appearances determined by the structures of the mind and not the *ding an sich* or the "things in themselves" as they exist in the phenomenal world. Things exist but also to us they are always constructs of the mind and inherently "unknowable".

> We have therefore wanted to say that all our intuition is nothing but the representation of appearance; that the things that we intuit are not in themselves what we intuit them to be, nor are their *relations* so constituted in themselves as they appear to us; and that if we remove our own subject or even only the subjective constitution of the senses in general, then all constitution,

all relations of objects in space and time, indeed space and time themselves would disappear, and as appearances they cannot exist in themselves, but only in us. What may be the case with objects in themselves and abstracted from all this receptivity of our sensibility remains entirely unknown to us. (Rohlf 2016, italics added)

Kant's fundamental idea is that of human autonomy, contending that human reason structures all of our experience and is the source of the general laws of nature and scientific knowledge. It is human reason that gives us morality and forms the basis for our belief in God, morality and freedom. In Kant's view, the natural world is separate and inherently unknowable; animals, plants and the abiotic expressions of nature are mere constructs of our rational minds that will remain forever alien to us.

The move from the linguistic animal and *animal rationale* definitions of human beings to that of the Enlightenment thinking thing has been characterized as "the quarrel between the ancients and the moderns" (Hollinger 1994: 21; Jones 1961). The accumulated knowledge of European indigenous peoples, along with the ancient Greeks, Latins, and the late medieval scholastics was centered on trial and error experience over long periods of time; however, their rigorous reflection was relegated to the dustbin by Enlightenment philosophers. In the ideal Enlightenment world of *the great dream of reason*, slowly-by-slowly all *cenoscopic* knowledge based on the interpretation of sense perception and common experience would be replaced by *ideoscopic* knowledge based on interpretation of empirical laboratory experimentation utilizing sense extending equipment and esoteric mathematical quantification (Deely 2010: 101; 2010a: 37).

Propelled by ideas of the Enlightenment and the scientific revolution, the industrial revolution emerged in England in the mid-eighteenth century to enhance further European colonialism and extend the global reach of modernity along with the concomitant Cartesian definition of human being. The development of the large-scale, separate and repetitious manufacturing production of goods and their redundant bureaucratic overseeing powered by massive fossil fuel extraction dramatically changed how modern humans sustained themselves and where they lived. Great masses of affected people had to move from rural areas and towns into crowded polluted cities and interact with landscapes increasingly devoid of plants and animals, even those domesticated species of the Neolithic era. Natural rhythms of day and night and the changing of seasons were replaced by the demands of the clock.

For modern humans to survive and thrive, the signs that required effective interpretation became man-made expressions of the factory and office. Refined sense perceptions that facilitated accurate semiotic interpretation which had evolved over millions of years for a life lived in the Paleolithic and utilized for millenniums in the Neolithic and ancient times were no longer essential for survival. Graceful bodily agility adapted for forest, plain, and mountain terrains, along with nuanced social skills formed through small kin-based intimacy were no longer essential attributes for survival. The din of the factory and the drone of the office made many of the remarkable evolutionary traits of our species, in the least, cumbersome annoyances, and in the most, demanding internal invectives caustically crying out for nuanced sensory attention and meaningful engagement with the natural world. Sewage systems, indoor plumbing, central heating and cooling of workplace and home and the inexorable march of other modern amenities allowed the indoor environment to prevail over outdoors.

The natural environment, where meaningful fulfilling experience had been located since the dawn of our species, became a remote backdrop to the human-built artificial environment for an ever-increasing number of the earth's peoples. Expressions of hundreds of millions of years of research and development by nature evaporated from the experience of modern humankind. Trees, flowers, insects, and birds along with their associated sounds, colors, textures, tastes, and smells moved from the foreground to the background of human semiotic engagement.

Anthropologist Gregory Bateson views this Enlightenment shift of modern Western culture and its globalization, what is being characterized here as a change in the definition of humankind from the Latin *animal rationale*, to be at the center of our environmental crisis and fostering an environmentally pathological monoculture around the planet (1972: 496–501). Applying a cybernetic approach that is also informed by a configurationalist orientation, Bateson maintains that culture is shaped by its dominating premises or fundamental assumptions (Benedict 1934: xvii), especially those concerning human interaction within nature. Centered around fundamental ontological and epistemological assumptions that define what it means to be a human being (Bateson 1972: 446–447, 456), culture arises and expresses itself through social communication. The different aspects of culture are further linked together through recursive "branching and interconnecting chains of causation" and reinforced through enculturation by self-validating and usually unconscious assumptions about "what sort of world it is" (Bateson 1972: 314).

For Bateson, the fundamental premises underlying culture are deeply embedded in the mind, that is, they are "hard programmed" and difficult to change (Bateson 1972: 336). Bateson states this in a way that relates directly to the ontological and epistemological thrust of this article, "all human beings (and all mammals) are guided by highly abstract principles of which they are either quite unconscious, or unaware that the principle governing their perception and action is *philosophic*" (Bateson 1972: 320, italics added).

The most important point here is that enculturation occurs in all cultures, including the globalizing modern West, through learned and shared self-reinforcing recursive communicative patterns of social interaction that express underlying assumptions, foremost of which is what it means to be a human being. Perceptions, symbols, meanings, values and the social behavior of the members of a culture arise out of the "integral relations of human beings in communication with each other and are a product of the field of communicative activity which their interactions construct. ... [Consequently] there are no social sanctions or arbitrary values external to the cultural communicative process from which they arose" (Harries-Jones 1995: 26). In other words, for Bateson culture is an interactive cybernetic system best understood and engaged by looking at typically unconscious "deeply embedded" assumptions about the world and the communicative patterns of social interaction that make them appear *true* and *natural* to the members of a culture experiencing them.

From this cybernetic conceptualization of culture gleaned through both theoretical reflection and extensive ethnographic fieldwork (Bateson 1958; 1971; 1972), Bateson formulated a cluster of six mutually reinforcing interrelated assumptions he saw as forming the ethos of modern Western Culture and lying at the root of the worldwide environmental crisis (1972: 496–501).

+ It's us against the environment.
+ It's the individual (or individual company or individual nation) that matters.
+ We can have unilateral *control* over the environment and must strive for that control.
+ We live in an infinitely expanding "frontier."
+ Economic determinism is common sense.
+ Technology will do it for us.

The underlying theme for Bateson in his modern Western cluster of ideas was *control* over nature based on the Enlightenment premises of the superiority of the rational human intellect over the separate, fallen, and unknowable natural world. These typically unconscious premises were seen as leading in an interactive cybernetic fashion to the modern overarching cultural attitude of hubris toward the natural world. Bateson maintained that the only way out of our contemporary environmental dilemma was to integrate humility into modern Western culture through an embrace of the traditional foraging cultural premise of the inherent *sacred unity* underlying the natural world and our embeddedness within it (Bateson 1991).

From this it can be concluded that for Bateson our sustainability is therefore dependent upon developing and propagating an ontological and epistemological orientation toward the natural world that stresses the pinnacle position of *relational being* or the development and maintenance of healthy accurate relationships with the natural environment that had effectively sustained us for thousands upon thousands of years.

Furthermore, Bateson saw the learning of humility as much more feasible to attain than the two other sustainability solutions typically most discussed, that of stepping back from technology, and population decrease. Finally, to accomplish this goal of making humility toward nature a premise of global culture he argued for aesthetics as the shortcut in this accomplishment. He contended that we needed to deeply engage with the communicative web of nature and then show to people of the world through both science and art (which he did not see as inherently separate) the exquisite beauty of the natural world. Bateson did not underestimate the challenge of this endeavor, feeling that it would be an even grander global enculturation project than what has occurred with modernity and its debasement of nature. However, he had a hopeful orientation toward the accomplishment of this grand task because he saw the evolutionary tendency of natural selection favoring the beautiful to be at play.

> There seems to be something like a Gresham's law of cultural evolution according to which the oversimplified ideas will always displace the sophisticated and the vulgar and the hateful will always displace the beautiful. And yet the beautiful persists. (Bateson1979: 5)

Bateson's cybernetic orientation toward evolution, culture and culture change provides the context for the next section of this article on the creation of the semiotic animal definition of human being by John Deely. Bateson's orientation further provides the context for what your author contends as arising from the creation of the semiotic animal definition of Deely, the launching of the Semiotic Age to bring sustainability to our species. Deely's definition is contrasted with and proposed as an antidote to the thinking thing definition of René Descartes; a definition that when globalized poisoned the well of human interaction with the environment on a worldwide scale through the creation of the Modern Age (Capra 1996; Horborg 2006).

5. Semiotic Animal, *Animal Semeioticum,* and The Semiotic Age

We interpret, therefore we live, Interpretamur ergo vivimus

The first use of the expression semiotic animal was in "passing" in 1990 by the prolific and visionary contemporary American philosopher John Deely in his *Basics of Semiotics.* He used it again on nine different occasions, including in a book titled *The Semiotic Animal* in 2004, written with two esteemed Italian coauthors, Susan Petrilli and Augusto Ponzio, before he authored the similarly named *Semiotic Animal* in 2010, which focused solely upon the concept. Two others had used the expression before Deely and one independently afterward used "the same expression without making a full theoretical development to establish the usage" (Deely 2010: xii). Due to the twenty-first century rapid embrace of semiotics in accordance with the growing awareness of the immense scope of semiosis as the action of signs, in writing *Semiotic Animal* Deely's aim was to

> thematize the notion and to establish conceptually its most proper usage … [and foster] the development of a semiotic consciousness … for the understanding of the human being as the only semiotic animal on earth … to show how semiotics provides the dawn of a new understanding of the human being as no mere 'thinking thing' but a verifiable part of the whole of nature, *a semiotic animal,* charged as such, for reasons that come more and more to the fore, even with the *care* of nature, the responsibility for the health of the planet as a whole ("semioethics") as it is turning out. (Deely 2010: xii)

This passage shows that Deely is well aware of the magnitude of his accomplishment in creating a new definition for human being to replace the modern definition in order to preserve life on earth as *we* know it and depend upon for our survival (Smith 2016). Your author maintains that this 2010 explication and clarification of the semiotic animal definition of human being by Deely is the first definition of human being to replace effectively that of Descartes's thinking thing after nearly 400 years of its continual expansion on the world stage. Nevertheless, Deely views the semiotic animal definition in relation to ushering in—rather than renaming the era itself—an "authentic" postmodern era in contrast to the postmodern era he dubs "falsely so called" (Deely 2010: 118). Deely contests the contemporary use of the term "postmodern" because, as mentioned earlier, he is in agreement with the popular understanding that postmodernity merely extends and expands upon modernity. Furthermore, popular postmodernism expands the idealist orientation of modernity especially in the crucial sustainability aspect of separation from the natural world, in which nature is often characterized as a "text" or a human cultural creation to be "read" and deconstructed (Derrida 1967). Cobley, articulates well Deely's work regarding modernity and postmodernity.

> Deely marshals a widespread and penetrating critique of modern thought, calling, in the process, for a renewal of philosophy through a greater understanding of its history which, ultimately, will lead to the birth of the truly *post*-modern world. In such a situation, what dawns is a new epic in which the shackles of the modern—nominalism, Cartesianism, *res cogitans*—are thrown off, giving way to a period in which knowledge of sign functioning rejuvenates thought. The history of philosophy is not left intact in such a way that academics can carry on doing what they were already doing and simply implement a new spin … [rather] it requires the development of a full-blooded semiotic consciousness or 'doctrine of signs'. (2009: 5–6)

There is full agreement by your author with Deely and Cobley that a new postmodern era is upon us, and with Deely's view of modernity as beginning when Descartes's thinking thing made a direct object of experience merely a construct of the mind (which will be discussed later in this section). Your author also agrees with Deely's view that the "authentic postmodern" era began in 1867 when Charles Sanders Peirce proposed his "New List of Categories" (Deely 2010: 19) (which is also discussed later in this section). However, following Deely's reference to the statement by Schmitz to him that "the term 'postmodern' is parasitic upon the meaning given to the term modernity" (Deely 2010:3), what is proposed here is that the development of the semiotic animal definition of human being by Deely is too consequential of a break from modernity to be only a modification of the era. The semiotic animal definition promises as great a break in the trajectory of our species' quest for survival as the thinking thing definition portended in the break from the European Middle Ages to the global Modern Age. Because of the magnitude of the creation of the semiotic animal, an entire new era must be proclaimed, the *Semiotic Age*.

While it may seem bold and too ambitious of a move to proclaim a new Semiotic Age, the outcome of the present nomenclature for the semiotic animal definition may at best involve a long drawn-out contest to become "the authentic postmodern expression" and at worse be designated as just another "postmodern*ism*" (Williams Deely 2016). Furthermore, Thomas Sebeok, Deely's mentor and friend, alluded to the need for a new term to designate the emerging era of semiotic consciousness as separate from modernity and postmodernity. Deely explains that "Sebeok once confided to me that he deemed the appellation, *postmodern* as 'so hopeless as better never to be used'" (Deely 2003: 30).

Moreover, after discussion of the Semiotic Age concept, which was first coined in the context of the end of modernity and postmodernity by your author in the collected papers of the 2015 Annual Meeting of the Semiotic Society of America (Smith 2016)—as mentioned earlier—Deely showed his approval of the notion at the Latimer Family Library at St. Vincent College in Latrobe, Pennsylvania. He volunteered his agreement with the assertion by stating to your author, "This is a great project that you have, defining the Semiotic Age" (Deely 2016).

Finally, the phrase, "We interpret, therefore we live", *Interpretamur ergo vivimus*, is presented by your author as an attempt to offer a summary expression for the semiotic animal and the Semiotic Age and also as a counter to "I think, therefore I am", or *cogito ergo sum* of Descartes. While brief support for the use of this phrase can only be made throughout this section, stated very concisely, the phrase is meant to emphasize that our species along with all other species engages in the semiotic process of *interpreting* our internal and external environment in order to live, while we are unique in our ability to reflect upon the semiotic process of interpretation and production of signs or semiosis that is life. This is in contrast to Descartes's definition, which views our species as made up of isolated individuals separate and distant from each other as well as from other species and our internal and external environment through our superior rational intellect.

The caveat mentioned in the introduction concerning support for the bold assertion of this article, that a way out of our pressing sustainability dilemma has become available and that a Semiotic Age is upon us, is only able to be touched upon due to the length restrictions of this venue, is most evident in this final section. That a more elaborate and thorough argument will occur in a future work must again be added to inform the reader of the opportunity that awaits your author and other interested scholars in their engagement with the assertion of this article. This opportunity for elucidation is present in regard to Deely's endeavor to thematize and to establish the proper usage of the semiotic animal notion that has been done directly only in what he describes as his "little book" (Deely 2010: xii). It is also present in the discussion concerning the establishment of a Semiotic Age, which is intended only as a brief introduction to this seemingly intrepid assertion—made so because of the magnitude of the cost of failure to address effectively the pressing sustainability challenge of our species that has arisen as a consequence of the Modern Age.

With these limitations in mind, this section gives a general chronological overview of key influences in the grand 2500-year history of semiotics that helped forge Deely's semiotic animal definition. For those who desire the "whole history of semiotic development in so far as such an exposition pertains to philosophy," Deely's 2001 definitive *Four Ages of Understanding* is the unquestioned best source.[5] The focus of this chronology is on the semiotic orientation within "the 'great conversation' which links philosophy across the graves of earlier generations" (Deely 2001: 585). This chronology is coined here by your author as the *great conversation within the great conversation* with two interrelated goals in mind. The first purpose of this particular semiotic chronology is to illumine how the work of previous semiotic scholars in-formed and eventually led to the semiotic animal definition of human being created by Deely, and to to what your author views as the establishment of a Semiotic Age. The second purpose of the following semiotic chronology is to clarify what Deely means by his semiotic animal definition of human being, especially in contrast to the thinking thing of Descartes and the establish-ment of modernity.

Even though this chronology will focus on individuals who influenced the work of Deely in his creation of the semiotic animal, it must be pointed out that these individuals, like Deely, stood on shoulders or stood shoulder to shoulder with others to develop their semiotic insights. Anthropology emphasizes that the individual is an expression of the culture or subculture in which a person lives; no human is "self-made" because it is the existence and transmission of culture that is an essential criterion for our species. As eminent anthropologist Herbert Spencer explains, "the genesis of a great man depends on the long series of complex influences. ... Before he can remake his society, his society must make him" (1896). While there is of course agency inherent in culture to allow for genius and invention to foster cultural change, the anthropological perspective is also summed up well by the saying attrib-uted to the Eastern mystic, Jiddu Krishnamurti, who rejected his ascribed status bestowed on him during adolescence as the chosen "World Teacher": "You think you're thinking your thoughts, you're not; you are thinking the culture's thoughts" (Krishnamurti 1970).

The "great man" theory of history (Carlyle 1841) notion is put at play immediately in the presentation of the work by the Greek physician, Hippocrates (460–377 B.C.), as the first individual who had a key influence on the development of the semiotic animal by Deely and the establishment of the Semiotic Age. Hippocrates was both the founder of semiotics and of Western medicine; he established semiotics as the scientific, rigorous and

---

5 In the timeline from the Greek, Latin, Modern, and Postmodern ages of understanding in Western Civilization of this epic work (Deely 2001: xxxi), the Semiotic Age is contended in this article as replacing the Postmodern Age.

systematic study of symptoms or signs of disease and health that focused on the complaints of the sick person. Hippocrates did this as a member of a school of medicine that formed in contrast to the dominant school of medicine at the time, and which emphasized the nature or causes of disease and health (Sebeok 2001: 73). Within his newly formed medical semiotics subculture, Hippocrates discerned a symptom to be a semion, or "a mark sign" that stands for, or indicates something about health to the semiotically trained physician (Sebeok 2001: 32). As Hippocrates states in *The Science of Medicine*, "the physician being unable to see the nature of the disease nor to be told of it, must have recourse to reasoning from the symptoms with which he is presented" (Chadwick and Mann 1950).

After acceptance of the medical semiotic approach of Hippocrates, a Greek physician's primary diagnostic task became to interpret accurately symptoms and signs of disease and health. Greek clinical practitioners defined *symptoms* (or subjective signs) as what the patient expressed to the physician verbally and non-verbally. Patient statements such as, *I have a pain in my chest* or gestures in which patients point to the chest area to indicate where their pain is being experienced, were defined as symptoms, or "objective" signs. What the clinician observed with his own senses was labeled "actual" signs. For example, if a patient complained of a sore throat to the physician, that symptom may mean a cold; if the patient complained of an area of itching skin, that symptom may mean an allergy; if the clinician perceived a dark bruise on a bent finger, that could be an actual sign of a broken bone (Sebeok 2001: 32).

In the Hippocratic approach to medicine, practitioners viewed symptoms as 'significant phenomena' (Heidel 1941: 62; Sebeok 2001: 73). Symptoms were "natural signs—those having the power to signify the same things in all times and places" (Sebeok 2001: 73). Hippocrates explains in his *Prognostic xxv*:

> One must clearly realize about sure signs, and about symptoms generally that in every year and in every land bad signs indicate something bad, and good signs something favorable, since the symptoms described above prove to have the same significance in Libya, and Delos and on Scythia. So one must clearly realize that in the same district it is not strange that one should be right in the vast majority of instances, if one learns them well and knows how to estimate and appreciate them properly. (Chadwick and Mann 1950)

It is crucial to specify the essential role of the external environment on human health and disease in the medical semiotics of Hippocrates; this is especially so in regard to the overarching sustainability and environment inclusion theme of this article. In *On Airs, Waters, and Places* (c.a. 400 B.C.), Hippocrates proposed the need for the integration of environmental signs such as the "weather, seasons, and prevailing winds; the quality of air, water, and food; and one's geographic location as influences on human health and disease" (Chadwick and Mann 1950). He asserted that environmental influences could disturb the balance required by the body and when taken to the level of populations, led to the onset of infectious diseases. Many of the notions proposed by Hippocrates regarding the role of the environment on human health, such as the association of waterborne infections with standing pools of water, remain credible today (Friis 2012).

With the medical semiotics of Hippocrates, the study of the symptoms and signs of disease and health, including environmental influences, were placed evermore "in the context of the great tradition" of Western medicine (Miller 1978: 184; Sebeok 2001: 66). The Roman physician of Greek ethnicity, Galen of Pergamon (139–199 A.D.), "whose one and only idol was Hippocrates" (Sebeok 2001: 32), several centuries later further ingrained semiotics, "ē sēmeiōtikē teknē or sēmeiōtikon"(the art of the signs), into medical practice. Galen accomplished this through his elevation of semiotics to one of the six branches of medicine in his classic work on medical diagnosis, published as *The Effigies of Galen* (Parey 1649), which rigorously codified the medical semiotic approach focusing on symptoms and signs to diagnose disease and health (Sebeok 2001: 4).

This cognitive model of semiotics in which something is understood as standing for something else to someone, in this case observation of the body in interaction with the environment that was uncovered by Hippocrates and first rigorously codified by Galen, continues to reside at the center of semiotic thought and Western medicine throughout these millenniums. This semiotic model of representation, centered upon the relationship between a knowing subject and a knowable universe, includes the present in what is the focus of this article, the formation of the semiotic animal concept by Deely and the establishment of the Semiotic Age.

The importance of this discovery of medical semiotics by Hippocrates and its codification by Galen *cannot be overemphasized* in regard to what it now means to our species and the resolution of our sustainability dilemma. Through medical semiotics the actuality of disease could be uncovered by rigorous investigation of the relationship between the physical expression of the body of the patient or symptom and what it represented in the context of the environment. In other words, by way of Hippocratic diagnosis, an attempt is made to *interpret* accurately the meaning of the expression of the body in regard to health and disease through the formation of a relationship between the abstract knowledge of the physician and the concrete bodily manifestation of the symptom. What Hippocrates uncovered as a consequence of his medical semiotics approach and what was systematically recorded later by Galen, was the *reality of relational being*. This was the same ontological and epistemological orientation discussed in detail earlier as the essence of animism or what lay at the center of the successful sustainability of our species throughout the 190,000-year Paleolithic era and in some areas into the 10,000-year Neolithic.

In the medical semiotics of Hippocrates, effective diagnosis is centered upon accurately interpreting the relationship between what will be called later by the Latins, *mind-independent and mind-dependent being* (Poinsot 1632), and by Deely in his concept of the semiotic animal as "suprasubjectivity" (2010: 58). This discovery by Hippocrates of a methodology to uncover relational being in regard to human health and disease can be realistically speculated to have occurred because of the importance of this domain of knowledge for humans. The importance of this domain existed for both the Ancient highly rigorous Greek physicians and for the highly imaginative Paleolithic shamans (Halifax 1979). For would not the most important intersection of mind-independent and mind-dependent being be found in the greatest achievement of the universe, the grandly complex and profoundly intricate human body engaged stochastically in a dynamic semiotic dance of homeostatic interaction between its internal and external environment? And is not the human body, including the brain which is in the body (Lanigan 2015), the ultimate expression of the process of what we have "heretofore called evolution" (Deely 2002: 125)?

Since the sustainability for our species is centered upon maintaining the health of our bodies, is it not in the domain of health and disease where the accurate interpretation of relational being is most required and most highly rewarded? This recognition of the importance of the medical semiotic interpretive process uncovered by Hippocrates continues in the practice of medicine today.

> Semiotics warns us that if we are to minimize errors in *interpretation*, we must remember that medical signs are but symbolic, often ambiguous proxies of truth whose meaning furthermore is shaped by its context and whose interpretation lies at the mercy of inference and the experience, and bias of the individual physician. (Burnham 1993: 939–943, italics added)

Finally, medical semiotics can play a major role in replacement of the thinking thing with the semiotic animal and establishment of a Semiotic Age to replace modernity. The reason is that the globalization of modern Western medicine in both clinical and public health is one of the driving factors of the "undeveloped" cultures of the world embracing modernity as superior to their way of life. Having a Western clinical medicine and public health infrastructure is a primary definition of a developed country (Connell 2010). Moreover, if the semiotic foundation that undergirds Western medicine could be appreciated, which is nearly unknown to modern Western health practitioners because of the Cartesian axiom to ignore "common" cenoscopic knowledge and reify "specialized" ideoscopic knowledge (Deely 2010: 20), an embrace of the sustainable semiotic definition would be greatly enhanced.

It was another Greek, none other than Aristotle (384–322 B.C.), who played a major role in the eventual creation of the Semiotic Animal and Age. While still embracing medical semiotics he was the first to study signs in non-medical terms. He saw signs as made up of three dimensions: (1) the physical *sign* itself, for instance the actual sound for the word cat; (2) the *referent* to which the sign calls attention, the category feline animal with fur and retractable claws; and (3) the evocation or calling forth of the meaning, what the referent conveys socially and personally. For Aristotle these three dimensions of the sign are not experienced individually but instead occur simultaneously. It is not possible to think of the sound "cat" without at the same time thinking of the type of animal to which it *refers*, a feline mammal—and without the experience of the social and personal meaning that the *referent* conveys.

With Aristotle, the study of signs moved away from a discipline solely involved in health and disease to become the study and categorization of natural signs (Sebeok 2001: 4) "deemed knowable antecedently to mind's activity" (Deely 2010: 42). In the philosophy of Aristotle the primary concern is with reality independent of the experience of the mind and how it can be effectively described (Deely 2010a: 75). This is shown vividly in Aristotle's famous treatise, *On Interpretation*, where he goes beyond logical syllogisms to explore the semiotic character of spoken and written language and how it is used to clarify the "real" world of things.

> First we must define the terms 'noun' and 'verb', then the terms 'denial' and 'affirmation', then 'proposition' and 'sentence.' Spoken words are the symbols of mental experience and written words are the symbols of spoken words. Just as all men have not the same writing, so all men have not the same speech sounds, but the mental experiences, which these directly symbolize, are the same for all, as also are those things of which our experiences are the images. (Aristotle 330 B.C.)

The next person in the chronology is Saint Augustine (354–430 A.D.), who was the first to develop a general notion of the sign. Before him, in an ancient world dominated by Greek philosophy the notion translated today as sign, σημεῖον or semeion, "should actually be translated rather as 'natural sign"', for this term sign in antiquity referred only to natural phenomena" (Deely 2002: xi). It was Augustine who originally distinguished between *natural* signs, such as symptoms and animal signals, in contrast to human made *conventional* signs (Sebeok 2001: 4). Moreover, in his theory of the sign, Augustine attributed a basic epistemic function to the sign as illustrated in his stating that "all instruction is either about things or about signs; but things are learnt by means of signs" (Jackson 1969). Thus, the line between things and signs and therefore the sign itself was defined epistemologically by Augustine rather than ontologically. That is, signs for him were used functionally to signify something. The general notion of the sign that Augustine developed was not designed for its own sake but instead "was proposed for a definite use", that of Christian Apologetics or in defense of the faith (Deely 2009: 15).

Augustine's general theory on the sign is recognized by Deely as the crucial juncture between ancient and medieval notions of the sign, which initiated the "dawn of the prospect of a semiotic consciousness. ... [One that] began with a *descriptive* definition based on observation" (Deely 2009: 7–58; Deely 2010: 20). Furthermore, the acceptance of Augustine's definition of the sign and its use in the introduction to Christian or Catholic sacramental theology at that time and up through the present day directly ties in with the Catholic theological orientation of Deely (2009: 17).

The Catholic focus of Augustine is of crucial importance to the development of the semiotic animal and also to the establishment of the Semiotic Age which emerged from this definition, given that the thinking thing definition that launched the Enlightenment and the non-sustainable Modern Age came as a replacement for the Catholic paradigm and Latin Age that was dominant in Europe at the time. Therefore, engagement with that replacement process by necessity includes familiarity with what was discarded intentionally and unintentionally in Catholic thought in order to see what was lost. This Catholic connection with the semiotic animal and age will be seen even more so in the next section on John Poinsot, or John of St. Thomas as he is known, the foremost "student" of Saint Thomas Aquinas.

The affinity between the medieval Catholic paradigm with the semiotic animal definition of Deely in relation to the establishment of the Semiotic Age is further demonstrated in the writings of the last two pontiffs concerning what it means to be human. Deely describes how papal writing supports his semiotic animal definition, which portrays

> a new picture of human 'being in the world', a picture amply illustrating Ratzinger's [later Benedict XVI] claim (1970: 132) that 'the undivided sway of thinking in terms of substance is ended; *relation is discovered as an equally valid primordial mode of reality*'. (Deely 2010: xv, italics added)

For Deely this ontological assertion of Benedict XVI "addressed the main subject presupposed to semiosis, namely, relation as a primordial reality of nature co-terminus with individuality." Deely sees further confirmation in the notions of Benedict XVI that human ethical responsibility toward protecting nature is "a global one" and that nature is only "at our disposal" based on our mastery of "a 'grammar'" that places humans *within the environment*. Finally, Benedict XVI asserts that only through accurately interpreting this "grammar" can human beings "separate wise use from reckless exploitation" (Deely 2010: xv).

The question arises: Why have these erudite insights concerning what it means to be a human being embedded in the environment that are so brilliantly articulated by Benedict XVI gone largely unappreciated? Perhaps the reason is that his appreciation of relationality, which to your author acknowledges and elevates the central characteristic of Paleolithic animism, was tempered by warnings from him that harken back to centuries-old conflicts between the Christian church and the natural world. In the words of Benedict XVI:

> Nature expresses a design of love and truth. It is prior to us, and it has been given to us by God as the setting for our life … as a gift of the Creator who has given it an inbuilt order, enabling man to draw from it the principles needed in order "to till it and keep it" (Gen 2:15). (Benedict XVI 2009)

However, Benedict stresses "that it is contrary to authentic development to view nature as something more important than the human person. This position leads to attitudes of neo-paganism or a new pantheism" (Benedict XVI 2009). Positions such as this by Benedict XVI have been pointed to as support for the link between Christianity and environmental decay (Vincentnathan 2016). The most cited work on this contention by far is that of the medieval historian Lynn White Jr. who published his much quoted "The Historical Roots of our Ecological Crisis" in 1967. According to White:

> Christianity is the most anthropocentric religion the world has seen. … [It] not only established a dualism of man and nature but also insisted that it is God's will that man exploit nature for his proper ends … the old [animistic] inhibitions to the exploitation of nature crumbled. What people do about their ecology depends on what they think about themselves *in relation* to things around them. Human ecology is deeply conditioned by beliefs about our nature and destiny—that is, by religion. … More science and more technology are not going to get us out of the present ecologic crisis until we find a new religion, or rethink our old one. [Italics added]

Amazingly, the solution White proposed for our environmental crisis in this seminal article was for Christianity to embrace the teaching of Saint Francis, "The greatest spiritual revolutionary in Western history … who tried to substitute the idea of the equality of all creatures, including man, for the idea of man's limitless rule of creation." How could White have imagined that after 800 years a Pope would finally take the name of Francis and strive to follow and promote globally to Christian and non-Christians the environmental teachings of Saint Francis aimed at enhancing the sacred relationship between humans and the natural world (Francis 2015)? Acting from his celebrated position as one of most admired persons in the world today by both Christians and non-Christians, the current pope, Francis, is encouraging replacement of the modern Cartesian ontology with its utilitarian environmentally nonsustainable definition of human. Because his bold statements on the need to protect the environment have been tied to defining what it means to be a human being, Francis has even been termed an "Environmental Anthropologist" by an esteemed Notre Dame law professor (Nagle 2016). In his paper he quotes from the Pope's environmental encyclical *Laudato Si*, "Praise be to you".

> Modernity has been marked by an excessive anthropocentrism which today, under another guise, continues to stand in the way of shared understanding and of any effort to strengthen social bonds. The time has come to pay renewed attention to *reality* and the limits it imposes; this in turn is the condition for a more sound and fruitful development of individuals and society. An inadequate presentation of Christian anthropology gave rise to a wrong understanding of the relationship between human beings and the world. Often, what was handed on was a Promethean vision of mastery over the world, which gave the impression that the protection of nature was something that only the faint-hearted cared about. (Italics added)

The Pope asserts the value of a Franciscan-centered environmental perspective that affirms the intrinsic sacred quality of the natural world as God's creation in need of appreciation and protection (Francis 2015), which is in consonance with the semiotic animal and Semiotic Age developments (Smith 2016). Furthermore, Francis has embraced a much more inclusive attitude towards different religious and spiritual environmental orientations than his predecessors including Pope Benedict XVI.

> When people become self-centered and self-enclosed, their greed increases. The emptier a person's heart is, the more he or she needs things to buy, own and consume. It becomes almost impossible to accept the limits imposed by reality. [Saint] Francis asked that part of the friary garden always be left untouched, so that wild flowers and herbs could grow there, and those who saw them could raise their minds to God, the Creator of such beauty. Rather than a problem to be solved, the world is a joyful mystery to be contemplated with gladness and praise ... all is not lost. Human beings, while capable of

the worst, are also capable of rising above themselves, choosing again what is good, and making a new start. (Francis 2015)

Perhaps this embrace of a Franciscan-centered approach to the natural world by the former Jesuit priest from Argentina came about in part because of his being the leader of the largest cenoscopic organization to have ever existed, the Catholic church, along with being an ideoscopically trained scientist. It could be that the combination of these two traditions (Deely 2010a: 55) helped him to appreciate the spiritual and scientific magnitude of the harm caused by climate change and the predictions of future cataclysmic devastation that affirmed the need to incorporate all environmental groups willing to work on this issue. Maybe it was his understanding of the impact of environmental decay inordinately affecting the poor and disenfranchised of the world whom Christ placed first among all (Luke 6:20–26). The key point is that the awareness of Pope Francis of the need to reject modern utilitarian environmental materialism bodes well for the acceptance of the semiotic animal definition; this occurs through the embracement of a loving, humble and sacred relationship with a *knowable* natural world centered on defining humans as embedded within nature and in need of caring for it for their survival (Francis 2015). This acceptance in turn can facilitate the propagation of the Semiotic Age and our species sustainability (Smith 2016).

Continuing with our chronology, the late-medieval philosopher who notably embraced the mantle of Augustine in the development of the sign is the Catholic Dominican mentioned earlier, John Poinsot (1589–1644). He is also the person possibly of greatest significance in regard to Deely's creation of the semiotic animal definition for human being that lived before Deely. Also known as John of St. Thomas, Poinsot built upon the fourteenth century semiotic epistemological and ontological work of Duns Scotus and that of the late-sixteenth-century Conimbricenses (Deely 2002: 8) to create an extensive philosophical system, the *Cursus Philosophicus Thomisticus*; included within it and of greatest importance to Deely was the 1632 seminal treatise on signs, the *Tractatus de Signis*.

Poinsot's treatise was basically ignored by modern philosophy until the 1920s when the Catholic philosopher Jacques Maritain "discovered" it. Maritain regarded Poinsot as perhaps the foremost student of Saint Thomas Aquinas, the greatest *realist* philosopher, or one who believes that the world can be known as it is (Deely 1988: 46–47). The treatise was discarded for these many years for two primary reasons. Firstly, philosophy chose the approach toward the difficult question of the character of reality and knowing (ontology and epistemology) of Descartes, which posited an immediate grasp of essences over the *semiotic problematic* of Poinsot that entailed the mediation of signs (Murphy 1991). Secondly, Poinsot's treatise was "lost" to philosophy because having chosen Descartes's approach, modern philosophy also followed his admonition toward Latin thinkers such as Poinsot, warning *"there is a considerable danger that if we study these works too closely traces of their errors will infect us and cling to us against our will despite our precautions"* (Descartes 1628: 13; Deely 2010: 10).

The influence of Poinsot on Deely was so great that he spent fifteen years translating and editing Poinsot's signature *Tractatus de Signis*, which when published in 1985, finally made the work available to contemporary philosophy. The renowned Semiotician Thomas Sebeok and mentor of Deely characterized Deely's work on Poinsot's *Tractatus de Signis* as

> the 'missing link' between the ancients and the moderns in the history of semiotic, a pivot as well as a divide between two huge intellective landscapes the ecology of neither of which could be fully appreciated prior to this major publishing event. (Deely 1982: x)

In Poinsot, Deely found the eloquent semiotic exposition that became the cornerstone of his semiotic animal definition, the ontological reality of relational being. Deely describes Poinsot as the

> first author who succeeded in giving voice to the underlying unity of *being in relation* upon which all actions of signs as such depends ... that the sign requires a standpoint superior to the division of being into what is and what is not independent of cognition, which translates, in modern parlance, into a standpoint superior to the confrontation of realism with idealism (Deely 2001: 694). [Furthermore] it was Poinsot who first explicated the point that *relation's singularity* [encompassing both mind-dependent and mind-independent being] *is the ground of the prior possibilities of semiosis*, and the essence of semiosis whenever an action of signs succeeds to occur. (Deely 2010a: 51)

For Deely, the grand achievement of Poinsot that "provided us with nothing less than a new starting point for the philosophical enterprise as a whole—a veritable 'new beginning' ... [was] establishing the sign as the key to a philosophy of experience" (Deely 2001:461), as demonstrated in the following passage by Poinsot.

> If the object of external sensation exists in something produced by sense itself as in an image or effect, then that object will not be something sensed immediately but rather something sensed in the image, which image itself rather will be that which is sensed. (Deely 2010a: 76; Poinsot 1632: 312)

In this passage Poinsot shows how humans as subjects are able through signs to experience a sense relationship with an image; they do not have the original sense experience portrayed in the image but instead with the image itself. For example, in the Blombos Cave at the tip of South Africa, where the oldest known art has been found and where the great *creative explosion* in human thought and behavior centered on symbols may have begun, an iconic image of an eland antelope or *Taurotragus oryx* is painted in color on the rock wall (Renfrew 2009). When the animal was viewed by an animistic Paleolithic hunter, the smell of the male eland, the unique sound of his hoofs spreading and clicking as he walks on the dry savanna landscape around him, and even the activation of saliva needed to digest a cooked eland could be experienced by the hunter. This is just as it is for a San Bushman hunter viewing the painting today.

Furthermore, the accuracy of the ontologically perceived and consequent epistemologically framed experience of relational being by the hunter is placed within a stochastically calibrated research and development process that equates success with nourishment and survival, and failure with hunger and starvation. There is a reality in the interaction or relation between the hunter as subject and the eland image as object that only living creatures can experience; it is an expression of *relational being*.

However, the path leading to a new beginning of the way of signs that Poinsot had marked out for Western philosophy, which harmonized with animism, was not taken. Instead, as we know, philosophy chose to follow the trail laid out by his contemporary, René Descartes, and his "way of ideas" in which the human is a "monad without windows" as Leibniz so bluntly pronounced (Deely 2002: xii, 7). Kant described the Enlightenment difference well when he stated, "Since every self-sufficient being contains within itself a complete source of all its determination, it is not necessary for its existence that it stand in relation to other things" (Kant 1747). Deely describes Kant's view in regard to relation as believing that

> the human mind works ... by forming mental representations behind and beyond which lay the reality of things (including that of other human selves). ... The development began, no doubt, with Ockham's doctrine that relation has no being of its own other than mind-dependent being. (Deely 2010a: 51–52)

Starting in the early 1600s, Descartes's definition acted as a deep ontological cultural assumption informing epistemology and spreading in cybernetic recursive feedback loops throughout European society and in turn the globalizing modern world. With England during the height of its global colonial expansion, the phrase "the sun never set on the British Empire" was used to point to the greatness of modernity and in turn the Western European definition of humanity. However, for the sustainability of our species it is imperative to make clear that the sun also never set on the worldwide enculturation process of modernity, a process fueled by Descartes's definition of human being that sees us as separate from nature. It is a global enculturation process that has inexorably continued to the present, gaining more and more momentum in terms of scale, scope, and velocity with ever-increasing marvelous technological innovation and concomitant massive environmental decay.

The next philosopher to be of major influence on Deely is frequently referred to as one of America's greatest, Charles Sanders Peirce (1839–1914), even though he was not recognized as such during his lifetime (Pencak 1995). Deely saw Peirce as the first of the modern philosophers to ignore Descartes's warning to avoid the Latins. For Deely, Peirce was responsible for clearing away "the underbrush to reveal from his Latin predecessors in semiotics a 'way of signs' ... [especially] in the synthesizing work of John Poinsot" (Deely 2010: 39, 40). Just as Deely viewed modernity as beginning when Descartes's thinking thing made a direct object of experience merely a construct of the mind, so Deely viewed a new postmodern era as beginning in 1867 when Charles Sanders Peirce proposed his "New List of Categories" (Deely 2010: 19).

> No longer, as in Aristotle, was the aim to classify all and only the possible modes of mind-independent being; and no longer, as in Kant, was the aim to demonstrate that only modes of mind-dependent being can be directly experienced and to determine what those modes are (the "a-prioris") [for Peirce]—the aim was to classify the manner in which mind-dependent being and mind-independent being interpenetrate and reveal themselves objectively through the weave and pattern of human experience as consisting of and constituted by the relations in which signs consist and through which the activity of signs, or semiosis, extends in principle to *the whole of being* as knowable. (Deely 2010: 6–7)

In Deely's perspective, with Peirce and his "new categories" addition to the doctrine of signs, the modern debate between realism and idealism was answered with a resounding "yes". Peirce agreed that "scholastic realism" was the essence of semiotics, however, adding also the important stipulation, *but not sufficient for semiotics* (Deely 2010: 7, 8).

This advance in the doctrine of signs by Peirce left no doubt "*that the inner human world, with great effort and serious study, may reach an understanding of non-human worlds and of its connection with them*" (Petrilli and Ponzio 2001: 20). Pierce also accounted for the large portion of reality that is *socially constructed* in general by the habits in animal life and in particular by the habits of human animal life, we know as "culture". Deely further contended that through the work of Peirce, semiotics had now gone *beyond* the primary debate that lay at the foundation of modernity and into the realm of postmodernity (Deely 2010: 8).

Moreover, Deely identified in the work of Peirce what he considered to be "his most dramatic move in semiotics" (Deely 2010a: 40). Building upon and then extending the work of Poinsot, which demonstrated even more clearly that signs depend upon triadic relations, Peirce devised his notion of the *interpretant*.

> I define a sign as anything which is so determined by something else, called its Object, and so determines an effect upon a person, which effect I call its interpretant, that the latter is thereby mediately determined by the former. (Peirce 1992: 478)

For Deely the distinction Peirce made between the interpreter and interpretant, "the meaning that one gets from the sign" through a "form of negotiation" by the sign-user that is made between the signifier or the physical sign itself and the referent or general object that the physical sign refers to (Sebeok 2001: 6) was seminal. Deely explains that Peirce's genius came in

> separating the third term in the sign relation from the order of finite mind, with his distinction between *interpretant* and *interpreter*, and the declaration that an interpretant *need not be mental*. This was the move that sets Peirce apart in the history of philosophy and semiotics as cenoscopic science; and this was the move that led to his famous proposal that 'the universe is per-fused with signs, if it does not consist exclusively of them'. (Deely 2010a: 40)

Deely explains that the interpretant notion is "crucial to understanding the action of signs as that follows upon the being proper to them" (Deely 2001: 375). He saw the inability to appreciate this third aspect in the triadic relations of the sign by philosophers, including those of the Latin Age, as blinding them from the fact that the problems concerning ontology, that is, determining what is real, are not simply problems about words, concepts, or things, but about signs "as mediating the difference between objective and physical reality at all times and in all dimensions" (Deely 2001: 375).

The key point here that relates directly to the semiotic animal concept of Deely and the Semiotic Age notion of your author is that through the in-terpretant component created by Pierce, the sign-based interaction between creatures and the physical universe in which they derive meaning is further refined and clarified. *Species success or sustainability becomes directly correlated with the accuracy of the meaning discerned through the interpretation of the signs in their environment.* In other words, the interpretant component of Peirce was a key steppingstone to the development of the semiotic animal definition of human being by Deely and the establishment of the Semiotic Age proposed by your author.

As the sole animal not only to engage in semiosis but also to possess knowledge of sign processes, including the relatively recently formed concept of the interpretant, we can now see the essential need to dramatically shift our attention away from the rampant exploitation of the environment. *Survival for the semiotic animal thus becomes directly linked to the protection and accurate interpretation of the environment from which signs crucial to our sustainability reside and arise.*

Because Peirce lived several centuries after Descartes at a time when the thinking thing definition and its expression in modernity was rapidly extending its dominance in all areas of American society, he was able to provide a direct appraisal of the results. His prescience for the coming sustainability dilemma we now face, as noted in his article "Evolutionary Love", was nothing short of brilliant.

> The twentieth century, in its latter half, shall surely see the deluge-tempest burst upon the social order—to clear upon a world as deep in ruin as that greed-philosophy [modern materialism] has long plunged it into guilt. (Peirce 1893)

Peirce viewed the modernizing society around him as centered upon a belief in the supreme value of greed. He rejected the modern Darwinian depiction of living creatures including humans as isolated, inherently self-serving individuals detached from their environment in ruthless competition with others for survival. This portrayal of evolution was characterized by Peirce as merely an expedient articulation of the dominant modern views on political economy. For Pierce it is love in the form of sentiment, or *agape*, not greed that propels evolution (Smith 2016).

> The movement of love is circular, at one and the same impulse projecting creations into independency and drawing them into harmony. … 'Our neighbor,' we remember, is one whom we live near, not locally perhaps but in life and feeling. (Peirce 1893)

The "Golden Rule" was not an abstraction for Peirce; evolutionary love centered on "the natural judgments of the sensible heart" related to actual beings, to "dear ones." Moreover, the notion of the circularity of love that Peirce articulates conforms with stochastic feedback processes of cybernetics and Bateson's formula mentioned earlier, of organism = biology + environment. This conceptualization makes the survival of the organism contingent upon being the one that *fits the best* into its environment.

The rejection by Peirce of evolutionary greed and environmental exploitation, and its replacement with love and environmental sentiment, is directly in consonance with the replacement of the thinking thing of Descartes with the semiotic animal of Deely; it is a straightforward step to envision how the replacement of the thinking thing and the globalization of a semiotic animal definition of humanity could act just as strongly on the sustainability of our species, but in the opposite direction to create a Semiotic Age centered upon love for all life including our fellow humans (Smith 2016).

Finally, the insights concerning *The Semiotic Animal* by the co-authors of Deely, Petrilli and Ponzio mentioned earlier in a 2005 work by that title focus on this economic aspect of modernity addressed by Peirce. Petrilli characterizes the development of the modern greed philosophy of Peirce in the present as "late capitalist society", manifesting especially in regard to communication. She sees capitalism as disrupting natural planetary communication or what is termed here by your author as *the communicative matrix of life* (Smith 2016: 111). For her, global capitalism "interferes not only with human life, but with life in general," on a worldwide scale (Petrilli 2005: 70). To stop the global destruction of the natural world, Petrilli believes that semiotics should not attempt to develop a specific economic ideological plan as a counter to modern capitalism. Instead, semiotics must concern

> our understanding of behavior in relation to the human being's unique responsibility as a 'semiotic animal' … a responsible agent capable of *signs of signs*, of mediation, reflection, and awareness with respect to semiosis over the whole planet. (Petrilli 2005: 74)

Both Petrilli and Ponzio define this orientation of responsibility for the *semiosphere* (Lotman 2005), or communicative matrix of life (Smith 2016: 111), as "semioethics" (Petrilli and Ponzio 2005: 87–88). To support this contention Petrilli (as explained by Sebeok) points out that when Peirce focuses on clarifying the action of signs he stresses his notion of the interpretant and how in the process of semiosis the interpretant is *produced*. Petrilli reiterates that "semiosis may be described in terms of *interpretation* … that it involves understanding or the teleonomic (that is, goal-directed) interpretation of signs" (Petrilli 2005a: 37). Therefore, she proposes that the modern global capitalist—or perhaps better stated, the modern global materialist—production of signs should be countered with a semiotic perspective that is just as extensive, inclusive and global. She believes that semiotics as it is practiced today is not ready for the task but that to undertake it the incorporation of a "truly" global perspective will be required (Petrilli 2005: 70). The expansion of the scope and scale of semiotics deemed necessary by Petrilli is being attempted in this article by your author through the assertion of the replacement of the thinking thing of Descartes with the semiotic animal of Deely and the Modern Age with the Semiotic Age. Furthermore, because for Peirce interpretants or the meanings of signs are produced or *socially constructed* by the habits of human life or culture, it becomes clearer how a radical alteration in the definition of human being in a society can facilitate large-scale cultural change.

This reflection on the notion of the interpretant by Peirce leads directly to Thomas Sebeok (1920–2001), the final individual who will be discussed in the chronology of semioticians informing the development of the semiotic animal definition of Deely and in turn the notion of the Semiotic Age by your author. It was Sebeok who played a key role by expanding the interpretant to the biological world and in so doing, moved the study of signs out of the approximate first three-quarters of the twentieth century detour it had taken into the linguistic camp of Saussure (Deely 2004: 3; 2004a: 4). Sebeok did this while integrating the pivotal concept of the umwelt or species-specific environment into semiotics, a concept that became central to Deely's work (Cobley 2009: 7).

Of all those living who influenced the work of Deely in regard to the semiotic animal, the honor of the one who had the greatest impact unquestionably falls to Sebeok, who eventually also became his mentor and close friend. No longer was Deely learning from the writings of the nonliving; instead his interaction was with a living "sign master" that included all the profundity and nuance an encounter with another living human in intellectual consonance with oneself entails (Kevelson 1983). Because of this level of importance Sebeok's personal history is presented in the context of some of the most crucial conceptual steppingstones leading to the semiotic animal definition of Deely. The description is in some detail just as personal steppingstones made during the lifetime of Deely will need to be discussed in a similar fashion in a future work.[6]

After elementary schooling in Hungary, in 1936 Sebeok came to England and enrolled in Magdalene College of the University of Cambridge. It was here where Sebeok formed the foundation of his academic career and where his eventual crucial influence on the field of semiotics and Deely found its beginnings. This occurred through his exposure to the celebrated communication theorists and semioticians I. A. Richards and C. K. Ogden, most noted for their seminal work on *meaning* (Ogden and Richards 1923). It was

---

[6] Deely has described Sebeok as a "Biologist Manqué" (Deely 2004) or someone who *missed* their opportunity as a biologist even though they had the ability to become one. Your author views Deely as an "Anthropologist Manqué".

also at Magdalene College that Sebeok first encountered the 1920 publication *Theoretische Biologie* or *Theoretical Biology*, and the work of the German biologist, Jakob von Uexküll that would later come to occupy the center of his contribution to semiotics, the semiotic animal definition of Deely, and to the vision of the Semiotic Age.

In 1939, Sebeok left England to enroll in the University of Chicago to major in linguistics. His primary influence there was the notable philosopher and semiotician Charles Morris, who steered him to anthropology, in which he completed his undergraduate degree in 1941. In his study of anthropology at the University of Chicago, Sebeok developed "a biological way of thinking" (Deely 2004: 2) that would remain predominate throughout his career and would come to steer semiotics back to its origin with Hippocrates as a life science. For graduate studies, Sebeok transferred to Princeton in 1942 where he earned a Master of Arts (MA) degree in anthropological linguistics in 1943; it was during this time that he received direction from the prominent philologist, or one who studies language in written historical sources, Roman Jakobson. In 1943 Sebeok joined the faculty of the University of Indiana at Bloomington. After completing his Ph.D. in Oriental Languages and Civilizations at Princeton, he came back to the University of Indiana in the Research Center for Anthropology, Folklore, and Linguistics that was abbreviated as (RCLS). Eventually as Chair he added semiotics to make it (RCLSS) (Cobley 2009: 192, Deely 2004: 2). In the period from 1960–1961, Sebeok was given a position at the Stanford Center for Advanced Study in the Behavioral Sciences, which offered him the freedom to continue developing his biological way of thinking.

With his background in linguistics, the most likely approach to the study of signs for Sebeok to follow would have been the dominant approach at the time, that of Swiss linguist Ferdinand de Saussure with its focus on language. However, Sebeok chose not to take this linguistic path, which as mentioned earlier, Deely later described as leading semiotics down a detour that took about "nine of the 20th century's ten decades to begin to commence to start to straighten things out" (Deely 2010: 15). In making this decision Deely explains that Sebeok

> never for a moment fell for the idea that semiosis could be adequately reduced or assimilated to a linguistic model of signifying, an idea he simply brushed aside as a "pars pro toto" fallacy—without denying that the semiological [linguistic] studies had a rightful place within the larger scope of semiotics proper. (Cobley 2009: 192; Deely 2004: 3)

In 1962 Sebeok took a major step in the development of the more inclusive paradigm for the study of signed-based communication (which he had begun through his work with Jakobson) than the prevailing linguistic model by organizing an Indiana conference on paralinguistics and kinesis. Deely saw the volume that derived from the conference, *Approaches to Semiotics*, as marking the beginning of the North American semiotic intellectual movement that additionally incorporated the seminal work of Charles Sanders Peirce (Deely 2004: 4).

In 1963 Sebeok coined the term "zoösemiotics" to include conclusively the study of animal communication in semiotics, which emphasized a broader orientation in his North American approach. To distinguish the human use of signs within the larger arena of zoosemiotics, in 1968 Sebeok established the term "anthroposemiotics." In 1975 he organized the first North American Semiotics Colloquium at the University of South Florida that led the next year to the establishment of the Semiotic Society of America and the first of its annual meetings. A few years later in 1981, under Sebeok's editorship of the international journal *Semiotica* founded by him, Martin Krampen introduced the term "phytosemiotics" for the action of signs among and between plants and animals from the position of plants. Through the development of these three concepts describing the action of signs in plant, animal and human domains, Sebeok applied his biological way of thinking to make the assertion that the action of signs was the *essential criteria of life* (Sebeok 1990).

As mentioned earlier, the integration of the work of theoretical biologist Jakob von Uexküll underlay Sebeok's contributions to semiotics and also to Deely's development of the semiotic animal. This was especially so for von Uexküll's concept of the umwelt.

> What is one to make of all this? It seems to me that, at the very least for us, workers in a zoösemiotic context, there is only one way to get through this thicket, and that is to adhere strictly to Jakob von Uexküll's comprehensive theses about signs. (Sebeok, 2001: 78,193)

A German term, *umwelt* dates back only to about 1800 with a variety of different meanings. Von Uexküll's meaning for the term was original, he used it "theoretically to illumine his biological research into the lifecycle of animals". For Sebeok, umwelt was not seen as a German term but as a "technical expression clarifying the requirements for the doctrine of signs pertaining to the life of animal organisms" (Deely 2002:127–128). Even though von Uexküll's work proved invaluable to semiotics and the semiotic animal definition of Deely, he was not formally a semiotician. Sebeok dubbed him a "cryptosemiotician" or one who works in secret with signs without being an actual semiotician (Deely 2010a: 30). It was through the integration of Von Uexküll's work into semiotics by Sebeok that the research by this cryptosemiotician and his concept umwelt entered into the field. Because of this Deely states in his attempt to define the term umwelt:

> I do so not as much on the basis of von Uexküll's own writings … as on the basis of those few recent works which develop the concept of Umwelt as Sebeok took it up for semiotics. (Deely 2002: 128)

What stood out most for Sebeok in the work of von Uexküll in his creative use of the concept umwelt was its focus inexorably on the "biological foundations that lie at the very epicenter of the study of both communication and signification in the human animal" (Sebeok 1976: x), "as well as every other species of animal" (Deely 2002: 128). Sebeok describes the umwelt as the phenomenal world that is observed by the observer. It is:

> the subjective world each animal models out of its 'true' environment (*Natur*, reality), which reveals itself solely through signs. The rules and laws to which those sign processes—namely, semiosis—are subject are the only actual laws of nature. (Sebeok 2001: 33)

Sebeok shows the umwelt to be an expression of the triadic process of sign interpretation by the observer or interpreter where the observed sign (S) and object (O) and the interpretant of Peirce (I) are involved in discerning "reality". The intuition of reality that makes up the phenomenal world by the observer becomes a consequence of the mutual interaction between the observer and the observed. For example, elementary sensations experienced by the observer (S) coupled to their meaningful transforms (O) become action impulses (I).

To elucidate further the umwelt concept, the South African eland antelope illustration mentioned earlier can be applied. The male eland hears a sound in the rustling of savanna grass near where he is standing (S). Through engagement with his species-specific environment or umwelt, the eland utilizes his sensory apparatus that coevolved in a communicative relationship with the semiosphere that is his surroundings along with personal experience gleaned while living, and transforms his perception into the general category of threat (O). Through this process of semiosis that happens instantaneously without conscious awareness, he makes his final interpretation. The interpretation becomes the eland's interpretant or his attempt through semiosis to accurately discern the nuanced character of relational being, or the "real" or suprasubjective meaning of the sound of the rustling grass; this gives rise to an action impulse (I), and the eland bounds away from the sound.

This complex elegant semiotic description of an animal subject engaged in a communicative relationship with its umwelt to facilitate its survival through knowing is contrasted with a modern simplistic reductionist description of a "meat machine" responding non-reflectively to a random external stimulus in *the environment*. From this contrast it becomes clear why Deely placed such high importance on the umwelt concept as refined by Sebeok, and why this concept is so integral to his development of the semiotic animal that replaces the thinking thing, and the consequent vision by your author of the Semiotic Age to replace modernity.

> I have found Umwelt to be a key term for the project of developing the epistemological paradigm proper to the way of signs, which overcomes in the process the modern paradigm definitive of the way of ideas [Deely 2002: 128]. ... This conundrum, this Gordian knot of "external reality," with which modernity had paralyzed the philosophers, was precisely what Sebeok cut. Faced with the dilemma of the modern implication of a maze of the mind's own workings, he found the way out. (Deely 2004a)

With the integration of Sebeok's refinement and utilization of the umwelt concept into semiotics, life becomes alive again; it becomes a connected and beautiful dance of interrelated knowing subjects as it had been for us before, when animism was our ontological orientation and epistemological expression. With this semiotic awareness we can appreciate that the quest, which our Paleolithic ancestors undertook of accurately interpreting relational being as integral to their long-term sustainability, is also integral to ours. By following the semiotic prescription of Deely "to reinstitutionalize cenoscopy, now *along with* the spectacular ideoscopic achievements of modernity" (Deely 2010a: 55) we are now prepared to continue the great adventure of our species, truly getting to know life on earth and how we can sustain ourselves by being an asset to it (Anderson 2005; Hornborg 2001; 2006; Smith 2016). We are now semiotic animals in a Semiotic Age!

6. Conclusion

> *For though there is of course a long history behind the semiotics of today, there is a sense in which semiotics is, as a widespread intellectual movement, a phenomenon more "of our time" than it is of any time past.*
>
> Susan Petrilli (2008: 3)

> *Aristotle remarks that speculative understanding by extension becomes practical.*
>
> Thomas Aquinas (c.1266)

Through the application of semiotic/ecological anthropology and cybernetics this article asserts that just as the thinking thing definition of human being of Descartes established the Modern Age and set us on an environmentally degrading nonsustainable trajectory, so the semiotic animal definition of Deely established the Semiotic Age that resolves our sustainability dilemma by setting us back on the 190,000-year environmentally embedded path of our Paleolithic ancestors. A shared characteristic that returns us to sustainability is the appreciation and ontological preeminence given to *relational being* in regard to our interaction with the natural world and the quest for its accurate interpretation. Another area of agreement between the Paleolithic orientation and the Semiotic Age that your author sees, as brought on by the semiotic animal definition of Deely, is the high esteem granted to cenoscopic knowledge, which is debased in modernity with its reification of ideoscopic knowledge. In the Paleolithic age this appreciation of relational being was expressed as an animistic orientation towards nature. In the Semiotic Age the appreciation of relational being refers to a semiotic or communicative orientation towards nature as expressed through the 2500-year development of the "doctrine of signs" that began with Hippocrates and found its establishment with the semiotic animal definition of Deely. In other words, your author contends that *semiotics is the great conversation within the great conversation, and the semiotic animal is the pinnacle and culminating expression of semiotics.*

There are two primary and important distinctions between the animistic and semiotic orientations that make the semiotic animal and Semiotic Age not a question of going back to a Paleolithic relational being consciousness but rather toward a new way of being in the world. The first distinction is that unlike animism, with the semiotic animal there is a conscious awareness of the triadic process of engagement involved in interpreting relational being. The second, which is intimately connected to the first, is that the power and profundity at the center of cenoscopic knowledge is found in the insight toward relational being provided primarily through the resonation of its figurative or aesthetic representation rather than its literal or descriptive interpretation. This is made evident through the requirement expressed by Deely in his semiotic animal definition of the need for the incorporation and integration of both cenoscopic knowledge and ideoscopic or modern Western scientific knowledge—guided by the recent development of the umwelt concept—to facilitate the grand purpose of our species to interpret accurately relational being (Deely 2010a: 55).

The reason for optimism that the Semiotic Age is not only upon us, but moreover that it will blossom to fruition and bring us back from the precipice of extinction is based on cybernetic understanding of cultural change as articulated by anthropologist Gregory Bateson and the cybernetic underpinning of the vast electronic global communication network that is today's Internet

(Smith 2016). In living systems and their expressions such as culture, change occurs through two primary influences, the negative feedback of pain and its avoidance along with the positive feedback of beauty and its attraction. Devastating environmental degradation in the form of climate change and massive biodiversity loss derived from modernity is providing the searing pain. Semiotics, in the form of a more elegant communicative model of knowable nature, which focuses on meaningful connection and stochastic processes rather than the random-chance separation from an unknowable nature model of modern classical physics, is providing the beauty.

This distinction between the Modern Age, founded on the thinking thing definition of human by Descartes and the Semiotic Age founded on the semiotic animal definition of Deely, is articulated well through an analogy of Bateson's. Borrowing from the Gnostics and Carl Jung, Bateson describes the distinction between kicking a rock verses kicking a dog (Bateson 1979: 6, 101). When a rock is kicked, a dyadic relationship occurs that can be predicted by classical physics based on universal laws discovered through ideoscopic knowledge. This is because the rock resides in the non-living domain of the "pleroma" where dyadic relationships occur devoid of knowing subjects. A stimulus in the form of the kick is followed by a predictable response; so much force applied to the rock will generate in turn so much movement by the rock. The rock as part of the physical universe is governed by entropy or the second law of thermodynamics that states that matter will gradually decline into disorder and decay. The rock sustains its existence by maintaining the rigidity of its form.

When a dog is kicked, a triadic relationship occurs of probability explicable through both cenoscopic and ideoscopic knowledge because the dog also resides in the living domain of the "creatura" that consists of knowing subjects engaged in interpretation of information. An act in the form of a kick is followed by a host of possible reactions; for a dog there are a myriad of "differences that make a difference" (Bateson 1972: 459). The response by the dog to the information received in the "message" of the kick could be a mild whimper, a fierce growl, a pounce, or a glance of uncertainty because of a previous relationship between the dog and the person. Maybe the kick was playful, or perhaps it was intended to move the dog out of harm's way with the dog realizing that it was done to protect him from injury. The dog is part of the rim of life clinging to the earth that is a *temporal distortion* of the third law of thermodynamics. Even though the dog is subject to the laws of physics, while it lives the dog makes order out of disorder and entropy is temporarily suspended.[7] The dog as well as all living organisms, including humankind, sustains its existence by accurately interpreting its species-specific environment in a stochastic process of calibration to facilitate systemic order or dynamic homeostasis founded on the reality of relational being.

Bateson says that the preeminence given to the pleroma by modernity in defining what it means to be a human being and how this definition separates us from the world of the dog or the creatura (as well as our bodies) is central to our sustainability crisis. While still subject to the laws of the pleroma, as a living organism the dog occupies a position in the creatura as belonging to the most elegant and beautiful expression in the known universe and is not treated as such within the modern Cartesian orientation. This glaring mistake in categorization clouds modern humans from understanding the profundity of life; it is what brings about the pain of environmental destruction (Bateson 1972: 492) such as climate change and massive biodiversity loss.

For Bateson, this dreadful ontological and epistemological error is what lies at the foundation of the pathology of modern society, impelling the insanity of continuing obviously unsustainable actions (Harries-Jones 1995: 199) such as the relentless use of fossil fuels driving climate change, and the release of more and more toxic chemicals along with ever-increasing habitat destruction that propels biodiversity loss. The madness of these environmentally devastating actions that increasingly separate modern humans from the natural world and their own bodies has made the exponential growth of the psychologically and physically debilitating disorders of depression and anxiety one of the most prominent results of modernization (Hidaka 2012; Schumaker 2001). It is like Shakespeare's Hamlet, who in the introduction of this article so vividly articulates the beauty of what it means to be human but later in the same soliloquy succumbs to the pathology of the palace intrigue around him by stating about humankind, "And yet, to me, what is this quintessence of dust? Man delights not me" (Shakespeare 1623: Act II, Scene II).

The semiotic animal offers a way to regain humankind's appreciation of the exquisite beauty and sacredness of life—a way to live in a world that is more connected, more meaningful, more alive. John Deely demonstrates this clearly by the pictures on the front and back cover of his appropriately titled book *What Distinguishes Human Understanding*. Evoking Bateson's rock and dog analogy, the pictures show Deeley with a large, light brown, formerly "wild" dog he appropriately named Beethoven, sitting on a bench

---

[7] Through reproduction an organism such as a dog can transfer its DNA or information for millennia to its offspring, thus continuing to "bring into form" its existence over a longer time period than some rocks (Hoffmeyer and Emmeche 1991).

next to him surrounded by books while Deely works on the manuscript that would eventually become the book. Originally a fearsome creature that greeted Deely and his wife with an ominous snarl when they first came to the house in Mexico where Deely wrote the book, the dog eventually moved into their home and back with them to America, where he took to sleeping on lace-trimmed pillows.

In the picture on the book's cover Beethoven looks quizzically at the manuscript, while the picture on the back shows him nuzzling against Deely's chin; the mutual activation and appreciation of the cognitive and emotional qualities of both *Homo sapiens* and *Canis familiaris* are obvious. These pictures show how Deely, as a semiotic animal living in a Semiotic Age, lives in a more beautiful and sustainable world of loving interaction between species, as does Beethoven.

When placed in the context of the 14 billion year old known universe, the 4.5 billion year old earth, and the 3.8 billion years of life existing on the rim of the planet, the awakening of humankind from modernity's globalization of the great dream of reason to the first rays of the dawn of the Semiotic Age derived from the semiotic animal definition of human by Deely is a momentous achievement to say the least. Through the semiotic animal, humankind as an expression of the universe allows the universe to know how life, its finest creation, works through the semiotic reality of relational being.

With this understanding of the semiotic animal and the establishment of the Semiotic Age, the greatest project ever engaged in by humans, how to sustain themselves on their earthly home, is now possible. Amidst the despair of environmental devastation hope can abound, because as Peirce and Bateson state so eloquently (Bateson 1979; Peirce 1893) and the universe attests through its semiotic expression of life—*through evolutionary love the beautiful persists*!

References

ANDERSON, Kat.
  2005.   *Tending the Wild: Native American Knowledge and the Management of California's Natural Resources* (Oakland, CA: University of California Press).

AQUINAS, Thomas.
  c.1266. *Summa theologiae*, in *S. Thomae Aquinatis Opera Omnia: ut sunt in indice thomistico*, ed. Roberto Busa (Stuttgart-Bad Cannstatt: Frommann-Holzboog, 1980), Vol. 2, 184–926.

ARISTOTLE.
    330 B.C.   *Poetics*, In *The Works of Aristotle*, ed. William David Ross and John
              Alexander Smith, Vol. 5. (Oxford, United Kingdom: Clarendon Press,
              1912).

BARKER, Graeme.
    2009.   *The Agricultural Revolution in Prehistory: Why Did Foragers Become
              Farmers?* (New York: Oxford University Press on Demand).

BARNOSKY, Anthony D.
    2011.   "Hast the Earth's Sixth Mass Extinction Already Arrived?", *Nature 471*,
              51–57. doi: https://doi.org/10.1038/nature09678

BARTHOLOMEW, George A.
    2005.   "Integrative Biology, an Organismic Biologist's Point of View", *Integrative
              and Comparative Biology* 45, 330–332.
              doi: https://doi.org/10.1093/icb/45.2.330

BATESON, Gregory.
    1958.   *Naven* (Redwood City, CA: Stanford University Press).
    1971.   "The Cybernetics of 'Self': A Theory of Alcoholism", *Psychiatry* 34,
              1–18. doi: https://doi.org/10.1080/00332747.1971.11023653
    1972.   *Steps to an Ecology of Mind* (Chicago and London: University of Chicago
              Press, 2000).
    1979.   *Mind and Nature: A Necessary Unity* (Cresskill, NJ: Hampton Press,
              2002).
    1991.   *A Sacred Unity: Further Steps to an Ecology of Mind*, ed. R. E. Donaldson
              (New York: Cornelia & Michael Bessie Book).

BENEDICT, Ruth.
    1934.   *Patterns of Culture* (Boston, MA: Houghton Mifflin Harcourt).

BIRD-DAVID, Nurit.
    1999.   "'Animism' Revisited: Personhood, Environment, and Relational Epis-
              temology", *Current Anthropology* 40.S1, S67–S91.
              doi: https://doi.org/10.1086/200061

BOIVIN, Nicole L. et al..
    2016.   "Ecological Consequences of Human Niche Construction: Examining
              Long-term Anthropogenic Shaping of Global Species Distributions",
              Proceedings of the National Academy of Sciences 113.13, 6388–6396.
              doi: https://doi.org/10.1073/pnas.1525200113

BURNHAM, John F.
    1993.   "Medical Diagnosis through Semiotics: Giving Meaning to the Sign",
              Annals of Internal Medicine 119.9, 939–943.
              doi: https://doi.org/10.7326/0003-4819-119-9-199311010-00012

BUSS, David M.
    2003. *The Evolution of Desire: Strategies of Human Mating* (New York, New York: Basic Books).

CAPRA, Fritjof.
    1983. *The Turning Point: Science, Society, and the Rising Culture* (New York: Bantam Books).
    1996. *The Web of Life* (New York: Anchor Books, Doubleday).

CARLYLE, Thomas.
    1841. *On Heroes, Hero-Worship, and the Heroic in History* (London: James Fraser).

CHADWICK, J., and W. M. MANN.
    1950. *The Medical Works of Hippocrates* (Oxford: Blackwell).

COBLEY, Paul.
    2009. *Realism for the 21st Century: A John Deely Reader* (Scranton, PA: Scranton University Press).

CONNELL, John.
    2010. *Migration and the Globalisation of Health Care: The Health Worker Exodus?* (Cheltenham, UK: Edward Elgar).

CRONON, William.
    1995. *Uncommon Ground: Toward Reinventing Nature.* Vol. 95. (New York: Norton).

DANESI, Marcel, and Paul PERRON.
    1999. *Analyzing Cultures: An Introduction and Handbook* (Bloomington: Indiana University Press).

DEELY, John.
    1982. *Introducing Semiotic: Its History and Doctrine* (Bloomington, IN: Indiana University Press).
    1988. "The Semiotic of John Poinsot: Yesterday and Tomorrow", *Semiotica* 69.1–2 (April), 31–127.
    1990. *Basics of Semiotics* (Bloomington, IN: Indiana University Press)
    2001. *Four Ages of Understanding: The First Postmodern History of Philosophy from Ancient Times to the Turn of the 21st Century* (Toronto, Canada: University of Toronto Press).
    2002. *What Distinguishes Human Understanding* (South Bend, IN: St. Augustine's Press)
    2003. "The Quasi-Error of the External World an Essay for Thomas A. Sebeok, in Memoriam", *Cybernetics and Human Knowing* 10, 25–46.
    2003a. "The Semiotic Animal", in *Semiotics*, ed. Rodney Williamson, Leonard G. Sbrocchi, and John Deely (Brooklyn, NY: Legas Press), 111–126.

2004.   "Thomas Albert Sebeok, 'Biologist Manqué'", Sebeok Memorial Essay International Association for Semiotic Studies 2004 World Congress, Lyon.

2004a. "Tom Sebeok and the External World", *Semiotica* 150, 1–21.

2009.   *Augustine & Poinsot: The Protosemiotic Development* (Scranton, PA: Scranton University Press).

2010.   *Semiotic Animal: A Postmodern Definition of Human Being Transcending Patriarchy and Feminism* (South Bend, IN: St. Augustine Press).

2010a. *Semiotics Seen Synchronistically: The View from 2010* (Brooklyn, NY: Legas Press).

2016.   From personal conversation with Alexander Schwartz, Maggie Stedman-Smith, and Richard Currie Smith, July 7, at Latimer Family Library Saint Vincent College (Latrobe, PA).

2016a. From personal conversation with Richard Currie Smith, Maggie Stedman-Smith, and Brooke Williams Deely, at home of John and Brooke Deely, July 7 (Latrobe, PA).

DEELY, John, Susan PETRILLI, and Augusto PONZIO.

2005.   *The Semiotic Animal* (Brooklyn, NY: Legas Press).

DERRICOURT, Robin.

2005.   "Getting 'Out of Africa': Sea Crossings, Land Crossings and Culture in the Hominin Migrations", *Journal of World Prehistory* 19.2, 119–132. doi: https://doi.org/10.1007/s10963-006-9002-z

DERRIDA, Jacques

1967.   *Of Grammatology*, trans. Gayatri Chakravorty Spivak (Baltimore: Johns Hopkins University Press).

DESCARTES, René.

1628.   *Rules for the Direction of the Mind*, trans. Dugald Murdoch in *Philosophical Writings of Descartes*, trans. and ed. John Cottingham, Robert Stoothoff, and Murdoch trans. 1985), I: 9–78.

1637.   *Discourse on the Method of Rightly Conducting One's Reason and Seeking Truth in the Sciences*, trans. Robert Stoothoff in *Philosophical Writings of Descartes*, trans. and ed. John Cottingham, Robert Stoothoff, and Murdoch trans. 1985), I: 111–151.

1641.   *Meditations on First Philosophy*, trans. John Cottingham in *Philosophical Writings of Descartes*, trans. and ed. John Cottingham, Robert Stoothoff, and Murdoch trans. 1985), II: 3–62.

1644.   *Principles of Philosophy*, trans. John Cottingham in in *Philosophical Writings of Descartes*, trans. and ed. John Cottingham, Robert Stoothoff, and Murdoch trans. 1985), I: 179–291.

1649.   *Les Passions de l'Ame* (1st ed.; Paris: Henry Le Gras); trans. Stephen H. Voss as *The Passions of the Soul* (Indianapolis, IN: Hackett Publishing Co., 1988).

DESCOLA, Philippe.
  1992. "Societies of Nature and the Nature of Society", *Conceptualizing Society*, 107–126.

DICK, Hugh, G., Editor.
  1955. *Selected Writings of Francis Bacon* (New York: Modern Library).

ELK, Black.
  1932. *Black Elk Speaks: Being the Life Story of a Holy Man of the Oglala Sioux*, as told to John G. Neihardt (Lincoln, NE: University of Nebraska Press).

FEHR, Ernst, and Urs FISCHBACHER.
  2003. "The Nature of Human Altruism", *Nature* 425.6960, 785–791. doi: https://doi.org/10.1038/nature02043

FRANCIS, Pope.
  2015. "Encyclical Letter: Laudato Si', On Care for Our Common Home". Online: <bit.ly/1GuiptI>.

FRANCIS, Saint, of Assisi
  1225. "Canticle of the Creatures", in Katherine Paterson, *Brother Sun, Sister Moon: Saint Francis of Assisi's Canticle of the Creatures* (San Francisco: Handprint Books, an imprint of Chronicle Books, 2011).

FRIIS, Robert H.
  2012. *Essentials of Environmental Health* (Burlington, MA: Jones & Bartlett Publishers)

FUENMAYOR, Ramsés.
  1991. "The Roots of Reductionism: A Counter-ontoepistemology For a Systems Approach", *Systems Practice* 4.5, 419–448. doi: https://doi.org/10.1007/BF01104460

GEERTZ, Clifford.
  1973. *The Interpretation of Cultures: Selected Essays* (New York: Basic Books).

GEROVITCH, Slava.
  2009. "The Cybernetics Scare and the Origins of the Internet", *Baltic Worlds* 2, 32–38.

HALIFAX, Joan.
  1979. *Shamanic Voices: A Survey of Visionary Narratives* (New York: E.P. Dutton).

HARRIES-JONES, Peter.
  1995. *A Recursive Vision: Ecological Understanding and Gregory Bateson* (Toronto, Canada: University of Toronto Press).

HAUGEN, Marty and St. Francis.
  1980. *Canticle of the Sun* (Chicago, IL: G.I.A. Publishers)

HEIDEGGER, Martin.
  1962. *Being and Time*, trans. J. Macquarrie and E. Robinson (New York: Harper & Row).

HEIDEL, William Arthur.
  1941. *Hippocratic Medicine: Its Spirit and Method* (New York: Columbia University Press)

HIDAKA, Brandon H.
  2012. "Depression as a Disease of Modernity: Explanations for Increasing Prevalence", *Journal of Affective Disorders* 140.3, 205–214.
          doi: https://doi.org/10.1016/j.jad.2011.12.036

HOFFMEYER, Jesper.
  2008. *A Legacy for Living Systems: Gregory Bateson As Precursor to Biosemiotics* (New York: Springer).

HOFFMEYER, Jesper, and Claus EMMECHE.
  1991. "Code-Duality and the Semiotics of Nature", in *On Semiotic Modeling*, ed. Myrdene Anderson and Floyd Merrell (Berlin and New York: Mouton de Gruyter), 117–166.

HOFMAN, M.A.
  2014. "Evolution of the Human Brain: When Bigger is Better", *Frontiers in Neuroanatomy* 8, 1–12.
          doi: https://doi.org/10.3389/fnana.2014.00015.

HOLLINGER, Robert.
  1994. *Postmodernism and the Social Sciences: A Thematic Approach* (Thousand Oaks, CA: SAGE Publications).

HORNBORG, Alf.
  2001. "Vital Signs: An Ecosemiotic Perspective on the Human Ecology of Amazonia", Σημειωτκή—*Sign Systems Studies* 1 (2001), 121–152.
  2006. "Animism, Fetishism, and Objectivism as Strategies for Knowing (or Not Knowing) the World", *Ethnos: Journal of Anthropology* 71, 21–32.
          doi: https://doi.org/10.1080/00141840600603129.

INGOLD, Tim.
  2006. "Rethinking the Animate, Re-animating Thought", *Ethnos* 71.1, 9–20.
          doi: https://doi.org/10.1080/00141840600603111

IPCC, INTERGOVENMENT PANEL ON CLIMATE CHANGE.
  2015. "Climate Change 2014 Synthesis Report: Fifth Assessment Report". Online: <http://www.ipcc.ch>.

JACKSON, B. Darrel.
  1969. "The Theory of Signs in St. Augustine's De Doctrina Christiana", *Revue d' Etudes Augustiniennes Et. Patristiques* 15, 9–50.

JONES, Richard Foster.
    1961.   *Ancients and Moderns: A Study of the Rise of the Scientific Movement in Seventeenth-Century England* (New York: Dover Publications).

JORGENSON, Andrew
    2006.   *Globalization and the Environment* (Boston, MA: Brill).

KANT, Immanuel.
    1747.   "Thoughts on the True Estimation of Living Forces", *Natural Science* (1929), 1–155.

KEVELSON, Roberta.
    1983.   "Thomas A. Sebeok, The Sign and Its Masters", *The American Journal of Semiotics* 2.1–2, 267–276.
        doi: https://doi.org/10.5840/ajs198321/28

KOTTAK, Conrad Phillip.
    2011.   *Cultural Anthropology: Appreciating Cultural Diversity* (New York: McGraw-Hill).

KRISHNAMURTI, Jiddu
    1970.   *The Krishnamurti Reader* (Westminster, London: Penguin Books).

KULL, Kalevi.
    1998.   "Semiotic Ecology: Different Natures in the Semiosphere", *Sign System Studies* 26, 344–371.

LANIGAN, Richard L.
    2015.   "Human Embodiment: An Eidetic and Empirical Communicology of Phantom Limb", *Metodo. International Studies in Phenomenology and Philosophy* 3, 257–287.

LEVIN, Simon.
    2005.   "Self-organization and the Emergence of Complexity in Ecological Systems", *Bioscience* 55, 1075–1079.
        doi: https://doi.org/10.1641/0006-3568(2005)055[1075:SATEOC]2.0.CO;2

LOTMAN, Yuri M.
    2005.   "On the Semiosphere", Σημειωτκή—*Sign Systems Studies* 1, 205–229.

MCLENNAN, J. F.
    1885.   *The Patriarchal Theory* (London, Macmillan)

MERCHANT, Carolyn.
    2008.   "'The Violence of Impediments': Francis Bacon and the Origins of Experimentation", *Isis* 99.4, 731–760.
        doi: https://doi.org/10.1086/597767
    2013.   *Reinventing Eden: The Fate of Nature in Western Culture* (Abingdon-on-Thames: Routledge).

MERTZ, Elizabeth.

2007. "Semiotic Anthropology", *Annual Revue of Anthropology* 36, 337–353. doi: https://doi.org/10.1146/annurev.anthro.36.081406.094417

MILLER, Jonathan.

1978. *The Body in Question* (New YorkRandom House).

MONTAGNINI, Leone.

2007. "Looking for 'Scientific' Social Science: The Macy Conferences on Cybernetics in Bateson's Itinerary", *Kybernetes* 36, 1012–1021. doi: https://doi.org/10.1108/03684920710777522

MURPHY, James.

1991. "Nature, Custom, and Stipulation in the Semiotic of John Poinsot", *Semiotica* 83.1–2, 33–68

NAGEL, John Copeland.

2016. "Pope Francis, Environmental Anthropologist", *Regent University Law Review* 28, 7–47.

OGDEN, C. K., and I. A. RICHARDS.

1923. *The Meaning of Meaning: A Study of the Influence of Language upon Thought and of the Science of Symbolism* (London and New York: Harcourt and Brace).

PALAGI, Elisabetta.

2006. "Social Play in Bonobos (Pan Paniscus) and Chimpanzees (Pan Troglodytes): Implications for Natural Social Systems and Inter-individual Relationships", *American Journal of Physical Anthropology* 129.3, 418–426. doi: https://doi.org/10.1002/ajpa.20289

PAREY, Ambrose.

1649. *The Works of that Famous Chirurgion Ambrose Parey* (London: Cotes and Willi Du-gard)

PEIRCE, Charles S.

1886–1913. *The Collected Papers of Charles Sanders Peirce*: Vols. I–VI ed. Charles Hartshorne and Paul Weiss (Cambridge, MA: Harvard University Press, 1958).

1893. "Evolutionary Love", *The Monist* 3, 176–200. doi: https://doi.org/10.5840/monist18933235

1992. *The Essential Peirce*, 2 vols., ed. N. Houser et al. (Bloomington: Indiana University Press).

PENCAK, William.

1995. "Charles S. Peirce: The Later Years and the Philosophy of History", in *Semiotics*, ed. John Deely, and C. W. Spinks (New York: Peter Lang), 401–406. doi: https://doi.org/10.5840/cpsem199514

PETRILLI, Susan.
   2005.   "From the Semiotic Animal to the Semioethic Animal: The Humanism of Otherness and Responsibility", in *The Semiotic Animal*, ed. John Deely, Susan Petrilli, and Augusto Ponzio (New York, Ottawa, and Toronto: Legas Press), 67–86.
   2005a.   "Human Responsibility and Life in the Universe of 'Global Semiotics'", in *The Semiotic Animal*, ed. John Deely, Susan Petrilli, and Augusto Ponzio (New York, Ottawa, and Toronto: Legas Press), 35–50.
   2008.   Sebeok Fellow Address to the Semiotic Society of America on 17 October at the SSA's 33rd Annual Meeting (Houston, Texas).

PETRILLI, Susan, and Augusto PONZIO.
   2001.   *Thomas Sebeok and the Signs of Life* (Great Britain: Icon Books).
   2003.   *Semioetica* (Rome: Meltemi).
   2005.   "Semioethics and Symptomatology of Globalization: Global Communication from the Perspective of Global Semiotics", in *The Semiotic Animal*, ed. John Deely, Susan Petrilli, and Augusto Ponzio (New York, Ottawa, and Toronto: Legas Press), 87–110.

POINSOT, John.
   1632.   *Artis Logicae Secunda Pars*, in *Cursus Philosophicus Thomisticus*, ed. B. Reiser (Turin: Marietti, 1930), vol. I: 249–839.

RATZINGER, Joseph (Pope Benedict XVI as of 19 April 2005).
   1970.   Introduction to Christianity (New York: Herder and Herder)
   2009.   "Caritas in veritate", Encyclical Letter June 29 (Vatican City).

RENFREW, Colin R., and Iain MORLEY.
   2009.   *Becoming Human: Innovation in Prehistoric Material and Spiritual Culture* (Cambridge: University Press).

ROCKSTROM, Johan.
   2009.   "A Safe Operating Space for Humanity", *Nature* 461.7263, 472–475. doi: https://doi.org/10.1038/461472a

RODRICK, Dan.
   2011.   *The Globalization Paradox: Democracy in the Future of the World Economy* (York: Cambridge University Press).

ROHLF, Michael.
   2016.   "Immanuel Kant", *The Stanford Encyclopedia of Philosophy* (Spring 2016 Edition), ed. Edward N. Zalta. Online: <http://plato.stanford.edu/archives/spr2016/entries/kant/>.

ROSENBLUETH, A., N. WIENER, and J. BIGELOW.
   1943.   "Behavior, Purpose, and Teleology", *Philosophy of Science* 10, 18–24. doi: https://doi.org/10.1086/286788

ROSZAK, Theodore.
  1975. *Unfinished Animal* (New York, NY: HarperCollins Publishers).

SACHS, Wolfgang.
  1993. *Global Ecology: A New Arena of Political Conflict* (London: Zed Books).

SACHS, Wolfgang, and Tilman SANTARIUS.
  2007. *Fair Future: Resource Conflicts, Security, and Global Justice* (London: Zed Books).

SCHUMAKER, John F.
  2001. *The Age of Insanity: Modernity and Mental Health* (Greenwood Publishing Group).

SEBEOK, Thomas A.
  1976. "Foreword". *Contributions to the Doctrine of Signs* (Lisse, Netherlands: Peter de Ridder Press).
  1979. "Prefigurements of Art", *Semiotica* 27.1–3, 3–74.
  1990. *Essays in Zoosemiotics* No. 5. (Toronto: Toronto Semiotic Circle)
  1994. "'Animal' in Biological and Semiotic Perspective", in *What is an Animal*, ed. Tim Ingold (New York: Routledge), 63–76.
  2001. *Signs: An Introduction to Semiotics*, 2nd ed. (Toronto: University of Toronto Press)

SHAKESPEARE, William.
  1623. *Tragedy of Hamlet, Prince of Denmark*, ed. William James Rolfe (New York: Harper and Brothers, 1891).

SMITH, Richard Currie.
  2005. *The Emergence of Ecological Restoration Through Perceptual Reframing: Applying Gregory Bateson's Living Systems Approach to the Minnesota River Basin Environmental Dilemma*, Dissertation (Minneapolis, MN: University of Minnesota Press).
  2010. "Semio-Epistemology: Fostering Sustainable Environmental Restoration Efforts", in *Semiotics 2010: The Semiotics of Time*, ed. Karen Haworth, Jason Hogue, Leonard Sbrocchi (Brooklyn, NY: Legas).
  2016. "Virtual Nature and the Sustainability of Life on Earth as We Know It", in *Semiotics 2015: Virtual Identities*, ed. Jamin Pelkey and Stéphanie Walsh Matthews (Charlottesville: Philosophy Documentation Center).

SPAARGAREN, Gert, A. P. J. MOL, and F. H. BUTTEL, Editors.
  2000. *Environment and Global Modernity*, Vol. 50 (Thousand Oaks, CA: Sage Publications).

SPENCER, Herbert.
  1896. The Study of Sociology (New York: Appleton).

STRINGER, Martin D.
  1999.   "Rethinking Animism: Thoughts from the Infancy of our Discipline",
          Journal of the Royal Anthropological Institute 5, 541–56.
          doi: https://doi.org/10.2307/2661147

STUTZ, Aaron J.
  2014.   "Embodied Niche Construction in the Hominin Lineage: Semiotic
          Structure and Sustained Attention in Human Embodied Cognition",
          Frontiers in psychology 5, 1–19.

SUTTON, Mark and E. N. ANDERSON
  2009.   *Introduction to Cultural Ecology*, 2nd Edition (New York: AltaMira
          Publishing).

TROSPER, Ronald L.
  2005.   "Emergence Unites Ecology and Society", *Ecology and Society* 10, 14.
          Online: <http://www.ecologyandsociety.org/vol110/iss1/art14/>.

TYLOR, Edward
  1871.   *Primitive Culture*, Volume 1 (London: John Murray).

VAN SCHAIK, Carel P.
  2003.   "Orangutan Cultures and the Evolution of Material Culture", *Science*
          299.5603, 102–105. doi: https://doi.org/10.1126/science.1078004

VINCENTNATHAN, Lynn, S., George VINCENTNATHAN and Nicholas
          SMITH.
  2016.   "Catholics and Climate Change Skepticism", *Worldviews* 20, 125–149.
          doi: https://doi.org/10.1163/15685357-02002005

VIVEIROS DE CASTRO, Eduardo.
  1999.   "The Transformation of Objects into Subjects in Amerindian On-
          tologies" Paper presented at the 98th Annual Meeting of the American
          Anthropological Association (Chicago, IL).

VON BERTALANFFY, Ludwig.
  1950.   "The Theory of Open Systems in Physics and Biology", *Science* 111.2872,
          23–29. doi: https://doi.org/10.1126/science.111.2872.23

WEISS, Gerald.
  1974.   *The Cosmology of the Campa Indians of Eastern Peru*. Dissertation (Ann
          Arbor, MI: University of Michigan Press).

WHITE, Lynn.
  1967.   "The Historical Roots of our Ecologic Crisis", *Science* 155, 1203–1207.
          doi: https://doi.org/10.1126/science.155.3767.1203

WIENER, Norbert (1894–1964).
  1948.   *Cybernetics: Or Control and Communication in the Animal and the Machine*
          (Cambridge, MA: MIT Press).
  1950.   *The Human Use of Human Beings* (New York: Houghton Mifflin).

WILLIAMS DEELY, Brooke.

2016.   From personal conversation with your author on July 8 at the home of John and Brooke Deely (Latrobe, Pennsylvania).

How Fit is the Semiotic Animal?

Stéphanie Walsh Matthews
Ryerson University

Abstract: How did the Semiotic Animal come to be? Do semiotic analyses of possible evolutionary trajectories allow us to understand how the Semiotic Animal developed a need for meaning in its life? This paper discusses what role built environments have on semiosis and how they might impact on what can be called semiotic fitness over time. Through the lens of evolutionary semiotics, biosemiotics and ecosemiotics, the question of "what is semiotic fitness?" will be dissected in order to understand what impact epigenetic fakeness and bloated signs might have on the Semiotic Animal.

Keywords: biosemiotics, evolution, semiosis, fitness

In various human sciences, the question of semiosis as a determining factor in shaping the world and our contemporary modeling of the Self has become paramount. Because of this, larger questions of semiotics and human evolution have come to the forefront in many fields, even though they may not be always identified as such. The main one, in my view, is: How did the Semiotic Animal[1] come to be? Does the answer lie somewhere within the evolutionary thrust from *homo sapiens sapiens*—to—*homo culturalis?*[2] Does any semiotic analyses of possible evolutionary trajectories allow us to understand how the Semiotic Animal developed a need for meaning in its life, rather than just a use of instincts? Do current semiotic frameworks provide a greater understanding of the influence of environmental conditions on species and does it shed light on on how our species has today become immersed in

---

[1] The term "semiotic animal", this special issue's eponymic title, was coined by John Deely. The term allows for a direct biosemiotic study of human signs within zoo-/anthropo- albeit bio-semiotics semiospherical frameworks.

[2] I use the term as Perron and Danesi do in *Analysing Culture* to discuss the human as producer and product of a semiotic environment infused with cultural symbolism that it can no longer be separated from (Danesi and Perron 1999).

ISSN 0277-7126

doi: 10.5840/ajs2016102514

Online First: October 26, 2016

The American Journal of Semiotics 32.1–4 (2016), 205–217.

the technopolis where we are processing information through multilayered textualities? Biosemioticians agree that the onus is on *semiotics* to provide the necessary insights to understand how meaning structures, sensory structures, and signifying codes now converge to produce the modern mind.

Through a synchronic lens, biosemiotics[3] can be understood as "the study of the action of signs in the living world" (Deely 2010a: 36) and that this study should include culture, which is a result of adaptive semiosis (ibid.: 44). Interestingly, few of us would consider evolution primarily in synchronic terms, because the object of interest is the understanding of human change; however, evolutionary semiosis and its specific processes can and should be the object of a synchronic investigation alongside a diachronic analysis, since one informs the other.

This paper aims to discuss the role of built environments on semiosis and how they might impact on what can be called semiotic fitness over time. If adaptive and co-optive environments are what shape semiotic phenomena at various ontological and epistemological levels, then what happens when these are no longer purely biospheric (built on firstness sensory processes)? In order to answer this, first we will look at the relationship between bio-semiotics and evolutionary theory in order to grasp what is meant by signi-fication and its cultural construction over time. We will thus discuss the role of bio-signaling systems as pre-semiotic features, that through adaptation, eventually develop into full-blown human semiosis. Through an ecosemiotic lens, we will investigate the diminishment of the natural environment today and the emergence of what can be called the bloated sign, which has been produced via fake environments, and its threat on eroding memory.

Biosemiotics: A Synchronic Diachrony

Biosemioticians carry out their primary inquiries into the nature of the rela-tionship between semiosis and evolution. Multiple apertures to investigate the connectedness of selection and adaptation mechanisms to internalized modeling capacities suggest the possible structural similarity of internal forms with respect to the representation of external environments. Ultimately, this theorizing refers to the semetic interaction with how the environment is forged through epigenetic landscaping (Andrade 2007: 392). Furthermore, it could

---

[3] As explained by Kalevi Kull, biosemiotics should be considered within a larger frame-work, namely that of ecosemiotics. As Kull points out, Deely had remarked already that human culture was only somewhat autonomous and that it shared structures with the greater biosphere (Deely 1990: 7; in Kull 1998: 348), and so Kull suggests the term ecosemiotics, one to which we will come back in our discussions of evolutionary semiotics (which, as we will see, is a mélange of biosemiotics, evolutionary semiotics, ecosemiotics, and cognitive semiotics).

be surmised that such interactivity involves an interpretative function within the selective process.

As many Biosemioticians will agree, a great deal of the initial framework for such an understanding is provided in Jakob von Uexküll's (1864) notions of *Umwelt* and *Innenwelt*. When discussing frameworks and structures through which the external world is experienced by way of models that are in turn internalized, *Umwelt* designates "the meaningful world of objects developed species-specifically by every animal" (Deely 2010a: 30) and the *Innenwelt* is the internal world of experiences of said species (Sebeok and Danesi 2000: 176). It is the dynamic creative process that informs the building of the representation of a possible external world into internalized processes. Forms of representation are then cast back onto the external environment. It is the revolving door—inside/outside/inside, etc.—that drives my inquiry into the immediate construction of perceivable realities of today. Additionally, questions into species-specific semiosis and the larger interactions between elements of the world constitute the essence of biosemiotics. Necessary connections between meaning and environment are more broadly discussed in ecosemiotics (or ecological semiotics.) Explaining exaptation through levels of perceivable nature as well as dyadic combination[4] feedback connections puts forth not an *a priori* built-in way to perceive, but a reciprocal system of information processing. Moreover, semiotic co-option (Maran and Kleisner 2010: 196) could provide additional clues to the bridging of what might be considered the cognition and culture gap, or what Dawkins refers to as the gene and the meme resemblance (Nöth 1990: 166).

In many instances, the role of space and time is emphasized in the construction of the "welts". Some might go so far as to state that semiosic processes are the product of diachronic constructions impacted onto the synchronic realm and that signs have no value outside of the realm of time. To this, I might add, the role of memory and our cognitive architecture are permanently hinged on temporality and I worry that this delicate balance might be threatened under current built environments.

The Semiotic Animal and Evolutionary Semiotics

In evolutionary theory, the notion of fitness is elaborated via Darwinism and Neo-Darwinism theories where natural selection is akin to survival of the fittest. As we shall see, the assumptions related to it support and are supported by a semiotic model (Andrade 2007: 389) however much it might

---

[4] Referencing the model Semiotic framework for evolutionary and developmental biology as introduced by E. Andrade (2007: 394)

seem to reject the notion of discrete selection at first blush. Even Epigenetic theories struggle with the notion of agency (Andrade 2007: 392) which calls into action a semiotic perspective to help in fostering agency within a larger sense of fitness. Although the discussion on *where does semiosis begin* is still in the infancy of debate, many have formulated a number of hypothesis that would distinguish human language and all other forms of cultural representation from other animal systems of communication. Humans have a unique ability to use signs.[5] More importantly still: this unique ability is one of our great strengths as it allows us to understand and redeploy the meaningful structures of experience through the use of signs. We are of the opinion that this semiosic activity is intrinsically linked to our evolutionary pathway.

In the Beginning, There Was the Code

When do meaning and the possibility of interpretation arise? It has been considered that communication and the transmission of traits and bio-information was initially done through codes. This "code-semiotics" is considered more simple and, as such, as preceding signs in evolution (Brier and Joslyn 2012: 151). What makes signs appear later in the evolutionary line is the fact that they require representation to function and therefore imply "a nervous system, because interpretation demands an intentionality to interpret one sign in one way and another in another, and we have no minds without nervous systems" (ibid.: 151–152). The notion of interpretation and representation are therefore the cornerstones of semiosis and most importantly are critical to the development and deployment of signs in culture (and, to that we should add, to the setting out of culture.)

Although numerous attempts have been made to equate the process of gene mutation (including adaptation, exaptation and co-option) with that of interpretation, there still needs to be a line separating early forms of interaction from that of interpretation (i.e., from code to sign.) For example, to demonstrate that what happens at the level of molecules and DNA parallels what happens at the level of the sign in the mind, Dawkin's analogy compares a gene to the meme. A gene is shared and passed along the same way memes are (culture signs) and that this is considered *imitation*. Through imitation,

---

[5] John Deely asks "why did it take so long for the human animal to realize that they are unique above all in being semiotic animals" (Deely 2010: 52). This underlines the homocentric occupancy of the discourse on semiotic animalness and semiosis although others (such as Maran and Kleisner 2010: 197), which positions semiotic co-option within the realm of animal conditions and meaningful social-communicative functions. Deely states that what the human semiotic animal does singularly is take sign interpretation out of the realm of the social and into the more elaborate and indirect bind of semiosis.

minds share memes in the same way genetic information is passed along through heredity (as stated in Nöth 1990: 166).

We can extract from this that the role of semiosis is linked to the ability to interpret and that signs are interpretable, shared, and can carry meaningful content provided there is the necessary context to support it. Semiosis isn't, however, imitation. It is interpretation.

Semiosis, as *homo sapiens sapiens* experience it, is part and parcel of the evolutionary trajectory the species has undergone. In some instances, some would argue that the divide between our current semiotic functions and that of our closely related apes is quite narrow (Donald 2014: 70) while others would go so far as to note that the capacity to interpret, design, and erect culture belongs to such genus as the *Macrotermes*, fungus-cultivating termites (Turner 2016: 85) where cognitive systems are essentially representational systems. One determining factor remains, which is clearly highlighted in the evolutionary semiotic writings of Barbieri, Joslyn and Brier, Allott and Andrade, is that the human species is unique in its representational symbolic practices characterizing language. Although Turner can demonstrate that species determine the structure of their interpretative function and Maran and Kleisner maintain that semiosis appears through semiotic co-option even in non-human species, our understanding of semiosis is here linked to the *homo sapiens sapiense's* particular mind and ability to produce and interpret meaningful signs. One irreducible fact is that only human language records and auto-represents others' representations over time, i.e., diachronically.

This, by no means, suggests that language is the ultimate point of evolution in semiosic terms. As Deely suggests, language is not the end point of the semiotic superorganism,[6] but merely a stepping stone towards the capacity to experience the world as we know it. As he notes, "linguistic communication is not the primary but the secondary modeling system within anthroposemiosis [... Language] arises as an exaptation rather than an adaptation" (Deely 2010a: 63). Such notions as adaptation and exaptation in the evolutionary trajectory are important as they determine, effectively or not, if semiosis is the result of our ability to use language and produce culture, or if semiosis is the result of our production of culture and language.[7] Regardless, many interesting hypothesis present themselves as helpful in our understanding of

---

[6] The term "Semiotic Superorganism" is borrowed here from J. Scott Turner.

[7] Maran and Kleisner suggest that the semantic organ developed through semiotic co-option is detectable in other animals as well. According to them, semiosis and semiotic selection do a great deal to determine the biological modelings and recombinations of animal structures and that "Semiotic selection allows more precise shaping of existing biological structures, based on the meaning relations present in the selector's Umwelt" (Maran and Kleisner 2010: 198).

the, now, symbiotic relationship between our cognition, the models we use for representation and the world as we experience it.

Let There Be Signs!

The notion of representations of the world in establishing the *Welts* and the ability to process them is most effectively discussed, as Deely points out, in Sebeok's—and later on in Danesi and Sebeok's—modeling systems theory. Deely discusses the idea of evolutionary success as an anthroposemiosic process that is anchored in a larger animal semiosic process. As Deely remarks, Sebeok's "ingenious" understanding and proposed theory based on von Uexküll and Lotman's work claims that our semiosic capacities are a result of exaptation (rather than an evolutionary trait), where culture is the realm in which the tertiary modeling system resides (Deely 2010a: 64).

What Deely is referring to is Modeling Systems Theory (MST) where is established through Primary Modeling System (PMS) a sensory based perception of the world. Through this, actions that are a direct result of the perceivable (transduced) world are established and give rise to a relation: This is Secondary Modeling System (SMS). Finally, when semiosis involves the relationship between a sign and its meaningful representation it is only through indirect association that it can unfold—producing the Tertiary Modeling System (TMS). The world as we experience it is therefore processed through internalized modeling that allows for the intake and interpretation of signs and their functions. Interestingly, modeling system theory is in line with other semiotic frameworks.

Mediation, Representation and Interpretations

Other biological and developmental semiotic theories posit that determining factors in our structural architecture are developed through a sequencing of external-internal events. Andrade considers two major forces that aid and shape the developmental process. They are: *Firstness*, an expansive force, and *thirdness*, a compressive force (Andrade 2007: 398–399). I would argue that Andrade's notion of the two major forces at work in semiotic evolution is closely tied with MST. Borrowing, as many biosemioticans have done, and do, from Peirce's universal categories, that is *firstness, secondness*, and *thirdness*, PMS corresponds with *firstness*, which Andrade states as being one of the two major forces in semiotic evolutionary and developmental biology and TMS with *thirdness. Firstness* is expansive, spontaneous, linked to inner drives, and most importantly, "associated with the production of evolutionary variations" (Andrade 2007: 393). He adds that *thirdness*, is an equilibrating force that mediates and generates "regularity and symmetry" where generalising tendencies may come to light (Andrade

2007: 393). Semiosis can (and could be) therefore notably situated (if it is to be situated anywhere) somewhere in the process of interpretation where signs are to be mediated, and their indirect causalities decipherable and mutable.

Even from different vantage points, the thinking is the same. Mediation of signs is where semiosis lies and semiosis is the product of an exapted co-relation of semiotic activity. The inner structures built to represent the outer structures are mutable and plastic and by definition so are the models that are to be constructed. We may also add what Maran and Kleisner argue that semiotics is proof that evolution functions outside a simple natural selection process and is rather an informing variable throughout evolution (Maran and Kleisner 2010: 398):

> In general we hold the view that semiotic processes cannot be subjected to the framework of natural selection. Semiosis is not the plain consequence of evolution; and correspondingly, memetics and other Neo-Darwinian approaches which try to describe signs as replicators, contradict semiotics in principle by being ignorant of semiosis as mediating and connecting meaning relation.

What is Semiotic Fitness?

What would then be "Semiotic Fitness"? Is there such a thing? We could estimate that somewhere in the concepts of selection, co-option, and exaptation, there would be the one key element in semiosic processes that allow for such a symbiotic relationship to develop between mind and world, body and mind. Mediation and representation, the ability to share, store, and recall the various signs that allow us to relate to the welts, seem to be at the helm of the height of semiosis. Effectively, all embodied experiences and their related cognitive outcomes must exist in a dialectical dance where there is a call and response between senses, representations and the ability to reference them in terms of a perpetual shifting performance edging new views on the world. Semiotic fitness could therefore be the legacy from which and through which we may share an *Umwelt* with the other animals of the semiosphere whilst all the while remaining capable of a very species-specific meaning system. This is supported by Sebeok's MST and is also reflective of all other evolutionary semiotic discourses. This capacity to represent collectively through autoreferencing suggests that it is necessary for the individual to collectivize management of the semiosphere. It should therefore be understood that semiotic fitness is necessarily a group engagement and that a cognitive collective[8] is basic to our species specific semiotic fitness. It is our anthroposemiotic

---

[8] The term "cognitive collective" is used here in the same way Merlin Donald references it in "The Digital Era".

strength and truly our remarkable biosemiotic specialty. Without it, we are not particularly fit for anything:

> Collectively, we may be very clever and able to achieve remarkable things; but individually, and especially when isolated from society, we are quite limited creatures. (Donald 2014: 70)

Fitness would be the plasticity of the mind combined with its rigorous underpinning. This is one of the strange paradoxical phenomena (remind you of anything?) once emerging from the dyadic structures of a strictly linguistic semiological framework. Regardless, paradoxes and idiosyncrasies plague evolutionary theory and are the binding stuff of hereditary mutations!

As Donald states, the brain is highly influenced and shaped by culture and technology—and I would add *in a diachronic way*,—but is also immediately altered in its architecture by the introduction of new mediated signs.[9] In other words, brain architecture is a synchronic and diachronic evolutionary ongoing system.

And so, semiotic fitness is acquired through a process of engaging with the world and representing it and being capable of generating mediating signs so that it may be understood individually, but shared collectively. The intelligence that comes from this design is truly the product of a collective effort, although intelligence is a characteristic often attributed to the individual. Furthermore, our semiosic ability is reinforced and shaped with each interaction with the welts. At first sensorium experience (PMS and *Firstness*) the unfiltered reality of the world becomes imbedded with structures needed to organize them. Then, through SMS and TMS, *secondness* and *thirdness*, we become capable of the full management of the newly designed semiosphere. But, let us keep in mind that the process is not "progressive." There is as much *firstness* in the experience of the past as there is *thirdness*. Motivated models such as TMS are influenced by signals that are PMS-based in their origins. The whole lot of universal experiences are the continuous blend of sense, law, and representation. *Thirdness* is no more escapable than is *firstness* and vice-versa.

Our evolutionary pathway erupted from the relationships to the *Welts*. What was once "out there" became embodied and represented. It is the experience of the world that allows for representations of it. For these reasons, our semiosic architecture allows us to retrieve, contrast and compare events within the mind. What we can recognize by surveying evolutionary semiotic theory is that it all happened in the world, first.

---

[9] Donald provides a number of examples where the introduction of reading on a person's mind alters the brain's circuitry (Donald 2014: 74). Cognitive architecture participates, in what I consider, a process of SMS through the acquisition of new signs.

So, what does happen when the world is so cleverly removed from representation?

Nature and the Relationship to Environment

Kalevi Kull suggests that "nature can never be supplanted" (Kull 1998: 352). In providing a very clear and poetic escalation of the Natures, Kull's Eco-semiotics[10] describe a semiotic ecology where human culture is brought into relation with internal and external natures and processes of interpretation are "imbedded in the semiosphere" (Kull 1998: 349). Slightly contrary to the anthroposemiotic belief that *homo culturalis* is best situated to interpret the signs of the semiosphere, Kull suggests that the semiotic animal, through metasemiosis, is capable of understanding *the how* of the modeling of the world by breaking through a dualistic interpretation of it. By not being espoused to the singular belief that culture is the mesh through which interpretation happens (although semiosis is highly informed by it) an evolutionary triadism through which all that is now interpretative can be and is formed. This is supported by Deely's proposal that nature exists in an autonomous yet related state to culture, and that culture relies on its environment. The relationship of environment to the building of representational forms is the panacea of all evolutionary semiotics (regardless of their separate epithets, i.e., anthropo, bio, eco, zoo, etc.)

Pursuant to this, Kull stresses that in living with nature (which is how culture is produced) is how a second nature is created replacing the first. To wit, Kull provides a breakdown of our relationship to nature, by suggesting that "Zero Nature" is "what we think outside the *Umwelt*" (Kull 1998: 355) and therefore "zero nature is nature itself." Nature is thus perceived first. Second is produced nature, the one that is interpreted; and third is a virtual nature (Kull 1998: 355). First nature onwards is thus filtered through human semiosis. Third nature, as it should be understood, is the image based on the image, it is purely virtual and is only mediated by previous forms of representation. It is safe to suggest that it is the furthest removed from "nature" itself and can be considered "postmodern". In summary (Kull 1998: 357):

0 Nature	Nature from Nature
1 Nature	Image from Nature
2 Nature	Nature from Image
3 Nature	Image from Image

---

[10] Kull proposes ecosemiotics as a part of semiotics of culture where biosemiotics would be different from the cultural semiotic field, but both survey from a semiotic lens (Kull 1998: 351).

The forms of representation are all interconnected. As Kull states, the semiotic ecology depends on this interconnectedness. Interestingly, as stated in the above table, the relationship between sign and object and representation in 3rd degree nature is removed so that the sign is a representation for another sign within the sign ecology construction. The relationship to nature is therefore only in the proposed diachrony of the sign itself.

As we move further and further along within a highly overmediated 3rd degree nature, to borrow Kull's terminology, the notion of grounded evolutionary semiotic fitness will have to shift from a co-relation with the *Welts* towards a more individually appreciated, albeit designed by the collective, representational experience that is not connected to the environment. This suggests that experiences that are mediated by a new *Welt*—one designed as a reflection of previous natures—will supplant the need of an original nature. These new *Welts* are not so new. They are, of course, the signs experienced through screens and the interactions grounded in a non-corporeal, disembodied interactions. They are atemporal and aspatial to best satisfy separateness and individuality. As such, they erode memory, physical and collective experience.

I should take the opportunity here to underline that our semiotic fitness includes the full embodied engagement of interpreting signs and that this function, although possibly exapted to another, would bring about a remarkably different form of our original state: the semiotic animal. After all, the most important element at stake here for the semiotic animal is not so much its *semiotiness*, but rather its *animalness*. If we have spoken of biosemiotics at all it is singularly because we share the semiosphere with all other species.

Epigenetic Fakeness and the Bloated Sign

As semiosic systems and the modeling of experience commence from the "*sensible* properties of things" (Danesi and Perron 1999: 70) that are then representational, we ask what might happen when the world is no longer a modeling of early sensory experiences, but always the experience of tertiary modeling systems (TMS)?[11] For the most part, we would say "fine" as it is the heightened result of our semiosic capacity. Donald argues, however, that the interfacing of over-mediated signs has an immediate impact on the mind. Direct and constant restructuring of the mind, already hyper-plastic, could result in an insurgence of contra-individuation and practiced reorganization

---

[11] It should be noted that many would argue that since the capacity to use and produce language, this has been the case.

of important cognitive abilities.[12] Our individual capacity to rememorate and organize signs is what allowed for the more complex ability to do so at a collective level. Hence, grounded sensory experiences are meshed in with all other levels of experience. Exterior forms of representation should not come and supplant the verifiably very animal engagement with the world that makes us unique in our semiosic properties. To have a purely mediated sign world would arguably change our semiotic fitness, but would significantly attenuate our animal side, the one that allows for such wonderful captivating systems of representation that strike home the most.

Our fitness depends on the ability to flexibly take on a wider and growing landscape of signification and a willingness to externally store it. We can still experience signs in all manner of ways, through different channels of experience, regardless if they come from "real" or "fake" environments. Epigenetic fakeness might allow us to continue being *homo culturalis* since for the most part we have been interacting with signs that slip and shift, that are interpretable and personal, cultural and tangible, for a long time. Signs have always been negotiable and malleable. The world on which the play of musement happens is "real" and is shared with other sensible (and sensitive) species, including our own. This should not be forgotten in this age of epigenetic fakeness and bloated signs. The world is still out there.

References

ALLOTT, Robin.
   1991.   "The Motor Theory of Language", *Studies in Language Origins* 2, 123–157.
   1994.   "Language and the Origin of Semiosis", in *Origin of Semiosis: Sign Evolution in Nature and Culture*, ed. Winfried Nöth (Berlin: Mouton de Grutyer).
   2001.   "Language and Evolution", in *The Origin of Language: The General Problem*, bit.ly/2c60mW9.

ANDRADE, Eugenio.
   2007.   "A Semiotic Framework for Evolutionary and Developmental Biology", *BioSystems* 90, 389–404.
            doi: https://doi.org/10.1016/j.biosystems.2006.10.003

BARBIERI, Marcello.
   2008.   "Three Types of Semiosis", *Biosemiotics* 2, 19–30.

---

[12] In his article "The Digital Era", Donald explains the need for proper governance of the internet in an effort to preserve independence and cultural co-existence in a favourable way.

BRANDT, Line, and Per Aege BRANDT.
  2005. "Cognitive Poetics and Imagery", *European Journal of English Studies* 9.2, 117–130. doi: https://doi.org/10.1016/j.pragma.2004.10.019
  2005a. "Mental Spaces and Cognitive Semantics: A Critical Comment", *Journal of Pragmatics* 37, 1578–1595.
    doi: https://doi.org/10.1016/j.pragma.2004.10.019

BRIER, Søren, and Cliff JOSLYN.
  2012. "What Does it Take to Produce Interpretation? Informational, Peircean and Code-Semiotic Views on Biosemiotics", *Biosemiotics* 6, 143–159.

DANESI, Marcel, and Paul PERRON.
  1999. *Analyzing Cultures: An Introduction and Handbook* (Bloomington: Indiana University Press).

DANESI, Marcel, and Stéphanie WALSH MATTHEWS.
  2015. "La Valeur dans la métaphore conceptuelle", *Valeur en Sémiotique*, 165–178.

DEELY, John.
  1990. *Basics of Semiotics* (Bloomington: Indiana University Press).
  2010. *Semiotic Animal: A Postmodern Definition of Human being Transcending Patriarchy and Feminism* (South Bend, IN: St. Augustine's Press).
  2010a. *Semiotics Seen Synchronically: A View from 2010* (Ottawa, ON: Legas.)

DONALD, Merlin.
  2014. "The Digital Era: Challenges for the Modern Mind", *CADMUS* 2.2, 68–79.

KULL, Kalevi.
  1998. "Semiotic Ecology: Different Natures in the Semiosphere", *Sign Systems Studies* 26, 344–371.

MARAN, Timo, and Karel KLEISNER.
  2010. "Towards an Evolutionary Biosemiotics: Semiotic Selection and Semiotic Co-option", *Biosemiotics* 3, 189–200.
    doi: https://doi.org/10.1007/s12304-010-9087-8

NÖTH, Winfried.
  1990. *Handbook of Semiotics* (Bloomington: Indiana University Press), enlarged trans. of *Handbuch der Semiotik* (Stuggart: J.B. Metzlersche Verlagsbuchhandlung, 1985).

O'NEILL, Shaleph.
  2008. *Interactive Media: the Semiotics of Embodied Interaction* (London: Springer-Verlag London Limited).

SEBEOK, Thomas A.
  1981. *The Play of Musement* (Bloomington: Indiana University Press).

SEBEOK, Thomas A., and Marcel DANESI.

    2000.   *The Forms of Meaning: Modeling Systems Theory and Semiotic Analysis* (Berlin: Walter de Grutyer).

TARASSOV, Valery.

    1998.   "Evolutionary Semiotics: Towards Agent-Based Semiosis", paper presented at the 1998 IEEE (Gaithersburg, Maryland), 605–609.

TURNER, J. Scott.

    2016.   "Semiotics of a Superorganism", *Biosemiotics* 9, 85–102.
        doi: https://doi.org/10.1007/s12304-016-9256-5

WHEELER, Wendy.

    2008.   "'Do Not Block the Path of Inquiry!' Peircean Abduction, the Tacit Dimension, and Biosemiotic Creativity in Nature and Culture", *The American Journal of Semiotics* 24.1–3.
        doi: https://doi.org/10.5840/ajs2008241/312

Teresa of Avila as Paradox of 'Perfection' across the Centuries: A Classic Case for Redefining the Human Being as Semiotic Animal[1]

Brooke Williams Deely

University of St. Thomas

Abstract: This essay explores new terrain in our era: Does the redefining of the human being as the "semiotic animal" have the potential to offer a point of departure historically by transcending in terminology—rather than replicating—long prevailing yet paradoxical philosophical dualisms such as rational/non-rational; culture/nature; public/private; active/passive; contemplation/action? As a historian I will put the definition of "semiotic animal" to the test in the laboratory of human experience, as illustrated by Teresa of Avila. Questions arise such as: Does this redefining of the human being as "semiotic animal" for the first time ontologically integrate the rational mode of knowing and the contemplative mode of knowing through love? Does the new definition thereby also intrinsically transcend those philosophical presuppositions deeply embedded in the older definitions of the human being as "rational animal" animal and "thinking thing" that privileged man *qua* male as more perfect than woman *qua* woman? Does the "semiotic animal", furthermore, deepen understanding of the human being as a *relational* being who is part of nature, thereby bearing ethical responsibility to nature as a whole?

Keywords: Teresa of Avila, semioethics, epistemology, mysticism, experience, gender

This definition of human being as a "semiotic animal" can help us in women's studies, and enlightens the case of Teresa with a new light.

Marie José Pérez, O.C.D.,[2] Carmelite monastery, Puzol, Spain

---

[1] Editor's Note: This monograph has been previously published in the SSA Yearbook, *Semiotics 2014.*

[2] From a letter to me (January 15, 2010). The initials "O.C.D." stand for "Order of Carmelites Discalced", the branch of the Carmelite Order reformed by Teresa and John of the Cross.

ISSN 0277-7126

doi: 10.5840/ajs2016321/43

The American Journal of Semiotics 32.1–4 (2016), 219–254.

Introduction

Why Redefine Human Being?

As the first historian to join the Semiotic Society of America, in 1978, I reflect on the new relevance across the centuries of Teresa of Avila as a classic paradox, one that illuminates a question transcending any one field of study, of how better to define the human being than heretofore in history. In what ways does "semiotic animal" indeed transcend the older definitions of the human being—the medieval "rational animal" and the modern "thinking thing"—both of which the postmodern era challenges as dualist? How do we move beyond this dilemma, as illuminated by the case study of Teresa not only within the terrain of women's studies, but in the wider vista of semiotics, as the study of the being and action of signs?

These questions are so interrelated that my reflections in exploring this ground move back and forth toward further mapping this terrain. I hope that, as qualitative research in "illuminating understanding" for further exploration (Shank, Brown, Pringle 2014: 30), the classic case study of Teresa can potentially open new avenues of research, whatever be one's particular cultural tradition or discipline.

Teresa's universal appeal across cultures is that she ventured to explore the mysterious depths of her own soul as a human being. In this sense, in drawing deeply from her own religious tradition in order to realize her potential as a human being, she transcended, by way of paradox, some inherited practices and values of her particular culture and thereby helped over time to transform it, by drawing on a universal human experience of mystical contemplation.

Before further exploration, I marvel at the mystery of human history as itself paradoxical. Who among us can explain it? Teresa speaks today, with the highest teaching authority of her own Roman Catholic tradition, as a "doctor of the universal church". Pope Paul VI, in 1970, proclaimed her so during debates as to whether woman, inasmuch as she is not embodied as man, could be so declared. The Pope's historic proclamation ended all debate. In 2015 the Church now globally celebrates the 5th centennial anniversary of the birth of this *Doctor Ecclesiae*.

1: Philosophical Context

Classification of "Mystical Contemplation"

In such a long-range view of past thought—in dynamic relation to the future development of thought—I explore with you how the life of Teresa, as a shining star within and beyond her own tradition as a Carmelite nun, exemplifies a two-fold paradox in bringing into play, as both a *woman* and as a *contemplative*, the mystical experience of transcendent love. Such experience is inaccessible to the human finite intellect and surely transcends gender, even though experience is always that of a gendered subject. "Learned men" during the Spanish Inquisition roped off mystical contemplation as dangerous territory, especially for women, as we will see.

To classify contemplation *philosophically* I turn directly to the great philosopher Jacques Maritain, also a figure in semiotics, whose work and life I have deeply pondered, also in relation to women's studies.[3] "There is no question", Maritain claimed, "but that mystical experience is absolutely independent of philosophy and gets along marvelously without it; and it is not among philosophers that great contemplatives are ordinarily found". As a philosopher with the soul of a contemplative and an artist, he drew from both Thomas Aquinas and from the lived contemplative experience itself of Teresa and John of the Cross, and from his lived experience of the Benedictine tradition. In relation to the Poinsot/Locke/Peirce philosophical tradition in semiotics, he lauds (1958: 74–75) Charles Sanders Pierce as great philosopher and says that John Poinsot,[4] especially, inspired his own work as a "dearly loved master" across the centuries (1958: 151–152).

Now in order to address a gap in semiotic research—how the nature of mystical contemplation is foundational to the quite speculative question of how we define the human being—I draw upon Maritain, for good reason, on the question of how to classify contemplation in the developing doctrine of signs. As a philosopher, he ventured into the theological domain of mystical contemplation but tells us—speaking as a philosopher—when he does so and why. Maritain had pondered not only Poinsot's *Treatise on Signs* but also his treatise (*De Donis Spiritus Sancti*, 1645, translated into French by Maritain's wife Raïssa) on mystical contemplation. John Deely, strictly as a philosopher, has stayed clear of this latter treatise. Yet here is ground to be explored in semiotics—a treatise on mystical contemplation written by a founder of the philosophical tradition in semiotics.

Suffice it to say, for the purpose of precision in my own research questions here, that Maritain (1932: 286, 349–350) classified the experience of contemplation as "suprarational" in that it is *above* nature, *above* reason,

---

[3] For Maritain's philosophy of history in relation to contemplation, see my book under Brooke Williams Smith (now Williams Deely), 1976: 82–85; 136–158; see also Williams Deely 1979: 28–35; 2013: 3–19; for the relation of Maritain's thought to feminism and semiotics see Williams Deely 1981.

[4] Maritain called Poinsot by his religious name, John of St. Thomas.

but not *outside* of nature, *outside* of reason, and as the "highest degree of knowledge". So I will refer to such contemplation precisely as a *suprarational* mode of knowing.[5]

Maritain would dismiss any thinker who would seek to understand the nature of such "contemplation", which is inaccessible to the intellect, without giving full credence to the testimony of what the mystics themselves say they experience. He minces no words in saying that (1959: 288) it is "a scandal to the intellect … to see psychologists and sociologists—or even philosophers and metaphysicians—lay hands on mystical experience in order to judge its nature by their own light, that is to say, systematically to misunderstand it". We can appreciate all the more Teresa's own lived experience during the Spanish Inquisition!

Within Teresa's own faith-based tradition, such a mode of knowing is grounded in union with divine love, rather than the knowing in the "human mode which proceeds according to the rule of reason" (ibid.). Maritain thus adheres to the view of John of the Cross in saying that such contemplation is an experiential, ineffable knowledge wherein the human mode of knowing must be renounced in that contemplation is "a ray of darkness for the intellect", a "night" in which the soul dispossesses itself of distinct ideas and formulated knowledge, and passes "beyond and above" the human mode of concepts to experience supreme knowledge. Maritain (1932: 349) borrows from John of the Cross in clarifying that so dispossessed one can say in truth: "*I was reduced to nothing and I knew no more. Beyond knowing? That is to say in love; in love transilluminated by the Spirit; compenetrated by intelligence and wisdom. For now my exercise is in loving alone.*"

Maritain further clarifies his use of the words "mystic" and "contemplation" (1940: 188) because of their misleading connotations. By mystic he does not mean to evoke "a procession of phenomena, ecstasies, and extraordinary gifts." Nor does he intend to connote the Greek notion of the contemplation of philosophers, whose end is intellectual knowledge. Contemplation, as he uses it, seeks to know God through the union with God in love.

Teresa as Paradox

My reflections take a "transcendent turn" in that I suggest there is a pressing need, in developing discourse in global semiotics, to classify this "suprarational" mode of knowing as a quintessentially human experience, therefore as integral to the terminological redefining of human being as "semiotic animal",

---

[5] For a definitive exposition see the Second Part of Maritain 1932: Chaps. VI–IX, 247–383.

rather than as screened out as in "rational animal" or "thinking thing". Hence it seems to me that the defining of the human being itself falls in the *speculative* dimension of the doctrine of signs. To relegate contemplation simply to the *practical* dimension, as derivative from the speculative dimension, misses the point that contemplation as the experience *itself* of suprarational love is a form of human knowledge *for its own sake*, prior to its overflow into the practical dimension. The contemplative mode of knowing, thus, *exceeds* the practical dimension of the doctrine of signs, while at the same time infusing it with wisdom: the definition "semiotic animal" begins to take on a life of its own more vitally *relational* than obtains in medieval and modern definitions of human being.

As Maritain would have it, I base my reflections on actual human *experience*, in the laboratory of human experience that Teresa represents (whether a given person's experience of the mystery of divine love be ordinary, extraordinary, or extraordinarily ordinary) as a unique human being acting in time as a human subject. Such lived experience itself, in my view, is integral to the redefining of human being.

Teresa herself sheds light on the paradox, first of all, as a woman who experienced the dire consequences of her presupposed lesser perfection in rationality, due to her embodiment as a woman. Philosophically challenging such a paradox lay in the far future of her lived presence in culture. Yet such a potential was there during her own lifetime, when, in her last words, she died "as a daughter of the Church" (Walsh 1943: 579). Her autograph copy of the book of her *Life*, which she wrote under obedience, was still in the hands of the Spanish Inquisition. She herself had never feared whatever be the outcome, even though a postmodern biographer (Gross 1993: 134) with good reason tells us: "I cannot but tremble at the thought of saying something about the status of women in Spain's Golden Age". From the vantage point of our era, we more clearly see the now famous paradox that Teresa suffered, especially as a woman, in her own time and place.

Her renowned translator in our era, Kieran Kavanaugh, O.C.D. (1980: 22–23), alerts the reader to patriarchal assumptions of her time, traceable to Aristotle and transmitted by the scholastics, in defining woman as generally less rational—hence less sound in judgment—than man.[6] Kavanaugh points out the dire consequences for women, given such a deeply rooted sign system. He also avers (1976: 28) that Teresa, in the specific context of her own time (wherein the Inquisition found suspicious whatever they deemed

---

[6] For an interpretative overview of this sign system, see the monumental work of philosopher Sr. Prudence Allen, R.S.M. (1985; 2002), third volume forthcoming.

as exaggerated or questionable forms of mystical experience) was the living presence of a "sign of contradiction". She struggled through her experience by reconciling "aspects of truth" in what might be termed her "reasonableness" in working with her own tradition, wherein she exemplified wisdom as the highest gift of divine love, as grounded in her dynamic integration of faith and reason.

In several essays in semiotics, I have addressed the relation of contemplation to developing feminist thought.[7] Here I explore further the need to see Teresa as such a "sign of contradiction", or paradox, not only in relation to female gender identity but in relation to contemplative experience itself as grounded in the suprarational way of knowing through love. These two senses of paradox, both in relation to woman and in relation to contemplative experience as transcending gender, are distinct but not separate: they need to be seen in *relation* one to the other in redefining the human being as "semiotic animal".

I presuppose Teresa's experience itself of mystical contemplation. In our postmodern era Kavanaugh's own introductions, as editor and translator of her complete works, as well as his hand in study guides on her,[8] introduce the reader to this subject as a critical frame of reference for further development of this vast inquiry across the centuries. My own task is simply to reflect on "where to go from here" in relation to my specific research question on why we need to integrate such contemplative experience in redefining human being as semiotic animal, given that the contemplative mode of knowing itself, as beyond discursive reasoning, is a suprarational mode of knowing experienced by human beings across gender and any given tradition. Hence, I argue that if anyone can shed new light on our understanding as to why redefine the human being human as "semiotic animal", it is Teresa herself.

My focus is thus on two senses of paradox. In the first sense of the paradox, I ponder how Teresa exemplifies, in her own words about her own experience, what it is to be a human being as irreducible simply to embodiment as a man or as a woman. Let me clarify that I am affirming, as well, her embodiment as a woman who remarkably exemplified femininity. That is not my own question. I am asking, rather: was this "self-actualized" human being really "less rational"—as a woman—than the learned men of her time, simply because

---

[7] See Williams Deely 1999; 2001; 2008; 2011. On this topic see also the Roberta Kevelson Award Essay, by Lauren Larson 2001, written under my direction at the University of St. Thomas, Houston.

[8] See, for example, Kavanaugh et al. 2010; and Alvarez 2011 provides a comprehensive overview of Teresa's life and work.

she experienced spiritual ecstasy of transcendent love, as well as wrote what we now consider great spiritual masterpieces of all time?

In the second sense of paradox, I explore new ground that renders the contemplative tradition *itself* as paradoxical in defining the human being as either rational animal or thinking thing. The question becomes: was Teresa— as test case—really less rational than, say, St. Augustine or St. Thomas Aquinas? Surely she was excluded, as a woman, from the scholastic schools of her time. Kavanaugh (2000: 115) gets straight to the point, in his laconic way of speaking: "Syllogisms were not her cup of tea", yet she evidences "a surprising logic and consistency", which "underlies" her writing, however at first seemingly "scattered" her thoughts may appear to be. Indeed, "through experience and questioning she got to know more about prayer probably than all the great theologians of her time".

I first reflect on a few episodes in Teresa's life that illustrate the paradox she represents within patriarchal and feminist (modern and postmodern) interpretative frameworks—as a paradox that sheds further light on the paradox of contemplative experience within the frameworks of older definitions of human being.

II: Teresa's Own Experience as Illustrative of the Paradox

Flight from Her Father?

Teresa's seemingly paradoxical "docility" and "determination", as I call the dynamic tension she exemplified both as a woman and as a human being, worked in complementary tandem throughout her life. I begin with her fleeing the home of her father (her mother had died some years before) to enter religious life, probably at age twenty. With her absolute resolution, she had stood up to her father to enter religious life. Devout as he was, he loved her greatly and opposed the idea, no matter who interceded for her.

As Teresa put it, "The most we could get from him was that after his death I could do whatever I wanted" (1565: 3:63). She was a dutiful daughter who greatly loved her father, so she was in a double-bind, or impasse, given her determination to follow her vocation in spite of the deep historical roots that sanctioned the headship of man. How could Teresa uproot the presupposition, for instance, in Gratian's codification of canon law: "Thus, it appears most evident that man is so much the head of the woman that she may not offer herself to God by any vow of abstinence or religious life without his permission." (Gratian c.1140: columns 1255–1256).

We know that Church authorities, including Augustine, had concurred with Aristotle that woman was the same species as human, given that she too was a rational animal. So was Teresa free to disobey her father by following her vocation as a nun? Her only defect was that she was less rational than man. At the same time she was fully human as a spiritualized animal,[9] and hence responsible for how she exercised her free will, right? Surely her "defect" would be perfected in eternity—as my Dominican friend Benedict Ashley used to reassure me.

Back to Gratian, whom I cite as a synecdoche for my reasoning why we need redefine human in a way that integrates as foundational to humanity contemplative experience, which springs so many surprises—seeming paradoxes—in transcending patriarchy and feminism in actual human experience. I reflect that for Teresa this world is merely passing, whereas eternity is forever. Should she wait for eternity to consent to the highest good of her inner vocation, or should she wait for her father, as ruling over her in this temporal order, to die first? The question that Teresa faced—even if subconsciously—was whether, like the Virgin Mary, she could directly consent to her vocation without the permission of male authority. Gratian himself had predicated his codification of canon law, in the case at hand, on the medieval distinction that, as a *female* human being per se, unlike a *male* human being per se, "woman is not created in the image of God."

A Carmelite nun in my 1994 course, "Gender Trap", challenged the English translation: "Did Gratian really say that? I want to see the Latin text!" Ah! I asked Fr. Ashley for the Latin text, which he sent in time for the next class meeting, with his short hand-written comment to the effect that some women were entering convents to escape male rule—hence the canon law. I handed out to my postmodern students the Latin text (as well as Fr. Ashley's comment): "*Mulier debet uelare caput, quia non est imago Dei*" (Gratian c.1140: 1255, column A), correctly translated in English as "woman is not created in the image of God".

Without male permission, shaking in her boots, so to speak, Teresa courageously ran away from her father to the Carmelite convent. Alas, the Mother Prioress refused to admit her without her father's consent. When her father saw her true determination, he gave his consent. She tells us that this victory was not without pain. She felt the separation from her father "so keenly that the feeling would not be greater, I think, when I die. For it seemed to me that every bone in my body was being sundered" (1565: 4:64).

---

[9] In contrast to the traditionally common designation of "embodied spirit": see Deely 2010.

No one noticed her struggle for detachment, and everyone thought she was pleased. And as soon as she took the habit, she experienced great happiness from then on at being in the religious life. When she would recall this joy, she tells us (1565: 4:64–65):

> there is no task that could be presented to me, no matter how hard, that I would hesitate to undertake. For I have already experienced in many ways that if I strive at the outset with determination to do it, even in this life His Majesty pays the soul in such ways that only the one who has this joy understands it.

Such was her human experience, as grounded in contemplative experience of hearing her own inner voice in acting as a human subject.

In reflecting on her "struggle for detachment", I point out that Teresa remained close in heart to her father to his dying day. Her vocation was distinct from her affection. Over her lifetime, she stands out for her warm, caring relationships with others; at the same time, she knew when to detach herself from relationships in the world that distracted her from her focus on her contemplative vocation, as centered in her dynamic personal experience with Jesus Christ as her nurturing source of wisdom, as her friend, relative, and spouse. Daniel Chowning, O.C.D. (2007: 56) emphasizes that such experience was "no abstract idea" but rather an encounter of a live friendship that eventually 'liberated" Teresa from undo dependency on others in seeking "a love that no human being can possibly give to another". Consequently, he concludes (2007: 56): "Teresa loved more freely, generously, without making excessive demands on others, realizing that ultimate satisfaction of heart is found only in God".

Thus, as sociable by nature as she was, she found what she herself termed a "detachment" from creatures indispensable to contemplative life. At the same time, I further reflect, she personified spiritual motherhood in its relational aspect of self-giving to others, while taking to heart the virtue of detachment from others precisely in order to receive God's love for her as the *source* of love that overflows into mutual relationships.

By such "detachment", Teresa thereby experienced such love as irreducible to a being simply in relation to others, as, for example, in the relations of wife, mother, or prioress, as a woman who is defined—in the abstract—as a rational animal who is a "relative being" in the anthropological category as "other" than (and inferior to) man. Her receptivity to God's love, as the source of her inner identity in her own lived experience eventually became the source not only of her extraordinary action in the world in founding monasteries and in writing spiritual masterpieces, but also the source of her mutual spiritual friendships. That is, her contemplative experience itself clarifies the distinction to be made between human altruism grounded in receptivity to divine love, which overflows into relation to others, and attachment to creatures per se as the primary source of love.

As she herself emphasizes in her *Way of Perfection* (1566: 8:71), in the dynamic relation between love, detachment, and humility, Teresa singles out detachment as embracing the other virtues as well: "Detachment, if it is practiced with perfection, includes everything". So also did her companion in monastic reform St. John of the Cross practice such detachment, while exemplifying spiritual fatherhood in the most nurturing sense, all his life, in his care of others, and he was also a man of action. He dug in the mud, and an aqueduct he designed still stands.

Building upon such knowledge, the further question underlying my own reflections remains to be explored in semiotic context: Was Teresa more rational or less rational than John? How measure that criterion for a "rational animal"? Or were they both nut cases—since neither considered the rational mode of knowing as itself the highest degree of knowledge, compared to the unknowing mode of knowing through love? What a paradox for both a medieval "rational animal" and a modern "thinking thing"! Indeed, the presupposed dualism of action/contemplation is itself paradoxical, in male-dominant discourse, in privileging as the highest mode of knowing the presupposed female side of the dualism, whereas the relation between action and contemplation, in such experience, is an integral one that transcends both patriarchy and feminism (in its multiple forms), while at the same time embracing embodiment of sex differentiation.

We encounter in Teresa good grounds for why modern secular feminists sometimes spoke of developing feminist consciousness as a "spiritual journey", whereby a woman could hear her own voice within, beyond that of male-identified dominant discourse. Both women and men, in every walk of life, across given traditions, say they learn from Teresa about human "wholeness". Surely such experience is beyond the boundaries of prevailing binary logic.

State of Her Soul?

Next let's stretch our historical consciousness regarding the state of Teresa's soul, as a woman, after her mystical life began when she was about forty. A burning question arose among spiritual and learned men she had consulted in her docility to her faith tradition. Not all spiritual men had kept confidences, so Teresa's extraordinary experiences were the talk of the town. Teresa had first consulted spiritual men who were terribly disconcerted as to what to think.

So she herself began to fear, given that, in all humility, she claimed no absolute certainty about the source of her direct experience. She wanted to distinguish between the workings of her own mind, wherein the "devil" (in the language of the time) might play tricks on her, and the work of God. In any case, her own critical self-reflection and detachment from her immediate experience came into play, and she never presumed she knew the answers to such questions. She thought it possible her prayer of quiet and of union might indeed be a "great illusion", and so she played safe through consultation, to put her experience to the test of informed inquirers, spiritual and learned men within her tradition. In the words of theologian Rowan Williams (1991: 149), "Teresa is not inclined to use her experience as evidence for what the universe is." Her mystical states are not a "paradigm of certainty", but rather have "authority only within a frame of reference which is believed on quite other grounds", given consistency with her specific religious tradition.

One of these men she so relied on, Francisco de Salcedo, arranged for her to consult a new authority, known especially for his holiness and learning as a theologian, Pedro Gaspar Daza. He and Salcedo agreed that her faults and imperfections and her favors from God were contradictory. Daza was perplexed. So he asked her to tell him all she could about her prayer. She broke into tears, as she could not express such an interior experience in words. She was failing—both as a rational animal and as a woman—to pass the test. In the words of one biographer (Walsh 1943: 117): "She was suspected by the two most holy people she knew of being the dupe of the devil." In this predicament she asked, with her genuine docility in seeking counsel, if she should give up mental prayer altogether, in order to avoid these dangers.

Spiritual men, having read the book she had written out of obedience— her *Life*—reached a verdict: her experience was of the devil. To make her saga short, she "saw danger everywhere" (1565: 206). At one point a friend and man of much clout in Avila urged that Teresa be exorcised. Her reputation became mud. She tells us that she found this experience excruciatingly distressing. She says, "I did nothing but weep" (1565: 244). Here is a person who, in her duress, identified with the humanity of Jesus, especially in his aloneness and suffering, as central to her spirituality. Constance FitzGerald, O.C.D. emphasizes (1988: 70) that Teresa over time increasingly identified with the "poor, suffering Jesus" for her inner source of affirmation and wisdom, in the face of such condemnation by learned men.

Teresa's predicament illustrates the paradox of defining woman as less rational than man and therefore under his rule. Teresa submitted, yes, to that rule (as did men under obedience), while at the same time increasingly trusting in her experience of the Lord's encouragement, which rendered her situation as a woman so paradoxical. There were enough persecutions she said (1565: 245) to drive her "insane".

She herself recognized the paradox: "For the opposition of good men to a little woman, wretched, weak and fearful like myself, seems to be nothing when described in so few words; yet among the very severe trials I suffered in my life, this was one of the most severe" (1565: 246–247). On the one hand, prayer itself consoled her with "new strength"; on the other hand, she knew that if she "contradicted" the learned men who were judging her spirit such contradiction would make matters worse for her, "since my doing so would appear to them as a lack of humility" (1565: 248)—they had already supposed she presumed to teach them as if she thought herself wise.

Her intention was not to teach but to be teachable—in her docility—in obeying the counsel of learned men, in her determination to follow Christ from within her own tradition. In her predicament God, too, seemed to be absent from her. Instead of consolation, she experienced, in her aloneness, a frightful helplessness. Finally, she heard a divine voice within, which dissipated her fear of the "demons".

My own interpretation (in consonance with FitzGerald 1988) is that Teresa, in her bout with "demons", seems to be experiencing a "dynamic tension" between her inner voice and the dictates of outer authority, wherein, with time, she increasingly integrated her docility and her determination in a holistic way that affirmed her own inner voice. In my view she thereby transcended, as a semiotic animal, both patriarchy and feminism. Inasmuch as she was both reasonable and experienced with contemplative prayer, some learned men in her own day listened to her in order to learn from such experience.

Finally, in 1560, when she was forty-five, a highly reputed Dominican, Pedro Ibáñez, weighed in on her behalf, contending that her visions were from God.

I muse that, in our day, Umberto Eco might write a best-selling novel on Teresa's highly cultivated self-reflexivity in discerning her own experience of visions, since he has shown that mystical contemplation is particularly problematic in its use of symbols (Eco 1982: 165–174). I simply point out that as a semiotic animal Teresa herself ultimately became so detached from her own mystical experience—for its own sake, that is—that she was not troubled further by questions about whether the ultimate source of an experience be "God" or the "devil" or her own "delusion", although she discerned the *effects* of such experience as indexical signs. As a wise human being experienced in the use of her reason, her point is that the purpose of the pure "gift" of contemplation—beyond human effort as a rational mode of knowing—was to bear good fruits of love of God and neighbor: that's all. The mystery remains.

The same can be said of John of the Cross, who was a learned man.

Reformer

At age forty-seven Teresa attempted to found her first Carmelite reform monastery, St. Joseph's, in Avila. She ran into virulent opposition from good Catholics, who saw no reason to found yet another monastery. Determined to fulfill her mission, she nonetheless gracefully—docilely again—let go of her attempt, obeying an order from her Carmelite provincial to go live in Toledo for a while, where she was out of sight and out of mind. With a wise detachment from outcome—an indexical sign of her underlying attitude—she set to work, again under obedience, to write her *Life*.

When the time came to resume founding her monastery, Teresa was under no illusions that she would not face hostile opposition. Indeed, the people of Avila, outraged with her plan, ridiculed her. The persecution of gossip and derision wore heavily on her and her lay woman companion in this innovative venture. It seemed to Teresa that her opponents were "partly right". Wearied, she left the matter to God:

> His Majesty began to console and encourage me. He told me that in this I would see what the saints who had founded religious orders had suffered, that I would have to suffer much more persecution than I could imagine, and that we shouldn't let it bother us. (1565: 282)

Teresa "marveled" at their new-found courage to withstand such opposition.

Then lo! The Carmelite provincial, who had heretofore supported the project, got cold feet in face of all the opposition and withdrew his permission. She tells us that this experience was the greatest trial she suffered during her foundations. Indeed, she says that her moving forward in her plan, given the support of the Bishop of Avila against the will of her superior, was—once again in her experience—like a death to her. Yet her determination saw her through this impasse. Her *determination* likewise encouraged her to resist the temptation to what she herself sometimes calls a "false humility" that could have caused her to back off such action—as only *male*-defined? At the same time, as remarkable as was her determination in this case, when she was under the fire of accusation from the Carmelite Provincial, instead of defending her disobedience, she actually won him over with her *docility* as grounded in her humility—as only *female*-defined?

Paradoxically, her combined determination and docility worked together, once again, in creative, dynamic tension, which so often in her life resulted in her own detachment from outcome—in overcoming roadblocks that at any given moment had seemed impassible. In her own lifetime, who could not resist the provocative question: "Who does she think she is"?

Indeed, to stop her reform effort, a Papal Nuncio, Philip Saga, once commanded her to confinement (some had suggested a prison cell in her monastery). In a favorite quote of mine showcasing the paradox of Teresa as a semiotic animal transcending patriarchy and feminism as limiting linguistic codes, he said (Sega 1577, as quoted in Sackville-West 1953: 85):

> She is a disobedient contumacious woman who promulgates pernicious doctrine under the pretense of devotion; leaves her cloister against the orders of her superiors ... and teaches theology as though she were a doctor [maestro] of the church, in contempt of St. Paul who commanded women not to teach.

Teresa herself, in pondering whether her opponents were right that she should not found monasteries, once wrote that the Lord said to her: "Tell them they shouldn't follow just one part of Scripture but that they should look at other parts, and ask them if they can by chance tie my hands." (1571: 393)

Little did she then know she would be founding throughout Spain fourteen monasteries—amid constant controversy and physical hardships, including her own precarious health—for the rest of her life. Nor did she know she would, between travels, be writing spiritual classics amidst volumes of business letters, into the early hours of the morning.

I reflect that her experience as a reformer does indeed shed new light on the paradox that a future pope surpassed in proclaiming Teresa a doctor of the church. Her own experience as a *contemplative* who also acted in the *public* domain as a *woman* provides an example that no longer presents a philosophical stumbling block in her way of perfection. Such philosophical dualisms as active/passive, public/private, and rational/non-rational become integrated with the shift to "semiotic animal" in that each side of the dualisms, while *distinct*, are no longer *separate*, nor essentially male-defined or female-defined. The new terminology has the potential of thereby deepening human understanding of the paradox of perfection across the centuries that Teresa herself experienced so deeply as a human being in her particular historical situation.

Way of Writing

Up to what point did Teresa put up with the prevailing modelling of the world wherein she as woman fell short of perfection as less rational than man? As a writer of classics in spirituality, wherein Teresa's own voice as a "doctor of the universal church" now also has teaching authority, could it be that, as a feminist literary scholar holds (Weber 1990), Teresa resorted to rhetorical deceit to win her way with the Inquisition? Or could it be, rather, simply that she wrote with the same kind of integrity that we see evidenced in her concern for her state of soul? Could it be she felt inwardly free to write in peace, sometimes even impishly about learned men, given her spontaneous sense of humor? Could it be, then, that she wrote without deception what she herself actually thought? As I interpret her texts, her consciousness truly did transcend patriarchal and feminist interpretive frameworks as useful only up to a point.

During her five years at San Jose, she revised and rewrote her *Life*, in obedience to her Dominican confessor Domingo Bañez, as well as wrote out of obedience, as always, *The Way of Perfection* (1566). Teresa wrote cautiously, it surely seems to me, out of her true humility wherein she realized that she could be mistaken, or at least she seemed unattached to proving herself right. According to Kavanaugh (1976: 27), furthermore, in his most critically informed reading of her, "the Inquisition was not the type of thing that could frighten her". He cites (ibid.) her own response in her *Life* (1565: 128–129) when some cautioned her in their own great fear that she might be accused by the Inquisition:

> This amused me and made me laugh … And I said they shouldn't be afraid of these possible accusations; that it would be pretty bad for my soul if there were something in it of the sort that I should have to fear the Inquisition; that I thought that if I did have something to fear I'd go myself to seek out the Inquisitors.

So she wrote openly about own experience. Although she herself approved of letting her nuns read her *Life*, her confessor forbade that as being too dangerous for women. As generally less rational than men, it would be safer, this confessor said, to throw the manuscript into the fire. At the same time he granted permission for her to write a book instructing her nuns, as they had requested, about prayer and contemplation, given due censorship. Fortunately for us, we have both the original and the revised (censored) manuscripts of the resultant book, *The Way of Perfection*.

Since women in her day were disallowed access to Latin learning, there is no way she could have written like a Latin-age scholar. She challenged learned men on the grounds of her own experience as a unique human being. Granted she knew how to fence with learned men in her own defense, given that, in the words of Gillian Ahlgren (1996: 8): "Teresa managed to overcome many disadvantages imposed on women by teaching herself through voracious reading and entering the male world of spiritual writing through her careful use of language and her skillful handling of opponents". In assimilating the Christian contemplative tradition, Teresa—by virtue of her own experience— intrinsically challenged the long prevailing definition of woman as less sound than man in her judgment, given her presumed lesser rationality. In the face of such devaluation of woman as a rational animal, Teresa stood her ground (1566: 51) in challenging even the public/private dichotomy as male-defined:

> Is it not enough, Lord, that the world has intimidated us ... so that we may not do anything worthwhile for you in public or dare speak some truths that we lament over in secret, without YOUR failing to hear so just a petition? I do not believe, Lord, that this could be true of Your goodness and justice, for you are a just judge and not like those of the world. Since the world's judges are the sons of Adam and all of them men, there is no virtue in women that they do not hold suspect. ... I see that these are times in which it would be wrong to undervalue virtuous and strong souls, even though they are women.

In her revision of *The Way of Perfection*, Teresa dutifully complied with the Dominican censor in deleting this passage, which she nonetheless had written in spite of her critics.

There are passages in Teresa's writings that directly confront the rational mode of discourse of learned men as being inapt to fathom divine mysteries, and that confirm this passage in the classic, *Imitation of Christ* (Thomas à Kempis 1441: 10), which Teresa herself read: "What will it avail thee to be engaged in profound reasonings concerning the Trinity, if thou be void of humility, and art thereby displeasing to the Trinity?" In ordinary matters, too, she says in her Prologue to *The Way of Perfection* (1566: 40), that her "love" for her sisters and her "experience in some monasteries" may help her, in speaking of ordinary things, to be "more successful than learned men". Nonetheless, she insists, in her *Meditations on the Song of Songs* (1575: 1:220), that women ought not to teach and "think they are right" without submitting their work to learned men. Indeed, she makes this point in this very work that one Dominican, Diego de Yanguas, thought highly improper for a woman to write.

In his "Introduction" to this work (1980: 211–12), Kavanaugh tells us that even though Teresa had written this manuscript with the permission of a former confessor, this "frightened" Dominican ordered Teresa and her nuns to burn their copies. She immediately threw her copy into the fire. Other copies exist to this day, however, including one her nuns had dared send away to the Dutchess of Elba, in safe-keeping for the future.

In *The Way of Perfection*, Teresa spoke directly to her nuns in instructing them to use their own judgment—based on their own experience—about this work: "If you find it all wrong, burn it" (1566: 90). She was addressing not the Inquisitors but her own nuns, and she spoke as their founder. Such comments are indicative of her detachment, of her own inner freedom to write the way she sees things, without *undo* deference to the critics.

Surely there are plenty of times she, in writing as a woman, is conscious of her critics. Yet the crux of my question is—as Virginia Woolf once pondered (1929: 106) about the integrity necessary for a great writer—whether Teresa "altered" her "clear vision in deference to external authority", or whether she took the "jump" and delivered what she had to say with "integrity," thereby giving us the "conviction" that "this is the truth"—that she had not "altered her values in deference to the opinion of others" (1929: 106).

Teresa, as a woman, often pens lines that ask for divine help right before she takes that jump. Does she not write in Woolf's poetic sense of the "contemplative" (Woolf 1929: 106) as signifying that "the power to contemplate" is "the power to think for oneself." Woolf (1929: 104) describes this contemplative state of mind thus:

> The whole mind must lie wide open if we are to get the sense that the writer is communicating his experience with perfect fullness. There must be freedom and there must be peace. Not a wheel must grate, not a light glimmer. The curtains must be close drawn. The writer, I thought, once his experience is over, must lie back and let his mind celebrate its nuptials in darkness. He must not look or question what is being done.

Teresa wrote her masterpiece, *Interior Castle* (1577), in the midst of great trials, between travels during her foundations, wherein her painstaking work of the previous fifteen years could now be suppressed because of raging jurisdictional disputes between Madrid and Rome (Kavanaugh 1980: 264). She herself tells us, in the Prologue (1577: 281), how she approached this daunting task:

> Not many things that I have been ordered to do under obedience have been as difficult for me as this present task of writing about prayer. First, it doesn't seem the Lord is giving me either the spirit or the desire to undertake the work. Second, I have been experiencing now for three months such great noise and weakness in my head that I've found it a hardship even to write concerning necessary business matters. But knowing that the strength given by obedience usually lessens the difficulty of things that seem impossible, I resolve to carry out the task willingly, even though my human nature seems greatly distressed.

Because of her ill health and other exhausting duties, she felt "a strong aversion" to this task (1577: 281); so all the more did she depend on God's mercy to "do the work" for her. We should note that she determined at least, in her true humility, to take the step of picking up her pen to write those opening lines. When she finished writing this work, she tells us that it has merit and that she is glad she has written it!

I turn now to her letters. The question arises, in relation to redefining the human being, whether such a lofty contemplative, who experienced levitation, was as reasonable in daily life as a wise man. I have read, ever so slowly a letter or two a day, both thick volumes of her surviving letters (Teresa of Avila i.1547–1577; i.1578–1582), an estimated small fraction of her letters, mostly business letters regarding her founding of so many monasteries.

Kavanaugh had candidly said to me, in 2011 during a friendly walk in Avila: "You have to read her letters—you can't be her friend without reading her letters!" I had thought I was already her friend, having perused his own translation of the first three volumes of her spiritual classics, and I can't recount how many other volumes about her. I followed his lead and found myself reading, in translation, his contemporary American English (thank goodness). I participated in this dialogue across the centuries, wherein Teresa's voice, Kavanaugh's voice as translator, and my inner voice dovetailed in my own experience. I had breathing space as a semiotic animal, in integrating reason and emotion as a good effect of such experience.

Through her letters one can glimpse her *in action, in daily life*, not only as a woman steeped in mystical contemplation. In Teresa's case contemplation and action, as we have seen, went hand in hand going beyond such a presupposed dualism as gender-identified (with action associated with male and contemplation associated with female). Bye-bye to this binary logic. I'm reflecting here on the *relation* between contemplation and action, in my second sense of paradox, inasmuch as redefining human being as "semiotic animal" does cast such a relation in a new light, beyond the boundaries of "rational animal" or "thinking thing".

I'm also impressed with how *reasonably* Teresa instructed learned men in negotiating not only real estate but also overlapping jurisdictions of all sorts. She was at once docile and determined (a sign of contradiction?), even in telling the King of Spain, Philip II, what to do and why. My point is that her letters exemplify the integration of the mode of knowing under the rule of reason and the mode of knowing under the rule of agape love, which worked together in moving her forward on the roads of Spain in founding monasteries.

In a letter to the King Phillip II (who favored her Carmelite reform), for instance, Teresa implored him to intercede on behalf of John of the Cross, who had just been taken prisoner by Carmelite friars deadly opposed to Teresa's reform. No one in Avila knew his whereabouts. "For the love of the Lord," she says at the outset in writing directly to the King: "I beg you to pardon me for so much boldness" (i.1578–1582: 578). Then she makes her plea, first pointing out—for good reason—this captive's saintly reputation in the town, before she adds that in her own "opinion" he is not only a saint but has been one "all his life" (i.1578–1582: 579). Her letter, as usual, explicitly evidences the voice of both reason and love. She points out that the captors—quite to the contrary—evidenced no concern for "what is reasonable" (i.1578–1582: 579), not even in juridical matters. She then expresses her own quite reasonable and loving concern (i.1578–1582: 580) in adding that he is "so weakened from all he has suffered that I fear for his life".

She writes, throughout her prolific correspondence about why, in a given situation, she is "distressed", "distraught", "disturbed", "worried", "anxious", or "fearful", yet with an inner peace. She lives through these emotions in a way that, rather than suppressing nature, surpasses it given her underlying attitude itself of love, detachment, and humility working in an integral way, as she teaches in her book, *Way of Perfection* (1566).

I reflect, in my own spiral of semiosis—which loops back and forth in time[10]—that she wrote numerous surviving letters after this book and also after she had written *Interior Castle* (1577), as an overflow from her own yet further experience of contemplation. This masterpiece guides us through states of soul and transformations leading to the supreme experience of union with God, as far as possible for a finite being still on earth. How did she get there, in her own spiral of semiosis? All she could do was persevere on the way of perfection, no matter what. Was she not human? Surely Teresa's teaching in her earlier book, *The Way of Perfection*, speaks directly from her own experience, as a semiotic animal, of her human emotions. For example, in regard to the key virtue of detachment she tells her nuns (1566: 187), with true humility:

> If it seems that the Lord has already given us virtue, let us understand that actually it has been received and that He can take it away, as in fact often happens, but not without His wonderful providence. Haven't you ever seen this for yourself, Sisters? I have. Sometimes I think I am very detached; and as a matter of fact, when put to the test, I am. At another time I will find myself so attached, and perhaps to things that the day before I would have

---

[10] I have in mind here the intuitive process of getting an idea, then developing it, and testing it against further experience, leading to further ideas, developments, and testings, and so on, making that web of relations we call "experience" over life's course. This dynamic process (abduction: getting ideas; deduction: developing implications of the ideas; retroduction: testing ideas, leading to further ideas, etc.) has come to be known as "the spiral of semiosis": see in particular Deely 2003c: 164, *inter alia*.

made fun of, that I almost don't know myself. At other times I think I have great courage and that I wouldn't turn from anything of service to God; and when put to the test I do have this courage for some things. Another day will come in which I won't find the courage in me to kill even an ant for God if in doing so I'd meet with any opposition. In like manner it seems to me that I don't care at all about things or gossip said about me; and when I'm put to the test this is at times true—indeed I am pleased about what they say. Then there come days in which one word alone distresses me, and I would want to leave the world because it seems everything is a bother to me. And I am not alone in this. I have noticed it in many persons better than I, and know that it happens.

Teresa is indeed a paradox—as both a woman and as a human being—who splendidly fails to fit either the medieval model or the modern model of human perfection in defining her as either a "rational animal" (with the focus on the human intellect) or a "thinking thing" (with the intellect as out of touch with embodiment in nature). Nor was she an "angel", as she herself so well knew in embracing her own humanity, in company with the humanity of Jesus. As Daniel Chowning, O.C.D. (2007: 38) comments: "Her spirituality has no room for an evasion of the body, time, or the present world. She supports all that is human and thus breaks through the Neoplatonism of her time with its distain for the body and material realities".

The underlying question I further explore is: how can we potentially overcome the long-prevailing philosophical paradox that the case of Teresa illuminates—as both a woman and as a contemplative—by our redefining the human being as "semiotic animal"?

III: Philosophically Grounding the Case for Teresa of Avila as "Semiotic Animal"

The Case in Historical Overview

We have already glimpsed how Teresa of Avila is a classic case of paradox against the backdrop of older definitions of human being. We begin to see where we might go in evolving human consciousness that transcends the heretofore male-identified culture/nature dualism, which had devalued *woman* as signifying nature to be dominated, rather than embracing collaborative stewardship for the whole environment of earth, inclusive also of life other than human. Such consciousness needs further philosophical grounding in relation to the two-fold paradox of perfection that Teresa presents.

Teresa was imperfect as a human being in relation to two historical usages of the word "imperfect". The first usage is grounded in the Western intellectual tradition wherein only the male human being is the perfect measure of rationality. The second usage is grounded in Gospel values, wherein all human beings are imperfect in falling short of perfect practice of the theological virtues of faith, hope, and love, as the "way of perfection" (in Teresa's tradition, to be understood here that no one is perfect in this sense of completion, wholeness, and fulfillment, even at death, except the Christ and his mother). Both these meanings of "perfection" need be distinguished in order to move beyond Western dualisms. As a "semiotic animal" Teresa escapes—at long last!—the gender trap wherein also learned men of her time were often enough snared, in the presupposed opposition between the rational mode of knowing and the suprarational mode of knowing by way of love in mystical contemplation.

In the first sense of "imperfect", in my reflecting further on the two-fold nature of the paradox at hand, Teresa was assumed to be "imperfect" precisely as a woman presumed to lack sound judgment, given that, by virtue of her femininity she is not-man. Only male human embodiment signified the perfection of rationality, as distinguished from the less perfect rationality of the female human. As a woman who suffered during the Spanish Inquisition from the dire consequences of this historically laden assumption, she tells us directly just how she suffered from this assumption. She herself sometimes seemingly accepted (was that simply her historical subconscious?) and sometimes explicitly challenged this assumption. She did so sometimes in pain and sometimes in play. Although such playful remarks got censored by learned men for revision, we have the original manuscripts that cast new light today on how she dared speak in her day of her own experience as a human being who was defined as a less-rational animal than "man", as the measure of embodied human perfection. Her lived experience translates in our day as signifying, rather, a semiotic animal beyond such faulty philosophical abstraction.

Surely we need not wait historically until Descartes's modern redefining of the human being as a "thinking thing" to see that discursive reasoning, in discourse across the centuries, is represented most perfectly by the human male. I have reflected that such a concept remains in the historical subconscious in late modern Western thought. Within Teresa's own Roman Catholic tradition, Jacques Maritain tactfully yet boldly attacked this paradox of perfection. He found it necessary first to correct (1967: 154–163) what Aristotle, followed by Aquinas and other doctors of the church, got wrong in conceiving of woman, *qua* woman, as "a man that nature accidentally botched up", as "a man that did not work out", a human who is not man (1967: 154).

Maritain made no attempt to dismiss or to disentangle earlier Catholic tradition in general (or Thomistic tradition in particular) from this erroneous assertion of "male superiority", which, as he put it (1967: 154), "seemed to go so clearly to the heart of the matter, alas, that St. Thomas thought he had to adopt this assertion".

Instead, Maritain (1967: 154) put his finger on the consequence "that in truth man alone corresponds perfectly to the definition of human nature (whose specific difference is to be endowed with intelligence and reason) … whereas woman is ordained to breed". Maritain told us (1967: 161) he was "sorry" for this "basic error that I have set out to attack, and which has played its role in the secular enslavement of women." Of this error both "the Ancients were guilty" and "our most venerable doctors for their part as well." Maritain insists (1967: 154–155) that the notion of "masculinity as the peak of human nature" continues "to exert its power in our subconscious".

Such an entrapped sign system does pinpoint Teresa's own predicament as a putatively less "rational animal" than man. By rejecting outright the deep-rooted error of his own tradition, as a Thomist Maritain established a historic turn away from past mistakes, and helped open the way for Pope John Paul II's own development of a discourse further integrating truly valid perennial truths in Aquinas and the larger Christian tradition. Indeed, as my compendium of Pope John Paul II's thought on women shows (Williams Deely 2014), the pope moved in a new direction, as did Maritain before him, toward transcending both patriarchy and modern feminism (early or late) in their mediations on this problematic sign system.

Remarkably—at the heart of the matter—both Maritain and this pope were profoundly influenced by John of the Cross's spiritual classics as well as by Teresa of Avila's own classics. Moving further into the terrain of mystical contemplation, we see that what got screened out in the older definitions of human as rational animal and thinking thing is *intuitive* knowledge, *especially* knowledge *by way of love*, in our shared humanity, in the receptive contemplative experience itself of divine love as a human subject, which overflows in mutual relation with the other as a subject (whatever be the species).

How best a human being integrates both natural reason and such suprarational experience of love, or, in the context of the most learned men of the Latin Age, both reason and faith as culminating in charity, is still a quest of our own time, wherein redefining human as "semiotic animal" transcends the medieval terminology of the "rational animal" and the modern "thinking thing" alike.

Developing Discourse in Semiotics

The presupposed dualisms of the older definitions of human being disappear—potentially—as the paradigm shifts to a semiotic perspective. We see that although we are not the only animals to use signs, we are the only ones who are aware of our use of signs precisely as signs. Indeed, we in semiotics have duly weighed and considered Thomas Sebeok's own steeped sense of history in his view that, in this respect, humans are unique among other animals here on earth in that we have the linguistic competence to model the world by transmitting and transforming human knowledge over time, in the dynamic relation of nature and culture (Sebeok 1984).[11]

We are beginning to "come to grips", in developing semiotic discourse, with how redefining the human being as "semiotic animal" might help us get beyond the impasse—or paradox—of older definitions of human that are right, at least, in recognizing that there is a difference not simply of degree but of kind separating humans from all other earthly animals. John Deely develops this point, in a novel way, by focusing on the distinctive manner in which human animals are capable of using signs. From this focus derives his term "semiotic animal" as he uses it for the first time in his *Basics of Semiotics* (1990: 1; 24, fn. 7; 124), and as he further develops this usage of "semiotic animal".[12]

After Sebeok, Eugen Baer, philosopher and a former president of the Semiotic Society of America, presented (2001: 3–12) a remarkable philosophical sketch arguing for what he terms "the foundation of the ethics of semiotics". In my essay (Williams Deely 2001: 19–20) that follows in that same volume, I place the problematic use of signs in mystical contemplation within the *speculative* dimension of the developing doctrine of signs and the ethical aspect of contemplation within the *practical* dimension of semiotics.

Susan Petrilli and Augusto Ponzio, in their landmark collaborative work, specified the term "semioethics" (2003) to highlight the relation of "anthroposemiosis" to ethics, as also unique to human beings, in that our evolving consciousness of the consequences of human activity entails an ethical responsibility for the use we make of things. Such responsibility extends to the common good of life on this planet in relation to, and as sustaining, human life itself in its wholeness.

The speculative and practical dimensions of the doctrine of signs are what I'd call "distinct but not separate", given the mediation of both speculative

---

[11] For my comprehensive overview of Sebeok's contribution both to the *semiotics* of history and the *history* of semiotics see Williams Deely 2011: 371–418.

[12] See John Deely 2001: 736–737; 2003: 207–221; 2004; 2005; 2005a; 2005b; 2005c; 2006; 2010. Also Deely, Petrilli, and Ponzio 2005.

and practical knowledge through the *sign*. John Deely has further developed this philosophical grounding itself of semioethics, as stringently derived from anthrosemiosis. He goes so far as to claim (2010: 105) that the contemplative tradition, wherein "care depends upon understanding's seeing of the whole" and follows from that seeing, proves to be the current underlying the overall movement of and development within nature that we call "anthroposemiosis".

My own reflections here remain within the domain of speculative knowledge, in that I seek to advance discourse on John Deely's precise usage of the terminology "semiotic animal" in relation to my particular research question as to why we need redefine human in this way that accounts at once for reason and emotion, as inclusive of the suprarational mode of knowing, in human experience. This terminological vantage point for the first time intrinsically transcends paradoxical philosophical dualisms.

Back to Teresa herself, we have seen that she—as our test case of paradox—so well exemplifies suprarational experience. The task ahead of further developing the usage of "semiotic animal" has the potential of deepening appreciation of such contemplation, thereby philosophically grounding an ethos of love in the very way we symbolize the human being as "semiotic animal". Since language structures our experience and consciousness, this move, in turn, sheds further light on the practical domain of semioethics.

Such an ethos overflows into any given social action, in the practical dimension, such as Teresa's founding of monasteries that welcomed all classes, even convert Jews (who were suspect during the Spanish Inquisition). At the same time, as I have attempted to clarify, this ethos *itself* falls within the speculative dimension of the doctrine of signs and vivifies the practical dimension of action. That is, contemplative experience of the divine source of love (not just any kind of love) as the prior highest degree of knowledge, can truly inform the redefining of human being as semiotic animal, however *imperfect* be the human being as such.

I have now entered into the terrain of the second sense of "imperfect"—as I move from my reflections on the Western intellectual tradition to the contemplative tradition. Perhaps St. Thomas Aquinas himself, in contemplating divine love, also stepped into this realm of unknowing when he commented that, compared to this experience, all his intellectual work was "so much straw". I once pointed out this comment to the great Dominican philosopher and theologian, Benedict Ashley (2012), who, at the age of 97, had just published a co-authored book with John Deely on the relation of reason and faith, *How Science Enriches Theology* (reviewed in Morrissey 2012). Fr. Ashley exclaimed to me in jest: "That was when St. Thomas was having a nervous breakdown!"

Aha! The paradox! I ask: what if we redefine Aquinas as a semiotic animal? Would that definition not better integrate what St. Thomas himself placed as the highest degree of knowledge, the *wisdom of the saints?* The terminology "rational animal", which has privileged the rational mode of knowing (especially in the paradoxical sense of woman defined as less perfect in this respect), gives way to an integral model of human experience embracing both rational and suprarational modes of knowing, thereby no longer visiting upon the definition of human being abstract absolute presuppositions that rule out human experience—in its wholeness. Such wholeness encompasses the relation of suprarational, rational, and emotional.

This dynamic relation (as experienced by the human being as a being in time), is beyond the confines of the finite intellect to fathom, however perfect be the measure of one's rationality. As our case study, Teresa's own suprarational experience transcends the anthroposemiotic mode of concepts, images, and analogy as the means of knowing. Maritain describes such suprarational experience (1922: 61) as "all spiritual" and hence "incomprehensible and ineffable" immediate knowledge of God. How unthinkable! Is that rational? Yet in another sense, he clarifies (1922: 261), the experience is not immediate, because (as we have seen, according to Teresa herself) God is still known "through His effects", as indexical signs. Hence, concepts are silenced but not suppressed, given that the suppression of concepts would be "contrary to the very nature of the intellect". At the same time, distinct concepts are all silent" (1922: 261). The terminology "semiotic animal" is thus all-encompassing for both rational and suprarational modes of knowing—as well as the *relation* between them.

In my second sense of the paradox of "perfection"—in relation to the contemplative tradition—Teresa was the first to say how imperfect she was as a human being, on the "way of perfection" in the imitation of Christ, as she developed, over time, through this the dynamic design of her life. She had a keen self-knowledge of her own imperfection, yet persevered in her attitude of love, detachment, and humility as the Gospel values of her faith-based tradition. Farouk Seif, in speaking of the nature of unfolding paradoxes of life, points out (2014) the "diaphanous interrelationship between the value of perseverance and the idea of design". Indeed, Teresa is a test case of his claim (2014): "To engage in design, one must develop the capacity for perseverance in order to thrive despite all odds in challenging situations".

In living with paradox, Teresa exemplifies the Christian mystical tradition for *both* woman and man, given her scale of values that transcend patriarchy and feminism as counter sign-systems. What is remarkable is her attitude of "perseverance", as in her counsel to her nuns (1566: 32:127) to be "strongly determined to persevere" in prayer as the prerequisite to the way of perfection. She bases her counsel on her own "experience", which is why, as she puts it, "I'm able to say, and do say, that no one knows how important determination is". Kavanaugh (1987: 46) clarifies that she had the freedom of spirit that comes with detachment from consolation, such as she practiced in her "persevering" prayer so as "to receive what God gives". Indeed, such *receptivity* is foundational to her Gospel-inspired way of perfection. Yes, paradoxically in linguistic expression, this "womanly" woman expected her nuns to be "manly" in their perseverance!

Thus both senses of the word "perfection", across the centuries—woman as deficient by gender, and human imperfection per se—illuminate a "paradox" that opens a new vista of research in relation to the underlying question of why redefine the human being as "semiotic animal". Without syllogisms, mystical experience itself, as a form of human knowing through love that is a ray of darkness to discursive reason, knocks the socks off the older definitions of "human" that privilege natural reason alone, and man *qua* male, as its highest perfection. We have, in the laboratory of actual human experience, the ultimate testing ground of the paradox of defining the human being as either "rational animal" or "thinking thing". We can see the vantage point of the semiotic perspective of "semiotic animal".

In such a laboratory of human experience, not only a woman, such as Teresa, followed the way of perfection of mystical contemplation, but so also did a man, her learned companion in her reform movement within the Carmelite order, St. John of the Cross, whom Teresa was unable to find and free after his capture. Secretly imprisoned and flogged for almost nine months, he composed some of the greatest poetry in the Golden Age of Spain, expressing in words his own experience of mystical contemplation, which he teaches as beyond the ineptness of words. Now he too is a doctor of the church, as is Teresa: such is the mystery of history.

Not only was John a great poet, but also a learned commentator on his experience of mystical experience as expressed in his poetry. So he used discursive reasoning in his explanation of the mystical, even though mystical experience itself, by its very nature, goes beyond all symbolic representation, or linguistic concepts, as he himself so aptly clarifies.

I muse what Farouk Seif, as artist and architect, might say, further, in shedding light on this crux of the question of paradox in relation to Design as a creative act. After all, the poet and the artist both draw from the preconscious of the intellect. Let me distinguish here the experience of the poet and the artist who progresses toward the Word (verbal or non-verbal), and the mystic, who, as Maritain says (1968: 19) "tends toward silence", which is the highest of all values:

> The fact is that when the poet passes from the state of poetic withdrawal, to the source of images and forms, to the mystical sleep, images and forms are lost, drunk up by the sea. The poet has perhaps lost his poem, but in the absolute scale of values this is an inestimable gain.

Given both the creative power of the word in structuring consciousness and such contemplative experience of the silencing of the intellect, if we define the human being as semiotic animal we gain yet further insight in distinguishing between the signs we use and the realities they signify.

For instance, mystical language has traditionally used sexual imagery to signify the passivity or receptivity of the soul—as irreducible to gender—in the union of the soul with divine love, as human participation in divinity. This experience itself is captive neither to sexuality nor to language. John of the Cross speaks of the soul as feminine, in a way wherein the contemplative tradition transforms male-dominant discourse in its privileging of the male side of the dualism of active/passive. A promising new insight, in my view, would be to challenge the connotation of "receptivity" (or passivity) as essentially female-defined, as opposed to "action" as essentially male-defined, which the case of both Teresa and John illuminates.

Consequently, redefining the human being as "semiotic animal" potentially calls for a deepened understanding of the values of the contemplative tradition. Teresa and John of the Cross point to the heart of the matter in our redefining the human being in terminology that transcends patriarchy and feminism. In the laboratory of human experience, which is the ultimate testing ground of this new terminology, we find the historical phenomenon that men—not only women—have freely submitted, out of the experience itself of agape love, to non-domination values as exemplified in monastic vows of poverty, chastity, and obedience. This monastic tradition showcases the paradox of historically inherited philosophical presuppositions that need no longer be replicated. By redefining the human being as "semiotic animal", we have a potentially new point of departure historically—in terminology as a promising beginning—that calls for integrating cognitive and affective (or "cathectic") modes of knowing as lived through human experience, since symbols are ways in which human beings structure knowledge and experience.

At the same time, such a definition opens onto the infinite, which is ultimately a mystery beyond our finite human understanding. The new definition transcends the historically problematic dualisms of rational/non-rational and culture/nature. These traditional dualisms only get in the way of an "integral" humanism that is grounded in nature while at the same time surpassing nature through the highest form of self-giving love experienced by both man and woman in our shared humanity. The classic case of Teresa, indeed alongside that of John of the Cross, offers a paradox that can shed further light on deepening human understanding, inclusive of a heightened awareness of our intrinsic ethical responsibilities for nature as a whole. In such holistic perspective "woman" is no longer represented as "less rational" than man and therefore as signifying "nature-to-be-dominated".

In the test of the centuries of the non-domination paradigm of the contemplative tradition, which Teresa herself exemplifies, we can now at least see how ironic is the paradox of editorially screening out the contemplative tradition as simply a way of perfection designed by monks and friars symbolically appropriating the female body, as receptive to divine love, in vows of poverty, chastity, and obedience, as well as in the practice of silence, in the imitation of Christ. Are men, such as St. Benedict and St. Francis who founded religious orders, therefore "unmanly"? Why did Teresa, who is said to be "womanly", insist on her nuns being "manly" in their determined perseverance? In the culture/nature false dualism, moreover, why must only woman's embodiment signify the temporal order of nature and only man's embodiment transcendence of the temporal order? A host of questions can become further clarified via our new definition.

Thus, we can better see the paradox accruing historically from the older terminology in defining the human being. This paradox need no longer be replicated (although it likely will be through a semantic lag), but rather intrinsically resolved, in the new light of "semiotic animal" as a promising paradigm shift, a new beginning in the development of future thought.

Concluding Reflection

Having taught women's studies in interdisciplinary context since 1976, including the course, "Semiotics of Feminism" at Indiana University, Bloomington, International Summer Institute for Structural and Semiotic Studies, 1983, I am well aware of the need to transcend historically inherited paradoxical dualisms with an alternative paradigm.[13] Here I address not any one school of feminism, postmodern French feminism included. I return, rather, to Simon de Beauvoir, in my spiral of semiosis toward developing future thought.

Teresa's starting point in experiencing—indeed embracing—her humanity was, as we have seen, her own embodiment in nature. Was she a masculine

---

[13] See also, for example, Christ 1980; Gatens 1991; Hollywood 2002; Beattie 2006; 2013.

type of woman, as the modern atheist existentialist de Beauvoir claimed in her classic opus, *The Second Sex* (1949), because Teresa's contemplative experience sent her into the world of God's "action" in self-realization transcending the anthropological category of woman as "Other" than man? De Beauvoir sees Teresa as a paradox, as a woman contemplative who acted upon the world of culture as does man, thereby transcending finite existence.

At the same time, de Beauvoir herself becomes entrapped in the male-defined either/or logic whereby "man" as human subject signifies action in the world—thereby transcending finite existence—whereas woman as anthropological "Other" than man signifies passivity (too bad for her) unless she can overcome her femininity by self-realization in the world of action. Teresa, as a "striking exception" among women contemplatives (1949: 674), acts thus as a human subject in founding of monasteries and writing spiritual classics. Therefore, according to de Beauvoir, the sole value of mystical contemplation in her case was that such experience led to action that gained Teresa recognition and self-realization in transcending her finite existence "beyond the sexual division" (1949: 674)

That is hardly the way the Carmelite tradition interprets Teresa's own texts. Kavanaugh conjectures (1985: 5):

> Teresa's reluctance to follow the Lord's urgings that she write about her foundations could have been due to her fear that others might think that they were her own accomplishments, an idea she disavows. The work was God's work. In addition, she dreaded taking up the task because of the lack of quiet time for writing. Tangled business matters, endless correspondence, persistent bad health, certainly none of these contributed to any spark of enthusiasm for the project.

Whereas we can all concur with de Beauvoir that contemplation did indeed result in Teresa's remarkable deeds that are irreducible to gender, at the same time Teresa's own grounding in love, detachment, and humility led her not to overvalue the opinion of others in her seeking first the kingdom of God within herself. Whether her good deeds were invisible to the world or visible to the world, for either condemnation or praise, became in time, in her lived through struggle with raging controversies and calumnies against her, "par for the course", so to speak. Hence she experienced an inner freedom in her practice of Gospel-inspired values, which vivified her intrepid action in experiencing her own tradition as a living tradition. That takes some doing.

Does de Beauvoir not put the cart before the horse in assigning male-defined action in the world as the criterion for Teresa's transcending of human finitude (as de Beauvoir says is the case also of John of Cross)? We see now that de Beauvoir herself—as a classic case of such paradox—got entangled in the active/passive, action/contemplation dualism as privileging the male as in the older definitions of human being, and as, consequently, devaluing the contemplative experience itself of love—in a universal sense beyond any given culture and in itself transcendent of gender.

The redefining of human as semiotic animal, therefore, does have the terminological potential to integrate in a higher synthesis the primacy of contemplative love, as prior to—and hence as foundational to—its overflow into relation with others. As semiotic animals, Teresa and John of the Cross transcend dualisms, in the true sense wherein de Beauvoir herself says (1949: 674) of Teresa:

> The truth is, as she herself understood, that the value of a mystical experience is measured not according to the way in which it is subjectively felt, but according to its objective influence. ... St. Teresa poses in a most intellectual fashion the dramatic problem of the relation between the individual and the transcendent Being; she lived out, as a woman, an experience whose meaning goes far beyond the fact of her sex; she must be ranked [as equal] with ... St. John of the Cross.

Thus, Teresa—as a classic case of paradox—does shed new light on women's studies, as well as on the related further question of our time of redefining the human being as "semiotic animal", toward a non-domination paradigm that embraces the interrelation of rational and suprarational modes of knowing in human experience. Do we need define rationality and contemplation as either male-identified or female-identified, or as reducible to sex complementarity per se? How do the virtues of love, detachment, and humility, in Teresa's own teaching, work in mutual relation to one another for both men and women in human fulfillment?

In reflection upon these questions, I conclude that it seems to me reasonable—even wise—to redefine the human being in a way that *comes to terms* with human experience (as the classic case of Teresa showcases) in its *wholeness*.

References

AHLGREN, Gillian.
>   1996.   *Teresa of Avila and the Politics of Sanctity* (Cornell University Press: Ithaca).

ALLEN, Sr. Prudence, R.S.M.
>   1985.   *The Concept of Woman: The Aristotelian Revolution, 750 B.C.—A.D. 1250* (Grand Rapids, MI; Cambridge, U.K.: William B. Eerdmans Publishing Company).

2002. *The Concept of Woman: The Early Humanist Reformation, 1250–1500, Vol. II* (Grand Rapids, MI; Cambridge, U.K.: William B. Eerdmans Publishing Company).

ALVAREZ, Tomás.
2011. *St. Teresa of Avila. 100 Themes on Her Life and Work*, trans. Kieran Kavanaugh, O.C.D. (Washington, DC: Institute of Carmelite Studies Publications).

ASHLEY, Benedict, O.P., and John DEELY.
2012. *How Science Enriches Theology* (South Bend, IN: St. Augustine's Press).

BAER, Eugen.
2001. "Semiotics of the Infinite", in *Semiotics 2001*, ed. Scott Simpkins and John Deely (Ottawa: Legas).

BEATTIE, Tina.
2006. *New Catholic Feminism: Theology and Theory* (London: Routledge)
2013. *Theology after Postmodernity: Divining the Void* (London: Oxford University Press).

BEAUVOIR, Simone de (1908–1986).
1949. *The Second Sex*, trans. and ed. H. M. Parshley (New York: Random House, Inc., 1989).

BUTLER, Judith.
1999. *Gender Trouble: Feminism and the Subversion of Identity* (New York: Routledge).

CHOWNING, Daniel, O.C.D.
2007. "Jesus Christ Friend and Liberator: The Christology of St. Teresa of Avila", in *A Better Wine: Essays Celebrating Kieran Kavanaugh, O.C.D.*, ed. Kevin Culligan. O.C.D. Carmelite Studies X (Washington, DC: Institute of Carmelite Studies), 3–61.

CHRIST, Carol P.
1980. *Diving Deep and Surfacing: Women Writers on Spiritual Quest* (Toronto: Fitzhenry & Whiteside Limited).

DEELY, Brooke: see under WILLIAMS DEELY and also SMITH, Brooke Williams.

DEELY, John.
1990. *Basics of Semiotics* (Bloomington: Indiana University Press)
2003. "The Semiotic Animal" (first systematic draft), in *Logica, dialogica, ideologica. I segni tra funzionalita ed eccedenza*, ed. Petrilli and Calefato (= itinerari filosofici; Milan: Mimesis, 2003), 201–219; also in *The Second Renaissance* (Milan: Spirali).
2003a. "The Semiotic Animal" (humanist version), presented in the Monday, 22 September 2003 'Metaphysical Session', of the International Con-

gress "Christian Humanism in the Third Millennium", Rome, 21–25 September 2003; web version posted on Congress site http://e-aquinas. net/pdf/deely.pdf.

2003b. "The Semiotic Animal" (definitional version), in *Semiotics 2003*, ed. Rodney Williamson, Leonard Sbrocchi, and John Deely (Ottawa, Canada: Legas), 111–126.

2003c. *The Impact on Philosophy of Semiotics. The Quasi-Error of the External World, with a Dialogue between a 'Semiotist' and a 'Realist'* (South Bend, IN: St. Augustine's Press). Spiral on p. 164.

2004. "From Semiotic Animal to Semioethical Animal and Back", in *Macht der Zeichen, Zeichen der Macht/ Signs of Power, Power of Signs* (Festschrift für Jeff Bernard; = Trans-Studien zur Veraenderung der Welt 3), ed. Gloria Withalm and Josef Wallmannsberger (Wien: Lit. Verlag), 120–136.

2005. "Why the Semiotic Animal Needs to Develop a Semioethics", in John Deely, Susan Petrilli, and Augusto Ponzio, *The Semiotic Animal* (Ottawa, Canada: Legas Publishing), 207–221.

2005a. "Defining the Semiotic Animal: A Postmodern Definition of Human Being Superseding the Modern Definition 'Res Cogitans'," *American Catholic Philosophical Quarterly* 79.3 (Summer 2005): 461–481. doi: https://doi.org/10.5840/acpq200579329

2005b. *Defining the Semiotic Animal* (Sofia, Bulgaria: New Bulgarian University 2005 Seminar Series Publication, Southeast European Center for Semiotic Studies).

2005c. "From Semiotics to Semioethics; or, How Does Responsibility Arise in Semiosis?", in *Semiotics 2004/2005*, ed. Stacy Monahan, Benjamin Smith, and Terry J. Prewitt (Ottawa, Canada: Legas, 2006), 242–261.

2009. "Why the Semiotic Animal Needs to Develop a Semioethics", in *Semiotics 2008*, ed John Deely and Leonard G. Sbrocchi (Ottawa: Legas), 716–729.

2010. *The Semiotic Animal: A Postmodern Definition of "Human Being" Transcending Patriarchy and Feminism* (South Bend, IN: St. Augustine's Press).

2012. "Toward a Postmodern Recovery of 'Person'," *Espiritu* LXI.143 (2012): 147–165.

DEELY, John, Susan PETRILLI, and Augusto PONZIO.

2005. *The Semiotic Animal* (Ottawa, Canada: Legas Publishing).

ECO, Umberto.

1982. "On Symbols", in *Frontiers in Semiotics*, ed. John Deely, Brooke Williams, and Felicia E. Kruse (Bloomington: Indiana University Press).

FITZGERALD, Constance, O.C.D.

1988. "A Discipleship of Equals: Voices from Tradition—Teresa of Avila and John of the Cross", in *A Discipleship of Equals: Toward a Christian*

Feminist Spirituality, ed. Francis A. Eigo. O.S.A. (Villanova, PA: The Villanova University Press).

GATENS, Moira.
1991. *Feminism and Philosophy* (Bloomington: Indiana University Press).

GRATIAN (Johannes Gratianus, ?–c.1160/78).
c.1140. *Decretum Gratiani*, in *Corpus Juris Canonici*, ed. Aemilius Friedberg on the basis of the 2nd Leipig edition of the text established by A. L. Richter (Graz, Austria: Akademische Druck, 1959).

GROSS, Jr., Francis L.
1993. *The Making of a Mystic: Seasons in the Life of Teresa of Avila*, with Toni Perior Gross (Albany, NY: State University of New York).

HOLLYWOOD, Amy.
2002. *Sensible Ecstasy: Mysticism, Sexual Difference, and the Demands of History* (Chicago: The University of Chicago Press).

HUGHES, Dominic, Translator
1951. *The Gifts of the Holy Ghost* (New York: Sheed and Ward), translation of Poinsot 1645.

KAVANAUGH, Kieran, O.C.D.
1976. "Introduction" to *The Book of Her Life*, in *The Collected Works of St. Teresa of Avila*, trans. Kieran Kavanaugh, O.C.D., and Otilio Rodriguez, O.C.D., Vol. 1 (Washington, DC: ICS Publications, Institute of Carmelite Studies, 1980), 15–51.
1980. "Introduction" to *The Book of Her Foundations*, in *The Collected Works of St. Teresa of Avila*, trans. Kavanaugh, O.C.D., and Otilio Rodriguez, O.C.D., Vol. 2 (Washington, DC: ICS Publications, Institute of Carmelite Studies), 15–36.
1980a. "Introduction" to *The Interior Castle* in *The Collected Works of St. Teresa of Avila*, trans. Kieran Kavanaugh, O.C.D. and Otilio Rodriguez, O.C.D., Vol. 3 (Washington, DC: ICS Publications, Institute of Carmelite Studies).
1985. "Introduction" to *The Way of Perfection*, in *The Collected Works of St. Teresa of Avila*, trans. Kieran Kavanaugh, O.C.D., Vol. 4 (Washington, DC: ICS Publications, Institute of Carmelite Studies), 3–82.
2000. "How to Pray: From the Life and Teachings of St. Teresa", in *Carmel and Contemplation: Transforming Human Consciousness*, ed. K. Cullen and R. Jordon Carmelite Studies, Vol. III (Washington, DC: ICS Publications).

KAVANAUGH, Kieran, O.C.D., Otilio RODRIGUEZ, and Carol LISI.
2010. *The Interior Castle Study Edition* (Washington, DC: ICS Publications, Institute of Carmelite Studies).

LARSON, Lauren.

2001.   "The Anomalous Assent: Contemplation as a New Semiotic", in *Semiotics 2001*, ed. Scott Simpkins and John Deely (Ottawa: Legas).

MARITAIN, Jacques (18 November 1882–1973 April 28).

1932.   *Distinguer Pour Unir: Ou, Les Degrés du Savoir* (Paris: Desclée de Brouwer). Page references are from the English edition, *Distinguish to Unite or The Degrees of Knowledge*, trans. from the fourth French edition under the supervision of Gerald B. Phelan (New York: Charles Scribner's Sons, 1959).

1938.   *Situation de la Poésie*, in collaboration with Raïssa Maritain (Paris: Desclée de Brouwer). Citation is from the English edition, *The Situation of Poetry* (New York: Philosophical Library, 1968).

1940.   *Scholasticism and Politics*, trans. Mortimer J. Adler (New York: The Macmillan Company).

1958.   *Reflections on America* (Charles Scribner's Sons).

1967.   "Let Us Make for Him a Helpmate Like to Himself," in *Untrammeled Approaches*, trans. Bernard Doering, Vol. 20 in *The Collected Works of Jacques Maritain* (Notre Dame, IN: University of Notre Dame Press, 1997), 151–164. Cf. "Faisons-lui une aide semblable a lui," *Nova et Vetera* 62.4 (October–December 1967): 241–254.

MARITAIN, Raïssa (12 September 1883–1960 November 4).

1950.   *Les Dons du Saint Esprit* (Poinsot 1645), traduction de Raïssa Maritain, Preface by R. P. Garrigou-Lagrange (Paris: Chez Pierre Tequi, 1950).

MORRISSEY, C. S.

2012.   "Pope Illuminates 'Reasonableness of Faith in God'", *The B.C. Catholic* (December 3, 2012).

PETRILLI, Susan, and Augusto PONZIO.

2003.   *Semioetica* (Rome: Meltemi).

POINSOT, John (9 July 1589–1644 June 17, aka "Joannes a Sancto Thoma", "John of St. Thomas").

1632.   *Tractatus de Signis*, disengaged from the *Artis Logicae Prima et Secunda Pars* (Alcalá, Spain) and published in a bilingual critical edition subtitled *The Semiotic of John Poinsot*, arranged by John Deely in consultation with Ralph Austin Powell (Berkeley: University of California Press, 1985). Available in electronic form (Charlottesville, VA: Intelex Corporation, 1992). A corrected second edition of this work, with new editorial materials, has been published by St Augustine's Press, 2013.

1645.   "De Donis Spiritus Sancti", *Tomus Quintus Cursus Theologici* (1645), disp. 18 (Vol. VI of the Vivès edition, Paris, 1885, 572–715). See Raïssa Maritain 1950 and Hughes 1951 for modern translations into, respectively, French and English.